Merry Christmas D[...]
from Elizabeth, Louise,
Eleanor, John &
Hugh.

FEET, SCOTLAND, FEET

THE GLASGOW **Herald** FULL 1991 WORLD CUP REPORTS

FEET, SCOTLAND

Edited
by
Derek
Douglas

FEET!

THE BOOK OF SCOTTISH RUGBY

Bill McLaren, Bill McMurtrie, Brian Meek and David Steele

MAINSTREAM
PUBLISHING

EDINBURGH AND LONDON

Copyright © *Glasgow Herald*, 1991

First published in Great Britain 1991 by
MAINSTREAM PUBLISHING COMPANY (EDINBURGH) LTD
7 Albany Street
Edinburgh EH1 3UG

ISBN 1 85158 425 0 (cloth)

A catalogue record for this book is
available from the British Library

Typeset in Sabon by Falcon Typographic Art Ltd, Edinburgh
Printed in Great Britain by Butler & Tanner Ltd, Frome

Acknowledgments

Many people have contributed towards the making of this book. First off, I must thank Adam Robson, Gordon Alston and John Davidson of the Scottish Rugby Union who facilitated multiple visits to the SRU's excellent library and museum at Murrayfield and allowed us to track down some early photographic material.

The assistance and co-operation of *Glasgow Herald* colleagues has also been much appreciated, particularly that of editor Arnold Kemp, deputy editor Harry Reid, news editor Bob Sutter, picture editor George Wilkie, sports editor Eddie Rodger and photographic librarian Robert Tweedie who withstood a constant bombardment of requests for pictures, and more pictures, with fortitude and forbearance.

Finally, on behalf of all the contributors, I thank most sincerely all of those who were interviewed and co-operated with us for what, I trust, will be a lasting memento of the Rugby Union game in Scotland.

D. C. A. D.
1991

Photographs by

ANGELA CATLIN, DUNCAN DINGSDALE,

BILL FLEMING, JAMES GALLOWAY,

CRAIG HALKETT, IAN HOSSACK,

ARTHUR KINLOCH, ALAN MACDONALD,

JAMES MILLAR, STUART PATERSON,

MARTIN SHIELDS and JAMES THOMSON

Additional artwork from the

OUTRAM PHOTOGRAPHIC ARCHIVE

and the

SRU LIBRARY AND MUSEUM, Murrayfield

Photographic research by

ROBERT TWEEDIE

World Cup 1991 photographs by

James Galloway and Alan Macdonald

Contents

Feet, Scotland, Feet!

A Caledonian Perspective

By BILL McLAREN

THERE HAVE BEEN many occasions since the earliest days of the Rugby Union game when Scotland's administrators have come in for heavy flak as being inflexible, perverse and refusing to move with the times, and some of that has been justified. No one, however, can deny that, even though they have taken their time to introduce change, they have created a Scottish rugby structure that is the envy of others and one that should see Scotland comfortably through the Nineties. Not only that but they have played a very important role in the evolution of the modern game whilst showing high integrity and principle in safeguarding what they have seen as the key features that have made Rugby Union such a distinctive sport.

Over the years Scotland's teams have experienced the humps and hollows of rugby fortunes in a series of lengthy hungers of comparative failure and short bursts of welcome and inspiring success. The Scots were giants in early days. They won or shared four of the first eight Championships in the 1880s during which time they were deprived also of four Triple Crowns by England at the last hurdle. They had a vintage spell at the turn of the century with four outright titles in seven seasons. They enjoyed memorable success in the Twenties with a Grand Slam in 1925, shared Championships in the following two seasons and a further outright title in 1929. In the past decade they have made a huge impact with 'Grand Slams' in 1984 and 1990 and a shared title with France in 1986. On the other hand, Scotland have been involved in 16 post-war 'wooden spoons' in very lean spells. Prior to their 1925 Grand Slam they had won only nine of their previous 26 games. Between 1934 and 1937 they won only three of 13 games and there was that miserable period from the 5–6 defeat by Ireland in 1951 to the 15–0 pasting from France in 1955 when Scotland lost 17 internationals in a row and all was sunk in deep dejection, to quote the words of a Hawick Common-Riding song!

That desperate spell was attributable in part, in my view, to the fact that Scotland always seemed to be short of brawn, ballast and altitude in the frontal exchanges. Opponents invariably were taller and heavier. I recall doing two radio commentaries for BBC in 1953 at the Ireland and England games, each of which Scotland lost by 8–26. They had virtually no line-out presence and I remember little Arthur Dorward of Gala, the Scottish scrum-half, being hurt at Twickenham because, not for the first time, he had to confront huge, rampaging English forwards. There was also some fearful lack of consistency in selection. Players were selected then discarded with alarming frequency and with detrimental effect on their own confidence. In the four games of the 1953 Championship Scotland called on 31 players. Fortunately the lesson was learned and one of the crucial factors in Scotland's recent triumphs has been selectorial good sense in appreciating the need for consistency of choice leading to continuity and therefore to a virtual club situation in the realms of team play and player rapport. The benefit to coaches hardly needs to be stressed in that where the broad nucleus remains constant, newcomers can be slotted in without much disturbance and with the huge advantage of having a circle of experienced, hardened colleagues to guide them along the way.

Of course, in those earlier times, exiled Scots sometimes were chosen for national trials on fairly skimpy evidence but progress has been made there too. From 1963 the Anglo-Scots had at least one fixture per season against a home district and from 1981, when the Anglos entered the district championship, the national selectors have had wider opportunity for running the rule over Anglo candidates in the four championship games they play each season.

Scots have had to compensate frequently for a shortage of really big men in their packs with superior fitness and mobility and a form of attack that suited their particular attributes and personnel. Hence the popularity with Scots of wheeling the scrummage and dribbling rushes, from the early days to the Second World War. Even in 1955 at the French match in Paris the Scottish pack wheeled several scrummages in order to dribble upfield. Unfortunately the pitch was firm and, virtually every time, dribble control was lost and the French scrum-half, Gerard Dufau, enjoyed himself hugely in gathering the bouncing ball to initiate counter-attacks. Scotland lost 0–15! It could have been many more.

Of course many of the great Scottish players of the Twenties and Thirties bemoaned the fact that their successors weren't skilled enough in keeping the ball close to their bootlaces in the dribble and they would be saddened to see that nowadays the wheeled scrummage is used mainly as a disruptive measure that disfigures the game. In its day the wheel and dribble was an innovatory tactic with a definite Scottish trademark and there have been other areas of the game in which the Scots have led the way. There was innovation and brilliant tactical preparation and application in the way they played the line-out in their greatest triumph – defeat of England at Murrayfield for the 1990 Grand Slam. But most of the bright ideas, ploys and style have emanated from France, the southern hemisphere and Wales, with the Scots very observant and clever at incorporating into their own patterns whatever was suitable from other airts.

Perhaps the one period when Scotland did field a pack big enough and rough enough to hold its own in every department was in 1961 when they fielded Hugh McLeod (Hawick), Norman Bruce (London Scottish), David Rollo (Howe of Fife), Frans ten Bos (London Scottish), Mike Campbell-Lamerton (Halifax), Ken Ross (Boroughmuir FP), John Douglas (Stewart's FP) and Ken Smith (Kelso). They beat Wales and Ireland but, significantly, when Mike Campbell-Lamerton could not play

at Twickenham, England denied Scotland a Triple Crown by 0–6. They have done that on five post-war occasions. The general feeling was that the selectors had erred in making three changes for Twickenham when one would have done. They broke up that formidable loose-forward trio by moving John Douglas to lock and Ken Smith to number eight and by bringing in John Brash of Cambridge University who was a skilful forward but one who tended to play a very loose type of game. The straight introduction of a natural lock would have been the better bet. That Bos-Campbell-Lamerton engine room was just one of several examples of big Anglo-Scots lending a bit of bulk to Scotland's frontal operations. Wilson Shaw's 1938 Championship-winning side had George Horsburgh (London Scottish) and Arthur Roy (Waterloo). Peter Stagg (Sale), all six foot ten inches of him, joined Campbell-Lamerton in the mid-Sixties, then Alastair McHarg (London Scottish) in the late Sixties. Scotland's 1990 'Grand Slam' owed much to the powerful play of Damian Cronin (Bath) and Chris Gray (Nottingham) who emerged in the Anglo-Scots side which beat the touring French in 1987, Gray later being regarded by New Zealanders as the outstanding Scottish forward on the tour there in 1990.

Throughout all of their varied experiences, and even in their darkest days, Scots have earned the highest respect for taking the rough with

Line-out action from the 1931 Scotland v France game at Murrayfield. Scotland, playing in white, unnumbered jerseys, won 6–3 the smooth in good spirit and for their unwavering commitment and, not least, their on-field attitude and behaviour. This surely stems in part from the very strict, authoritarian attitude of the early administrators who set standards and insisted that everyone adhered to them. Scots certainly have learned from the past although it frequently took them longer than their rivals to initiate progress.

In early times Scotland were fortunate in that their best players, indeed their only players, were centred on a small group of clubs and the international side therefore was drawn from that small pool, all of whom had played the game at school under the guidance of great men of vision and stature. Indeed it makes folk boggle today at the thought of schoolboys playing in the senior international side, but in the earliest days that was the case. Ninian Finlay and Charles Reid were Capped when just 17 years and 36 days old and still schoolboys at Edinburgh Academy. Scotland's first international side, 20 of them, were drawn from just seven clubs, with Glasgow and Edinburgh Academicals providing six each. As more clubs were formed the available talent became more widely spread but it was still the stronger clubs who provided the bulk of the national side. Scotland's successes in the early 1900s were gained by a side based heavily on the powerful Edinburgh University and Edinburgh Academicals sides of that period and the 1925 Grand Slam team included the entire Oxford University threequarter line, while the half-backs were partners at Glasgow Academicals.

In the modern era Scotland's talent has been too thinly spread and the series of 'friendly' fixtures between traditional rivals did not provide stern enough tests, week in, week out, for Scotland's top players. The introduction of a district championship competition in 1953–54 did

Hawick's Jock Beattie, at the centre of the picture, leads a Scottish foot rush against the Welsh at Murrayfield in 1932. Wales won a bruising encounter 6–0

provide a bridge between club and trial stages, at least for the home Scots, with the Anglos joining in 17 years later, and the creation of a National Leagues structure in 1973–74 has given players a regular series of encounters carrying additional pressure that fits them out the better for the trials, tribulations and strains of the higher spheres. There still is a feeling that the gap between top and bottom of the 14-team divisions can be too great and there have been proposals to reduce the number of teams in the top divisions to eight, playing home and away, but that so far has not gained the necessary approval. What isn't in doubt is the value of the National Leagues system in the blooding of players to serious rugby where the results do matter in contrast to former times when, for instance, defeat did not carry the strain of possible relegation. At the same time it is to be hoped that the overpowering desire to win does not adversely affect the quality of spectacle that games have to offer, especially in times when the professional Rugby League is gaining converts through the exciting fare it provides with its basis very much on handling and running and with the use of the boot strictly limited.

One big change in the Scottish situation has been the elimination of the 'old school tie' system where national selection is concerned. Of course it is hardly surprising that resentment was created among emergent clubs, especially those in the Borders, that former pupils of well-established schools were given preference. But the game in Scotland started in the great boarding schools. The High School of Edinburgh, Edinburgh Academy, Loretto, Merchiston, Fettes, Dollar, Glasgow Academy and Glenalmond all gave early impetus to the rugby game and it stood to reason that, as the former pupil clubs began to form, led by Edinburgh Academicals in 1858, the administrators would be men of learning and

'The struggle for possession' was how this picture from the Scotland–England game at Murrayfield in 1933 was captioned in the *Glasgow Herald* of the time. England won 3–0. Contemporary reports indicate that England had the better of the forward exchanges which was just as well because during the game, it is reported, both centres – D. W. Burland and R. A. Gerrard – 'went lame'

Getting in the tackle . . . this shot from the Scotland v The Rest match at Melrose in 1934 clearly shows the stand at The Greenyards, with its 'eagle's eyrie' Press box perched atop the roof

standing in their communities and themselves with strong allegiance to the schools.

It has to be remembered too that the early international matches were played before Border clubs were established and there can be no doubt that when Borderers did begin to challenge their city rivals they were regarded as taking the game far too seriously and being an uncivilised lot into the bargain! So it wasn't until 17 years after the first international was played, and until the 37th Scottish international, that a Border player was Capped, Adam Dalgleish, the Gala forward. Some of the resentment was a bit overdone. At the same time there was handed down from one Hawick generation to another, for example, the widely held complaint that injustice had been done by the Scottish selectors in failure to play together in the national side Mattha Elliot and Davey Patterson who were recognised in their day as the outstanding quarter-back partnership in the country. One also was brought up to believe that, but for the 'old school tie', that Hawick giant, Bill Kyle, would have gained far more than his 21 Caps had he gone to Loretto, Fettes or Merchiston. Yet an examination of the record shows that he was Capped as a 20-year-old and played 16 matches in a row, was left out for six, played four, missed one and played his last against Wales in 1910. That doesn't seem unfair recognition of his considerable ability. In any event the 'old school tie' accusation, whether justified or not, has had no part in Scottish selection for many years. All that matters to Scotland's selectors nowadays, lucky enough to have had as their recent conveners Robin Charters (Hawick), Bob Munro (Leith Academicals) and Duncan Paterson (Gala), is whether a player is good enough to fit in to the pattern of the national side. It matters not whether he was educated at Gordonstoun or expelled from Langholm Academy!

In one other area the Scottish game has seen the light and brought about a huge change in attitude and that is in its treatment of the media.

There was a time when the SRU seemed to delight in withholding information from the Press. On one occasion they staged a match at Murrayfield in which several proposals relating to changes in the scrummage law were to be tested. Prior to the match John Robertson, spokesman for the Press, asked a Union committee man politely if he could give the Press an idea of what the proposals were and what they might look for. The reply was: 'Use your bloody eyes.' Nowadays there is genuine co-operation between the Union and media with regular Press briefings for up-to-date information and Press conferences after training sessions and international games. Those are much appreciated by the Scottish rugby correspondents, who have the good of the game at heart, and they are of considerable benefit to the Union as well in the dissemination of information and in providing their generous sponsors with valuable media mention and coverage.

There has been a particular Scottishness created by Scotland's international players over the years. Initially they were depicted as undersized tearaways, 'ill tae keep in order', to quote another Hawick Common-Riding song, unceremonious and liable to hack at anything above the ground but, despite lacking the ballast and stature of some opponents, magnificent in spirit, prepared to run all day and always deadly when it came to putting opponents on the floor. They have come through various evolutionary periods to their current high standing in world rankings as a side of multi-talents with a clear imprint of the type of game that suits their personnel and supported by a coaching back-up with gifts and depth which set it apart as being very special. Some of the adverse comment directed at Scotland has been quite unfair. He was a Welshman, I believe, who first levelled the charge that if it had been left up to Scotland, handling never would have been legalised! Perhaps the thinking behind this was based on the fact that Scots in the early days and, indeed, in later times, pinned much of their faith in rousing forward play in which wheeling of scrummages and rip-roaring dribbling rushes were at the very heart of their style. Of course the earliest games were contested by 20-a-side and involved prolonged periods of mauling and hacking the ball forward or, if not the ball, hacking at an opponent's shins. Scots were good at it, so much so they struck fear into opponents' hearts with the ferocity of their rushes. Eventually they so developed the art of footwork that their supporters invented that famous war-cry of 'Feet, Scotland, Feet!'

In some of the early meetings with England the battle often centred on Scotland's tough forwards and their dribbling rushes against England's faster backs but reports of those games often referred to stoppages for injuries – always to Englishmen! The Scottish hierarchy were very loath to part with the scrummage wheel and dribble and were espousing the value of the 3–2–3 scrummage formation, from which the break at the knuckle and foot rush technique was easier achieved, when the other rivals all were embracing the 3–4–1 formation that has now become the norm with an occasional variation of 3–3–2. There is no doubt that Scottish forwards made the dribbling rush very much a Scottish speciality and in the Twenties and Thirties they employed the tactic to devastating effect.

Indeed I remember once bumping into the legendary Irish back Eugene O'Davy at Landsdowne Road and he recalled the Triple Crown decider there in 1933 when Ireland scored two tries to none but the Scots sealed the Crown with two drop goals, then worth four points to just three for a try. Scotland won 8–6. That great Irishman described with some feeling how the clinching drop goal by Harry Lind climaxed a rousing foot rush by the Scottish players virtually from their own line.

Even allowing for that Scottish tactic, however, who can point the finger at Scots for holding back the development of handling attack? Doctor H. H. Almond, Headmaster of Loretto School for 40 years to 1902, and a guiding light in the early days of Scottish rugby, was the real inventor of line handling. Mind you, at one time if a player passed the ball he was 'despised as showing fear'. Almond had to force the Loretto boys to pass because it was regarded as 'funking'. There was that famous occasion in 1879 when an Englishman carried the ball over his own line and touched down at Raeburn Place and 'was loudly hissed by the Scottish crowd of ten thousand not because it lost a rare chance to Scotland but that it showed want of pluck not normal with Britons'.

Almond, however, was a man of vision and courage who, having given a controversial decision in the very first Rugby Union international between Scotland and England at Raeburn Place in 1871, proffered the sage advice that 'when an umpire is in doubt I think he is justified in deciding against the side which makes most noise. They are probably in the wrong'. On such secure foundations was the early Scottish game erected! So Almond encouraged passing at Loretto and although the English laid great store by the handling success of the Oxford University sides of the 1880s what they didn't stress was that it was the influence exerted by former Lorettonians on those university sides that was the crucial element.

T. A. Kemp (St Mary's) brought down by G. B. Horsburgh (London Scottish) in 'a real Scots tackle', wrote the photographer who took this 1939 shot of the Scotland v England game at Murrayfield

For the most impressive outcome to handling attack one need only refer to Scotland's first Grand Slam success in 1925. In their four victories against France (25–4), Wales (24–14), Ireland (14–8) and England (14–11), Scotland had an incredible haul of 17 tries of which 14 were shared by their wings, Ian Smith (eight) and Johnny Wallace (six) and only two by forwards, Sandy Gillies and David McMyn, the other being by scrum-half Jimmy Nelson. In those days Scotland arguably had the finest back division in the world with their famous Oxford University threequarter line, the Glasgow Academical halves, Herbert Waddell and Nelson, and a superb full-back in Dan Drysdale, the first of the eight Heriots FP full-backs to have played for Scotland. They didn't get 14 tries from their wings without handling of the highest quality!

There have been occasions when the Scots have played very conservatively. Time was, especially in the late Fifties and Sixties, when defenders were permitted to place claustrophobic pressure on attackers and it was virtually suicidal to attempt handling attack from set pieces. So Scotland had a succession of powerful stand-off halves who could punt far and accurately – Tom McClung (Edinburgh Academicals), Gordon Waddell (London Scottish) and David Chisholm (Melrose) were outstanding examples – and even in modern times John Rutherford (Selkirk) and Craig Chalmers (Melrose) have proved influential figures with the accuracy of their punting in Scotland's Grand Slams of 1984 and 1990. Scotland thoroughly deserved their 1984 triumph but the only time they really spun the ball wide was when the game against Ireland was in their pocket and Peter Dods flew in from a wonderful switch move by Keith Robertson. Scots have shown astute tactical awareness in their use of punting as a means of combating heavy defence pressure and of keeping handling error to a minimum, although there were signs in

Scotland v England at Murrayfield in 1939 and the England scrum-half executes a classic diving pass

H. B. Toft (Waterloo), the England captain, awaits line-out ball with outstretched arms. The game was Scotland v England at Murrayfield in 1939 and England won 9–6

their successful tour of New Zealand in May and June of 1990 that they are coming closer to a genuine total rugby style in which every section of the team is constantly involved and continuity of action, through keeping the ball alive, is set alongside unfettered commitment by every player to copybook tackle chores.

No one can deny that Scots have proved highly suspicious of change over the years and deeply thirled to what they knew and were used to. Yet in several departments of the game they have built a proud record in leading the way and lending a tone by which others have set their own models.

Whereas, in the past, full-backs were essentially defenders concerned with catch, touch kick, fall and tackle, the modern game prides itself in the emergence of full-backs as influential figures in attack with Andy Irvine (Scotland), Serge Blanco (France) and J. P. R. Williams (Wales) as the prime examples. Scotland indeed has spawned several outstanding exponents including Keith Geddes (London Scottish), Ken Scotland (Heriot's FP), Arthur Brown and Peter Dods (Gala) and now Gavin Hastings (Watsonians). Irvine scored a then record ten international tries from the full-back position. There is evidence to suggest that, back in the game's beginnings, Scotland actually produced the first attacking full-back in Harry Stevenson (Edinburgh Academicals), although that was by chance. He had been an automatic choice for Scotland at centre in seven internationals but took a dislike to the rather static long-passing game in vogue and so was shifted to full-back. But there was no curbing his attacking instincts and time and again he dashed upfield to initiate unexpected strikes.

Those thousands of rugby folk all over the world who enjoy the drama and vivid action of seven-a-side play have Scotland, and especially the Melrose Club, to thank, for it was at the Greenyards in 1883 that the idea, hatched by Adam 'Ned' Haig, became the first ever sevens tournament. How 'Ned' would be amazed today to see the worldwide spread of his abbreviated version and how, even to this day, the distinctive aspect of sevens, sudden death in extra time, prevails just as it did on that very first occasion when Melrose pushed off with the Cup despite protestations from Gala that they had played only ten of the agreed 15 minutes of extra time in the final. On such firm foundations were the seeds of sevens success created! Hardly surprising then that a Scot was instrumental in launching the prestigious Middlesex Sevens at Twickenham, the biggest tournament in the world – Dr J. A. Russell Cargill, an Edinburgh Academical, whose name adorns the winners trophy.

Scotland were first in the field with a ground of their own when Inverleith was opened in 1899. They switched to spacious Murrayfield in 1925 where the biggest crowd ever for a Rugby Union international, 104,000, was accommodated at Scotland versus Wales in 1975.

The huge popularity of short tours, not only by international parties but by clubs and districts as well, owes everything to the farsightedness of Scottish rugby administrators who arranged the first ever such tour to South Africa in 1960. It was a venture into the unknown but an immediate success for there always has been a close rapport between the two countries and from that inaugural event has developed a Scottish reputation for being ideal tourists – modest, friendly, fair and extremely well behaved. That first tour party had a perfect blend in managership

Jock Beattie of Hawick, one of Scotland's greatest pre-war forwards, is in the thick of the action and has the ball at his feet in this shot from the Scotland v All Blacks game at Murrayfield in 1935. The New Zealanders proved victorious 18–8

Hands aloft . . . Scotland v
New Zealand at Murrayfield
in 1935 and all eyes are
on the ball

from Wilson Shaw and Charlie Drummond and although the itinerary that
called for playing the Test match first was clearly unwise they lost that
by only 10–18 and won their provincial games against Griqualand-West
(21–11) and East Transvaal (30–16). The party comprised ten backs
and 11 forwards as follows: Gordon Waddell (London Scottish), captain,
Tom McClung (Edinburgh Academicals), Robin Chisholm and Alec Hastie
(Melrose), Ron Cowan (Selkirk), Brian Shillinglaw (Gala), Arthur Smith
(Cambridge University), George Stevenson (Hawick), Ronnie Thomson
(London Scottish), Pat Burnet (Oxford Greyhounds), Norman Bruce and
Frans ten Bos (London Scottish), David Edwards and Bob Tollervey (Heriot's
FP), Oliver Grant and Hugh McLeod (Hawick), Hamish Kemp (Glasgow
High School FP), Brian Neill (Edinburgh Academicals), David Rollo (Howe
of Fife), Charlie Stewart (Kelso) and Wat Hart (Melrose). Scotland since have
toured in Canada '64 and '91, Argentina '69, Australia '70 and '82, New
Zealand '75, '81 and '90, Far East '77, France '80, Romania '84, North
America '85 and '91, France and Spain '86 and Japan '89.

It was in 1959 that Scotland recorded another first – when their
'electric blanket' was installed at Murrayfield, thanks to the generosity of
Dr Charles Hepburn. Some 44 miles of electric cables, nine inches under
the surface, ensured thereafter that Scotland had rugby when the rest of
Britain was frozen off.

In the early Seventies Scotland led the way again with an official
national club competition and the first ever international sevens tournament. Not that leagues were new to Scots. After all, Borderers had set up
their own domestic League in 1901, although this appears to have been
done much against the wishes of the SFU. Of course the Union committee

men already had come to regard Borderers as difficult to handle. When Border clubs began to play the game in the 1880s, the Union hierarchy were concerned about 'the rough language, robust play, standards of umpiring and intense local pride' in the Border game. One story tells of the first city referee to have charge of a Border club game who, on being asked on his return home how he had fared, snarled: 'Fared? It's not a referee those people need, it's a missionary!'

Border desire to stage their own league competition, about which the parent body weren't all that happy, was typical of the problems created for the Union by Borderers at various times. Jed-Forest had already been reprimanded for leaving the field before the referee had blown for no-side in a game with Hawick where Jed-Forest felt aggrieved about the award of a penalty to their opponents. Gala were suspended after the referee had complained about behaviour at a match against Watsonians. The Melrose club and captain were suspended following behaviour at a match against Royal High School FP. Later Gala and Hawick were suspended for 'abusive behaviour by their supporters to referees'. The Union were concerned about the presentation of goods as prizes at sevens and decreed that only medals or badges could be awarded. At one time Borderers threatened to set up their own South of Scotland Rugby Union in protest at having just one representative on the Scottish Football Union. The intention of starting a Border League was another irritation for the parent body but the Borderers went ahead, their League inaugurated in 1901 and a cup for the winners introduced in 1907. Curiously the Union provided 75% of the cost of the cup although six years previously the offer by W. S. Lang (Edinburgh University) of a cup for competition had been declined

Scotland v England at Murrayfield in 1937 and at the centre of the picture W. R. Logan and J. A. Waters (both Scotland) contest possession with R. J. Longland of England. Logan, the Scottish scrum-half, was reported to have had a particularly good game. Nevertheless, England won 6–3

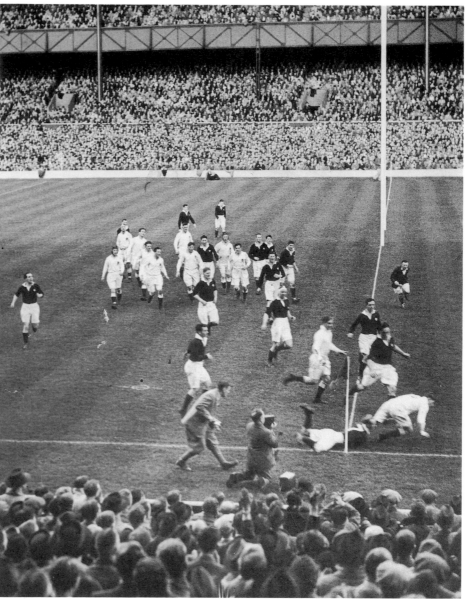

The England stand-off P. L. Candler (St Bart's) goes over for England's second try in the 1936 game against Scotland at Twickenham which England won 9–8. Contemporary reports stated that Scotland wing-threequarter K. C. Fyfe (Sale) marked his opposite number, the dangerously elusive runner, Prince Obolensky, out of the game

by the Union because 'such competitions are injurious to the welfare and purity of the game'. Borderers clearly didn't agree and even had the cheek to invite the Union's strong man, J. Aikman-Smith, to present the trophy for what has remained the oldest league competition in the British Isles.

Murrayfield was the venue in 1973 of the first ever international seven-a-side tournament held to mark the centenary of the Scottish Rugby Union. It was contested by eight countries: Scotland, England, France, Wales, Ireland, Australia, New Zealand and a President's seven, and England beat Ireland in a thrilling final.

To some extent the progress of the game in Scotland has been retarded by some of the early administrators and their unwillingness to move with the times. They could prove an awkward lot. It was said that whenever

Scottish rugby officials had to discuss a new proposal their instinctive reaction was to say 'no', then hasten very slowly along the road of consideration! It is hard to believe in this day and age that at one time Scotland refused to number their players in internationals. Wales and England wore numbered jerseys in 1922, Ireland in 1926, New South Wales in 1927 and France in 1929 but it wasn't until 1933 that Scotland fell into line. Indeed the story goes that when King George V asked Scotland's rugby secretary, J. Aikman-Smith, why the Scots were not numbered, that die-hard conservative growled: 'This is a rugby match, not a cattle auction.' Aikman-Smith was one of those early *obergruppenfuhrers* in Scottish administration during the formative years, domineering, dogmatic, yet forthright and unswerving in his belief in the high quality of the Scottish game and utterly opposed to any form of professionalism. How, one wonders, would he have reacted to the recent International Board proposals to liberalise the amateur regulations over communication for reward which would permit players to benefit directly from the game? How, indeed, would such strong characters as Herbert Waddell, Alf Wilson and Charlie Drummond? Perhaps some of the attitudes of the past were a bit extreme but those old-time officials dealt in clearly etched lines. There were no fuzzy areas and they certainly meant what they said. For instance, when a testimonial was set up for the

G. D. Shaw (Gala) kicks for goal during the 1937 Wales v Scotland game at Swansea. Scotland, playing four number eight forwards in the pack (as they were to do again 50 years later), won 13–6. Shaw converted two of Scotland's three tries

Ireland had the upper hand in this 1936 encounter with Scotland at Murrayfield. Scotland lost 10–4

Welsh international player, A. J. Gould, in 1895, the SFU (it didn't become the SRU until 1924) protested and then cancelled the fixtures with Wales for 1897 and 1898. Ten years earlier the three Hawick players, A. J. Laing, W. Burnett and R. Burnett, who had taken part in the original tour to Australia and New Zealand in 1888 were called before the Union to make sure that they hadn't made any money out of it! When a French club advertised in a Scottish newspaper for a stand-off with the promise of a business situation the Union took steps resulting in the club president and his committee being suspended. Jed-Forest once were refused permission to make a grant from their club funds to a player who had had his leg broken in a game.

The business of numbering players wasn't the only area in which Scotland were a bit tardy in getting in on the act. In 1958 they turned down the idea of having schools internationals but changed their minds in 1967. They were against replacements in internationals but became the first country to benefit when Gordon Connell was replaced by Ian MacCrae against France in 1969 – and MacCrae was instrumental in setting up Jim Telfer's injury time try for a miraculous 6–3 win, the last time Scotland won in Paris. They were well behind Wales in getting coaching going too but, to their credit, once in they set about the task with vigour and good sense.

Coaching, indeed, represents the major development in the Scottish game since the Sixties. Actually the first SRU Coaching Conference for some 148 schoolmasters was staged at Fettes College in September 1955 and was followed by the publication of a skills booklet, *Raise the*

Hectic action from the
Scotland v England encounter
of 1935

Standard, compiled by Herbert Waddell. There is no doubt that Scotland's abysmal 17 consecutive defeats inspired this coaching movement. Every encouragement has been afforded clubs and schools in the creation of coaching structures. The Scottish Schools Rugby Union was formed in 1968 following a national course for referees and schoolmasters. Coaching in Scotland owes a big debt to the two conveners of the Scottish Rugby Union's coaching committee, George Thomson and Tom Pearson. In 1969 the first national course for club coaches was staged, John Roxburgh became the Union's technical administrator in 1974 and Douglas Arneil his assistant in 1981. Mini-rugby was launched in 1974 and the first annual youth rugby camp was staged at Bruar in 1978. Initially the Union were lukewarm about appointing a coach to the national squad and there was not universal approval of the invitation in 1970–71 to Bill Dickinson of Jordanhill College to assist the captain during training. But, as 'adviser to the captain', Dickinson was highly successful in his seven seasons during which Scotland won 16 of 21 internationals at Murrayfield, including a run of ten home wins in a row.

Dickinson was instrumental in forcing the rugby world to reassess its approach to scrummaging through creating in the Scottish side perhaps the most formidable scrummaging pack of all time. He was a devoted student of the mechanics of scrummaging and the lore he imparted to his Scottish forwards enabled them to make their scrummage a powerful attacking force as well as a disruptive one. He did this with a pack that included a loose-head prop in Ian McLauchlan (Jordanhill College), initially regarded as far too small and too light for international play, and a lock, Alastair McHarg (London Scottish), who was regarded by many of the *cognoscenti* as a loose number eight being played out of position at lock. Dickinson created a close rapport with McLauchlan, one of his physical education students at Jordanhill College, and made him into one of the most successful loose-head props in the world, and for all McHarg's eccentricities in positioning, he clearly did his bit at the scrummage, partnered as he was by one of the great scrummaging locks in Gordon Brown (West of Scotland).

The Scotland packs of the early Seventies with McLauchlan and Sandy Carmichael (West of Scotland) as props, McHarg and Gordon Brown in the boiler house, Nairn MacEwan and Peter Brown (both Gala), Roger Arneil (Leicester), David Leslie (Dundee High School FP), Mike Biggar (London Scottish) and Jock Millican (Edinburgh University) and with Frank Laidlaw (Melrose), Quentin Dunlop (West of Scotland), Bobby Clark (Edinburgh Wanderers) and Duncan Madsen (Gosforth) as hookers, set a new standard in scrummage work and Scotland frequently finished the livelier because of the steam their scrummaging had taken out of their opponents. More than once McLauchlan hung far heavier props up to dry in scrummages or forced them to operate at uncomfortably low levels.

There was that amusing story concerning McLauchlan after Scotland had gained their first Twickenham win for 33 years in 1971 with the prospect of playing England again a week later at Murrayfield to celebrate the centenary of the first ever Rugby Union international. One

The white-shirted England players outnumber the Scots in this shot from the match at Murrayfield in 1935 which Scotland won 10–7

English forward complained at the post-match dinner about Scotland's unceremonious scrummage method with the comment: 'We just don't play like that down here.' Growled McLauchlan: 'Well, pal, you have a bloody week to find out how to do it.' A week later Scotland won 26–6!

After Scotland's pack had out-scrummaged Wales in the 1974 Cardiff match which Wales won 6–0 with a disputed try by Terry Cobner, even that rugged Welshman, Clive Rowlands, said to me the following day: 'You know, we're getting far too blinking technical about our scrummaging.' Never had Clive said a truer word and everybody began to get 'too blinking technical' as they followed Scotland's and Dickinson's lead. The Scottish game always will owe a lot to that tough old nut, Dickinson, who laid the first guidelines in coaching the national side to be followed by Nairn McEwan, Colin Telfer, Jim Telfer, Derrick Grant and Ian McGeechan so that presently Scotland are the envy of the rugby world with their quartet of World Cup coaches, Ian McGeechan, Jim Telfer, Derrick Grant and Douglas Morgan, all on the same wavelength and all revered by everyone in Scotland's squads and with splendid back-up as well from Richie Dixon, David Johnston, Ian Barnes, Bruce Hay and others.

No one needs to remind Scots that there have been very hard times – several post-war wooden-spoon 'whitewashes', that 44–0 humiliation at the hands of the Springboks at Murrayfield in 1951 that stood as a cruel reminder in all the record books as the biggest-ever hiding in a Cap international until Ireland, who have been at one with Scotland on numerous occasions over the years, ran up 60 points without reply against Romania at Lansdowne Road in 1986. Nor do any of those who

Scotland v England in the Sixties . . . a Murrayfield line-out tussle

Front-row union . . . Sandy
Carmichael, Frank Laidlaw,
Ian McLauchlan

experienced it ever want to dwell on the national gloom during those 17
consecutive defeats that ended in such unexpected fashion with a 14–8
triumph over a star-studded Wales at Murrayfield on 5 February 1955,
a match distinguished by one of the greatest individual tries ever seen
at Murrayfield when Arthur Smith (Cambridge University) was launched
by Adam Robson (Hawick) at half-way. Smith, of the silken grace, was
hemmed in but his marvellous control of pace took him to the Welsh
full-back, A. B. Edwards. He chipped over his head, tapped the ball on
with his foot, then swooped to pick up and dive over. When I handed over
the microphone to the inimitable Andrew 'Jock' Wemyss for his closing
comment on BBC Radio, there was a tear in his eye and he began: 'I can
hardly speak for we've come out of the long dark tunnel into the warm
sunshine.'

Scotland learned as the sun shone again for it was that catastrophic
sequence that pushed Scots into the coaching sphere with its slow but
admirable improvement in the national fortunes. Over the piece, for a
small country with limited resources, Scotland has a proud record but not
only in on-field peaks that came to a never-to-be-forgotten crescendo with
that 13–7 Grand Slam triumph over England at Murrayfield on 17 March
1990 but in fields of administration and in the leadership qualities of so
many of our top men. They were taking charge and imposing their own
sense of discipline and sensible application in the very beginning. Three
of the first six British Isles tours were captained by Scots of giant stature
– W. E. Maclagan (Edinburgh Academicals and London Scottish), Mark
Morrison (Royal High School FP) and 'Darkie' Bedell-Sivright (Cambridge
University and Edinburgh University). Alf Wilson, Doug Smith and George
Burrell figured as tour managers with the British Lions, Jim Telfer and Ian
McGeechan have been Lions coaches and Arthur Smith, Mike Campbell-
Lamerton and Finlay Calder have also captained the Lions on tour. Some
55 Scots have played in one or more Test matches for the British Lions.

Scotland have been Five Nations Champions outright on 13 occasions, have shared the Championship eight times, been Triple Crown winners ten times and have been thwarted only at the last Triple Crown hurdle by England virtually as often and they have swept the boards for Grand Slams on three occasions – 1925, 1984 and 1990. In the World Cup they were the only country capable of holding the mighty All Blacks to just two tries. When Wales were having their second 'golden era' from 1969 to 1979 they had most trouble from Scotland who, in three consecutive games against them at Murrayfield, held them to 18–19 then beat them 10–9 and 12–10. Scotland have played 36 games against national tour sides and are well in credit with 20 wins, 14 defeats and two draws. They have beaten the touring Wallabies five times, the touring Springboks three times and have held the touring All Blacks to a draw on two occasions. The mighty 1964 New Zealanders, led by Wilson Whineray, lost only one of 34 games and had beaten Ireland, Wales and England and went on to beat France in Paris. But this Scottish side refused to be overawed and held them to a 0–0 draw: Stewart Wilson (Oxford University); Christie Elliot (Langholm), Jim Shackleton, Iain Laughland, Ronnie Thomson (all London Scottish); Gregor Sharp (Stewart's College FP) and Tremayne Rodd (London Scottish); Brian Neill (Edinburgh Academicals), captain, Norman Bruce (London Scottish), David Rollo (Howe of Fife), Bill Hunter (Hawick), Peter Brown (West of Scotland), Jim Telfer (Melrose), Oliver Grant (Hawick) and Pringle Fisher (London Scottish).

Every decade has spawned Scots of such brilliance as to justify fully the tag of world class and, indeed, they still lead the world in certain areas. Colin Deans (Hawick) is the world's most Capped hooker with 52 appearances, John Rutherford (Selkirk) and Roy Laidlaw (Jed-Forest) hold the world record of 35 Cap international appearances as a half-back partnership, Gavin Hastings (Watsonians) is joint holder of the record of six penalty goals in an international, G. C. Lindsay (London Scottish) is equal holder of the record of five tries in a Cap international, Johnny Wallace (Oxford University) is one of only four players who have scored a try in each of the four internationals in a Five Nations Championship and the famous 'Flying Scot', Ian Smith, shared the record of eight tries in a Five Nations Championship and, until three years ago, held the world record of 24 tries in Cap internationals until that mark was beaten by Australia's David Campese. Probably the most exciting Scottish player of the post-war era, Andy Irvine (Heriots FP), once even scored five tries from full-back for the Lions against King Country/Whanganui in 1977!

The future looks promising too. The Scottish Rugby Union's Coaching and Youth Development subcommittee seek to promote a style of play 'that can be taught, coached and played at all levels of the game and which is best suited to the circumstances of rugby in Scotland'. It takes into account the Scottish climate and the characteristics of Scotland's playing personnel, and the basic elements from the background to Scotland's playing philosophy – skill, aggression, pace, fitness, discipline and positive attitude. This last element is aimed at developing positive rugby, 'not the promotion of foolhardy, devil-may-care play but an encouragement of players to exploit every reasonable attacking opportunity and to develop the fitness and skills necessary to recognise such opportunities and to approach the game in a positive, attacking frame of mind'.

The game in Scotland is in good hands. The coaching fraternity includes several highly respected international stalwarts. On the morning of the Scotland versus Argentina game on 10 November 1990 the back pitches at Murrayfield were flooded with mini-rugby players – 560 of them from over 50 clubs who enjoyed a series of friendly matches prior to being guests of the Scottish Rugby Union and of the sponsors, Adidas, at the international in the afternoon. What a kaleidoscope of youthful enthusiasm, endeavour and good spirit it presented, all organised by Douglas Arneil and the Scottish Rugby Union's Youth Development Officers under the encouraging eye of John Roxburgh. Those youngsters represent the future of the game in Scotland and assuredly, in time, will emulate their illustrious predecessors in putting their own special brand on the rugby game to the continuing admiration of friend and foe alike.

Big Al . . . Alastair McHarg
dresses for the weather!

Have Notebook, Will Travel

A Rugby Tourist's Tale

By BILL McMURTRIE

AUCKLAND'S DOMESTIC AIRPORT is not exactly the crossroads of the world, though it was probably not all that strange that, one morning in June 1990, I crossed the path of David Bishop, the New Zealand referee. I was on my way into Auckland from Palmerston North after the Scottish touring team's hard-won 19–4 victory over Manawatu the previous day, and he was heading home to the South Island from Buenos Aires, where he had refereed Canada's World Cup qualifying win over Argentina. The previous time we had spoken was three months earlier, just after he had refereed Scotland's 13–7 win over England in the winner-take-all Grand Slam decider at Murrayfield.

In that same airport, even more germane to the tale that follows, I met another New Zealander, Terry O'Connor, the likeable man from Pukukohe who had been the 1981 Scottish touring team's baggage manager and general factotum. He had turned up at the airport to see if the Scots were on the early-morning flight from Palmerston North, and he was back later in the day, when they did fly in.

Inevitably, the conversation with Terry revolved round the current tour rather than the one in which he had been involved and, exacting critic though he was, he was full of admiration for the Scots. The tourists had gone undefeated in all of their provincial games, which the previous Scottish teams in New Zealand had not done in 1975 and 1981, and their performance in Palmerston North especially appealed to Terry. He complimented the Scots on how they had stood up for themselves in that bruising encounter, touching the borderline of violence, and that, most significantly, was by the tourists' second string. Only Kenneth Milne, the Heriot's hooker, and the two utilised replacements, Scott Hastings and Damian Cronin, were to take the field the following Saturday against the All Blacks in the second Test, the final tour match. By their performance, resilience, and courage the Scots reserve XV set the tone for the Eden Park international. They provided the back-up for the first-choice XV to come back from the 31–16 defeat in the first Test the previous Saturday at Carisbrook, Dunedin.

Rarely, as they did at Eden Park, can a Scottish XV have done so much to deserve victory without achieving it. Only seconds before the interval they led 18–9. Scotland's first win over New Zealand was in sight, only 41 minutes away. Dead-eye Grant Fox, however, kicked a penalty goal in the last minute of the first half, and he chipped the All Blacks to a 21–18 victory with three more after the interval. So it was that three decades of international tours were completed with Scotland showing only one Test win in the southern hemisphere. That one light was the 12–7 victory over Australia at Ballymore in 1982.

It is a tale of touring that began 30 years earlier in Port Elizabeth, South Africa. In that time Scotland have visited 13 countries. I have had the honour to be with them to record the tours in ten of those for the *Glasgow Herald*, and among the players Peter Dods, the Gala full-back, has the phenomenal record of having been on nine of Scotland's past ten tours. He missed the 1989 visit to Japan as he was with the Lions in Australia later that year.

When Gordon Waddell led Scotland to South Africa for three matches in 1960 he was the captain of an expeditionary force who travelled a roundabout way to the opening match in Port Elizabeth – via London, Frankfurt, Lisbon, Las Palmas, Windhoek and Johannesburg. Never had any of the tour Home countries previously gone solo on tour to a major rugby nation. Yet here the Scottish Rugby Union, so often accused of holding back, were leading the way. Others have followed on short tours around the world, though none has been abroad as often as the Scots, certainly not since 1980. The only year Scotland have missed since then was 1983, when the Lions were in New Zealand.

Gordon Waddell . . . captain of a Scottish expeditionary force

Lift-off . . . the young
Melrose giant Doddie
Weir reaches for the sky
against the Argentinians at
Murrayfield. 1990

David Sole on the charge
against the Pumas. 1990

Referee David Bishop awards
a penalty in Scotland's
favour against the Welsh at
Murrayfield. 1991

Derek White crashes through the Welsh defence to score Scotland's first try during the 32–12 victory at Murrayfield. 1991

The Edinburgh Academicals' hooker John Allan made a big impact before falling victim to a rib injury and making way for Kenny Milne. 1991

Damian Cronin rises
above the rest. 1991

David Sole, Paul Burnell,
Chris Gray and Derek
Turnbull watch intently as
Welsh scrum-half Robert
Jones gets away his
pass. 1991

England's Wade Dooley is thwarted by the combined efforts of Damian Cronin and Derek Turnbull. 1991

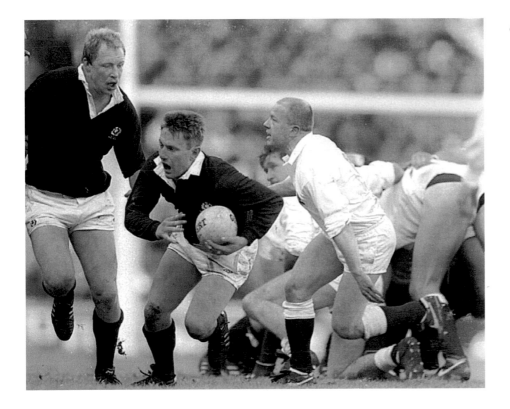

Gary Armstrong, who was in the eyes of many the player of the season, evades Richard Hill in order to make one of his sniping runs. 1991

Ireland's Brian Robinson takes the low road to try success despite the best efforts of Gary Armstrong and John Jeffrey. 1991

David Sole is well held by the Irish defence. 1991

Panic over . . . Scotland's right-winger Tony Stanger thwarts Irish intentions as the ball ricochets over the Scots' line from a corner flag line-out. 1991

Scott Hastings pulls down Brendan Mullin just a yard short of the Scottish line and averts a certain Irish try. Brother Gavin lends tactical support. 1991

Touchdown . . . a try for
Tony Stanger as the Hawick
winger puts the finishing
touches to a well worked
move off the back of
a scrum. 1991

The one that got away . . .
Phil Matthews makes ground
despite the best efforts of
John Jeffrey. 1991

Such was the novelty of a short tour that in 1960 the Scots started with the international against South Africa. Perish the thought that any schedule should be drawn up that way now. As it was, South Africa won by 18–10, but the Scots went on to win their two provincial matches, 21–11 against Griqualand West and 30–16 against East Transvaal. The late Arthur Smith scored three tries in that last match, still a record for a Scot on tour in any of the senior rugby-playing countries though three others have surpassed that figure in Canada and Zimbabwe.

Norman Bruce, the London Scottish hooker, scored a try for the tourists in the first minute of the Test. The late Arthur Smith converted, but what hopes the Scots had of expanding that lead were knocked back when George Stevenson, the Hawick centre, was injured soon afterwards. He struggled on, but by the time Smith scored and converted it was only to cut the final margin back from 18–5.

Four years later Scotland went on a less demanding tour, winning all five matches in Canada. In only two other tours have the Scots had a 100% record – 1977 in the Far East, and 1988 in Zimbabwe.

Ontario gave the Scots a stuffy game as the opener in Toronto, the tourists winning 17–10. Before they left Toronto, though, the Scots had added a 75–0 win over Ontario Universities, and there followed victories against British Columbia by 21–0, Western Canada 14–3, and Quebec

Peter Dods . . . Scotland's tourist of the decade

Hector Monro . . . the Dumfriesshire MP was forced to cut short tour management duties in order to fight a snap General Election

45–3. Keith Bearne, the Liverpool back-row forward, had five tries against the Ontario students, and Sandy Hindshelwood, the Stewart's wing, followed suit in the Montreal match against Quebec. To score five tries in a match remains a record for a Scot on tour, though 24 years later David Leckie, Edinburgh Academicals' number eight, equalled it against the Goshawks in Mutare, Zimbabwe.

At the time of the 1964 tour 15 of the Scots were Capped. Seven of the eight others went on to play international rugby. The one exception was John Buchanan, the Jordanhill College forward. On that tour only Brian Neill, the Edinburgh Academicals prop who led the Scots, wore a jersey with a thistle. All the others had to make do with the plain dark blue, and it was not until the 1969 tour to Argentina that a tour tie was introduced. The right to wear the tie was retrospective, and those who had been on tour to South Africa and Canada were invited by the SRU to purchase one – £2 plus 1s 6d for postage and packing.

Inside less than nine months, between September 1969 and June 1970, Scotland went south on two tours, first to Argentina and then to Australia. Between those ventures, as well as the Five Nations Championship, Scotland's cosmopolitan programme included also a 6–3 win over South Africa, the Springboks' last appearance to date at Murrayfield.

Duncan Paterson, later to be Scotland's World Cup manager for 1991, was on both tours, and he cited the Argentinian venture as the harder, even though Caps were not awarded for the two Tests against the Pumas. Dunc also recalled that Jim Telfer, the Melrose forward who was Scotland's captain in Argentina, had a subtle way of ensuring that his fellow players did not lapse into the Argentinian habit of taking wine with every meal. As soon as he realised that the bottles were to be regularly on the table he simply asked his Melrose and Gala friends that, however much they were used to taking wine with their meals, they should desist for the benefit of those not used to such niceties.

On the field the Scots won their four provincial matches, though none by large margins, but they suffered a 20–6 defeat in the first Test in Buenos Aires, the Pumas scoring three tries to one by Mike Smith, the London Scottish wing. In that match, after Alex Travaglini's opening try, Ian Murchie, the powerful West of Scotland centre, suffered a broken collarbone, an injury that was to hamper his future career.

Bruce Laidlaw, the Royal High stand-off, replaced Murchie at centre for the second Test, also at Buenos Aires, and the Scots, more settled than they had been two weeks earlier, recovered from the loss of an early score to win by 6–3. Telfer started the scoring move around halfway, and after about half the team had handled Sandy Carmichael went over for the try. Colin Blaikie failed with the conversion but kicked a penalty goal before the interval, and the half-time score remained unchanged to the end.

On the Australian tour that followed, the Scots beat Victoria, New South Wales Country, and Sydney but lost the harder games against New South Wales and Queensland as well as the Test. The Wallabies scored six tries in their 23–3 win, Scotland's only response being a Wilson Lauder penalty goal. Lauder, the Neath flanker, emerged from the tour with a personal achievement that stood for 20 years. He scored 56 points in his five matches on tour, a figure that Andy Irvine equalled in his four games in New Zealand in 1981. The tally was the most any Scot scored on tour in a major rugby-playing country until Peter Dods surpassed it with 58 in his four games in New Zealand in 1990.

During the 1970 tour the Scots were deprived of their manager, Hector Monro, in unique circumstances. As MP for Dumfriesshire, he had to return home to fight a snap General Election. George Burrell took over, and in the course of the next seven years he was to be manager of two teams visiting New Zealand, the Scots in 1975 and the Lions in 1977.

Scotland's 1975 tour to New Zealand was the first on which they had a specifically designated coach: Bill Dickinson. The Scottish Rugby Union had enlisted him five years earlier as the first coach for the national

Andy Irvine . . . captain in New Zealand

team, though he was acknowledged by the euphemistic title of 'adviser to the captain'.

That tour started with a runaway win, the Scots beating Nelson Bays by 51–6 at Trafalgar Park and Andy Irvine scoring a try, eight conversions and a penalty goal. His total of 23 points was at that time the most by any Scot in a tour match. Defeats followed at the hands of Otago (19–15) and Canterbury (20–9), but the Scots swung into gear with wins over Hawkes Bay (30–0), Wellington (36–25), and Bay of Plenty (16–10). Jim Renwick, John Frame, and Ian McGeechan scored the Scots tries in the highly creditable win over Wellington, and Douglas Morgan converted the lot as well as kicking six penalty goals. His 24 points passed Irvine's record in the opening match.

Above all else, however, the tour will be remembered for the water polo Test at Eden Park, Auckland. More than four inches of rain had fallen in less than 12 hours, and conditions were so bad, with the ground almost a lake, that it was even suggested that the match might have to be cancelled; it could not be postponed because of the Scots' flight home the following day. More than 45,000 braved the weather, and the match went ahead.

Scotland had to face a torrential gale in the first half, and at the interval, down only 0–6, they felt they had a chance. The icy wind, however, swung almost 180 degrees, and the Scots had to face it. New Zealand won 24–0 with four tries – all, incredibly, converted by Joe Karam.

Bruce Hay, now the Boroughmuir coach, had cause to remember that match with regret. It was his first Cap, but within quarter of an hour of the kick-off he had a broken arm. Irvine had to switch to his usual position at full-back, and Billy Steele took over as replacement.

Two years later, with Nairn McEwan doubling as player and coach, Scotland swept through a Far East tour, winning all five matches and

Alan Lawson . . . Liberace's shadow

Fin and Jim . . . the Calder twins were joined in Australia by brother John

finishing off with a 74–9 victory over Japan in Tokyo, though they led only 16–3 at half-time. Bill Gammell, still then with Edinburgh Wanderers before joining Heriot's, scored four of the 11 tries against Japan, and Colin Mair, the West of Scotland full-back, kicked nine conversions and four penalty goals. Over the tour Gammell had ten tries, Mair kicked 63 points, and for some of the games Brigadier Frank Coutts, president of the SRU that year, piped the Scots out on to the field.

Humidity on the day of the opening match against Thailand in Bangkok – an 82–3 win – was such that the Scots realised they would need to replace fluid while play was going on. So they spaced supplies of water and fruit down each touchline to replenish themselves at any stoppage, much to the consternation of the Thai referee.

Another referee, Peter Hughes, now Lancashire representative on the Rugby Football Union committee, accompanied the Scots, and in the first game he had charge of he must have forgotten where he was. For the initial 20 minutes he spoke in French!

When Scotland visited France in 1980, even though for just three matches, with Jim Telfer as coach, it was the true beginning of the era of touring. Telfer, Ian MacGregor, convener of the selection committee, and others with fingers on the pulse realised by then that the one way our small nation's rugby could develop was for it to be tested against the best. In successive years the Scots visited not only France but also New Zealand and Australia. The opposition was the best, and it was on those tours that Telfer laid much of the foundation of the Grand Slam that was to follow in 1984.

Scotland's record in their three 1980 matches in France was not good, with a draw and two defeats, but with Roy Laidlaw, Colin Deans, and David Johnston scoring tries they contributed much to an entertaining contest in which they lost to the French Barbarians by 22–26 in Agen. It was the first game the new French invitation club played, and for the occasion they trotted out most of their country's 1977 Grand Slam team, even if that meant that Jean-François Imbernon had to play with his legs so wrapped in bandages that he appeared almost to be tied together.

Peter Dods – his name will appear frequently from now on in this brief history – scored the only points with penalty goals in the two other matches, both against French XVs, a 20–6 defeat in Bordeaux and a 6–6 draw in a thunder-and-lightning storm in Brive.

Scotland were short of regulars for that French tour, mainly because of the Lions' visit to South Africa, but the following year, with Andy Irvine as captain, they mustered almost the full complement for the visit to New Zealand. John Beattie, already a Lion at the age of 22, was a notable absentee because of severe knee damage, an injury he received in training for the tour, but the door was opened for two young number eight forwards, Iain Paxton and Derek White. Ironically, a knee injury during the tour removed White from the competition for the international berth vacated by Beattie, and Paxton was left to win his first Cap in the Dunedin Test.

Three years later Beattie and Paxton were to return to New Zealand as the Lions' number eight forwards, and they were also in Scotland's Grand Slam squad the following year. White had to wait until 1990 to savour a Grand Slam.

In the opening game of the 1981 tour, scoring 24 points against King Country in Taumarinui, Andy Irvine, Scotland's captain, matched the record Morgan had set five years earlier in Wellington. The Scots won that Taumarinui match comfortably by 39–13, and Irvine repeated the 24-point tally in the 32–9 win over Wairarapa-Bush at Masterton.

On the Saturday between those games the Scots fell to Wellington by 15–19, and Roy Laidlaw lost his deputy as scrum-half. Gordon Hunter's jaw was broken in that game, and Alan Lawson had to be called out from home. Hunter's tour T-shirt carried the nickname 'Liberace' because of his habit of playing the first three bars of Beethoven's *Moonlight Sonata* on every piano he encountered, and, inevitably, Lawson when he arrived was presented with one bearing the legend 'Liberace's Shadow'.

A week after the Wellington game the tourists beat Canterbury 23–12 at Lancaster Park, Canterbury, with a performance that Jim Telfer, as coach, described as the best he had seen by any Scottish team abroad. The Scots were heeding the lessons of how to compete in New Zealand rugby.

In the first Test in Dunedin the Scots proved they were learning, though handicapped by the conditions, with sheets of rain sweeping the ground. Colin Deans scored their only try, exploiting Graeme Higginson's loose line-out tap on a hack and chase that was mainly all his own work, but others were agonisingly close. Steve Munro was across the line, though penalised for reputedly lifting the ball over. Irvine twice dropped awkward passes, David Leslie was recalled from the posts for being offside, and the All Blacks won by 11–4.

New Zealand had a far wider margin in balmy conditions in the

Jim Aitken . . . suffered first defeat as skipper on tour in Romania

Sean McGaughey

second Test, winning 40–15, their biggest score then in international rugby, though less than ten minutes from the end the Scots were still in with a shout, only seven points adrift. They might even have been closer had not Munro been caught by Bernie Fraser as he was escaping into wide space on the right. A fully fit Munro might well have made the long run to the line, but the Ayr wing had been confined to his room earlier in the week because of a virus; its aftermath was still affecting him. In the last seven minutes New Zealand scored three tries all converted by Allan Hewson. 'What was the influence behind that surge?' I asked Graham Mourie, the All Blacks' captain. 'We felt threatened,' he replied. 'We had to step up our game.' It was both a backhanded compliment to Scotland and a commentary on a vital ingredient in any top-notch team.

Before the Canterbury match the Scottish District Championship flag, a Saltire with inscriptions, was paraded round the ground by a couple of kilted supporters – it was its first appearance in public since it had mysteriously disappeared from a Border club's flagpole earlier that year. Naturally, Ken Smith, the tourists' manager, himself a kenspeckled Borderer, wanted it back in official hands, and eventually it was returned, though only after a travelling supporter, the late Eric Donaldson, at that time an Edinburgh selector, had negotiated a ransom. The price was two tickets for the Auckland international.

A year later Scotland, again led by Andy Irvine, were back on the trail to the southern hemisphere, their departure from Heathrow delayed by more than 12 hours. As we boarded the bus taking us to an airport hotel for the unscheduled overnight stop-over, Iain Milne asked, rhetorically of course: 'Does that mean we get an extra day in Australia?'

By the time they arrived in Brisbane they were fully 24 hours behind schedule, but three days later, after a two-and-a-half-hour flight into the outback, the Scots comfortably won their opening match. Led by Alan Tomes, the Hawick lock, the Scots beat Queensland Country by 44–16 at Mount Isa.

Their stay included a visit to the depths of the earth in the huge mineral mines there, but the official party had to decline a match-day invitation for three to join the local flying vet on a trip across the state line to a cattle station in Northern Territory and a different time zone. Two scribes and a supporter, Mike Dawson, whose voice is known to millions as the regular announcer at Murrayfield, filled the empty seats in the vet's plane for the flight out of Mount Isa before dawn. Breakfast was steak straight from a pot on an open fire. Work done, the vet flew us back to Mount Isa in time for lunch and the Scots' late afternoon kick-off.

Back to reality after the up-country win, the Scots lost to Queensland by 7–18 at Ballymore and by 13–22 to Sydney, but a midweek win in Melbourne's cool, damp air, a sharp contrast to Mount Isa, restored the tour to its intended course. Led by another lock, Bill Cuthbertson, the Scots beat Victoria 38–3. John Calder, the Stewart's Melville forward, scored two tries in that match only three days after he had arrived as a replacement, joining his brothers, Jim and Finlay, and as if that were not enough the newcomer had another brace in the 44–3 win over New South Wales Country in Singleton the following midweek.

When John Calder arrived the players' fines committee decreed that the brothers would have to forfeit three dollars each if they were ever photographed together. It was a picture that had to be taken sooner or later, and it cost one Sydney newspaper the princely sum of nine dollars (about six pounds at that time) as a contribution to the players' fund.

Between those matches, back at Sydney Cricket Ground, the tourists avenged one of their earlier defeats. With a much-improved game, especially by the forwards, the Scots won by 31–7 against a New South Wales XV which included no fewer than 13 of the Sydney team who had beaten the tourists. It was a result that drew Ian MacGregor, the Scottish manager, to comment on how the forwards had played much more like a touring pack. Scotland led only 9–7 at the interval, but in the last ten minutes the surging forward domination was turned into a convincing weight of points. Jim Telfer's work with the forwards was paying off, and Andy Irvine was back on form with his kicking, converting two of the three tries as well as scoring four penalty goals.

On the day after that match the Scots had one of those interludes that breaks the strain of travelling and training. The coach journey from Sydney north to Singleton included a stop for a barbecue lunch at one of the Hunter Valley vineyards, a memorable meal, not only for the accompanying wine but also for its setting against the background of the quaintly named Broken Back mountain range.

After Singleton, with the Scots' 44–3 win over New South Wales Country, they returned to Ballymore and a famous victory, beating Australia 12–7. It was Scotland's first – and, so far, only – win in the

Opposite:
Hawick's Alastair Campbell

southern hemisphere, a fine way to mark Andy Irvine's 50th Cap. Gerry McGuinness, the West of Scotland prop, and Rick Gordon, the London Scottish centre, each remember it as his first international.

As a contest, the Test was too close and tight to be memorable. Mistakes littered the match too often. Scotland erred less frequently. Their game was more resilient: they weathered a Wallaby storm in the first half, and latterly the Scots merited success through mounting pressure.

Scrummaging made the Scottish try. Twice in succession the Australians lost possession on their own goal-line. First the Scots forced a ragged heel from which Roy Laidlaw caught his opposite number, Philip Cox, and then Colin Deans nicked a tight-head strike. Laidlaw drifted to the right, John Rutherford threw out a long pass, and Keith Robertson went over in the corner. Irvine's touchline conversion took the tourists to 9–3 with 12 minutes gone in the second half.

It had been a different story in the first half. With 20 minutes gone the Scots had been in the Australian half only once, but that was the occasion for Rutherford's drop goal to open the game's scoring.

Nine minutes after Robertson's try Michael Hawker replied for Australia, exploiting a rare defensive lapse by the Scots, but Irvine made sure with a penalty goal from all of 45 metres after Tony Shaw had punched Colin Deans. Six months earlier the same Shaw had felled Bill Cuthbertson at Murrayfield; Scotland had won then, too.

After a 22–4 win over Australian Capital Territory in Canberra the Scots felt the Wallabies' backlash. Australia made three changes with the return of the Queensland trio, Paul McLean, Roger Gould, and Peter Grigg, and the Wallabies' revenge was sweet with a 33–9 win. Irvine scored Scotland's points with three penalty goals, all for scrummage infringements, two for offside and one for a collapse that prevented a pushover try. It was small consolation that those nine points carried his tally to over 300 in international rugby – 273 for Scotland and 28 in Tests for the Lions.

Scotland did not tour in 1983. Instead, eight Scottish players went with the Lions to New Zealand, as did Jim Telfer as coach. It was a sorry tour, the Lions losing all four Tests as well as the games against Auckland and Canterbury. But the Scots profited later. The eight Lions formed the basis of Scotland's 1984 Grand Slam XV and within months Telfer's sadness turned to jubilation. It was appropriate that the deciding win against France was on his birthday, 17 March, as was the Grand Slam win over England six years later.

Two months after the Grand Slam in 1984 Scotland, ever eager to break new ground, had a three-match tour in Romania, and it was quickly apparent that it would not be plain sailing. The first game was played in a thunderstorm, the slippery surface was laked with pools of rainwater, the ball was liable to squirt out of seemingly firm grasps, and the Scots beat a Bucharest XV by just 6–3. The only scores were two penalty goals by Peter Dods.

In the second game the Scots, profiting from a stern downfield wind, pulled back from a 3–15 deficit at half-time and beat South-East Romania

28–18 in Constanta on the Black Sea coast. Even such a high-scoring match had only two tries, both by the Scots, the first by Peter Steven and the second by Douglas Wyllie. Dods kicked 17 points, but the honours among the Scots belong mostly to Sean McGaughey, the Hawick breakaway forward, who celebrated his 21st birthday with driving play that was the pack's catalyst.

McGaughey was duly selected for his international debut the following Sunday. So was Gary Callander, the Kelso hooker, standing in for the absent Colin Deans. McGaughey celebrated his selection by climbing over the balustrade of his hotel room's balcony and doing exercises hanging outside – 12 or 13 storeys up! Callander later went on to captain Scotland, but the Bucharest game was to be McGaughey's only Cap. The fearsome promise he showed in Constanta was not fulfilled. We had thought there that we had seen the next David Leslie.

Jim Aitken led Scotland for the seventh time in the Bucharest international, and it was to be his first defeat, after a Twickenham win to open his captaincy, the incredible 25–25 draw with the All Blacks at Murrayfield, and the 1984 Grand Slam. In unaccustomed conditions, with a May sun grilling the August 23 Stadium, the Scots tried and let slip a 19–12 lead to fall by 22–28. Aitken admitted afterwards that his tongue was so dry that it all but stuck to his mouth, and he could hardly raise a whisper to urge his Scots on.

Even in defeat Dods passed a personal international milestone. His 15 points with a try, conversion, and three penalty goals included his 100th for Scotland: he was only the second Scot to reach three figures in international rugby, following Andy Irvine.

Scotland returned to Canada in 1985, 21 years after their first visit, and one game across the 49th Parallel was thrown in as extra spice. It was, however, not the best of tours. For one reason it was the wrong way round. It started with the harder half of the Canadian section in British Columbia, and the Scots paid the penalty. British Columbia beat the tourists 22–13, scoring three tries in the last quarter of an hour, whereas the Scots finished the trip with a record 79–0 win over Alberta in Calgary.

First signs of uneasiness were to be seen when Scotland needed tries by David Leslie and Iwan Tukalo in the last five minutes of the opening match against Vancouver Island in Victoria. Victory by 20–10 was thus salvaged, instead of the draw to which the game was heading as injury time loomed. Island's defence was exceptional. They were more like a red wall than the Crimson Tide, their *nom-de-guerre*, and even Iain Milne was cut down three times close to the Islanders' goal-line, twice by Guy Prévost, a brave little centre about 100lb lighter than the Bear. It was also the match of the ripping jerseys. No fewer than 13 jerseys were so badly torn that they had to be replaced. The quality of the material fell far short of what the Scottish Rugby Union expected, and the embarrassed suppliers sent out replacements in time for the match against British Columbia over on the mainland at the picturesque Brockton Oval, overlooking Vancouver Harbour and the backdrop of the Rockies.

Scotland's back play against British Columbia did not reflect the command their forwards achieved in the first hour, and when the heart latterly went out of the tourists' pack British Columbia added another notable scalp to their collection. The 1966 Lions lost to British Columbia, as did the 1958 Wallabies.

After that defeat the Scots retreated across the border to play against the United States' West Coast Grizzlies in Seattle. The Scots, though down 0–6 early on, won by 32–6, and they then adjourned to Alberta for two comfortable wins. They beat the Wolverines' invitation XV by 62–6 at Ellerslie Park, Edmonton, and then won against Alberta by 79–0 at Kingsland Rugby Park, Calgary. Peter Dods, playing on the right wing to allow Gavin Hastings in at full-back, scored 43 points in that last match, including four tries, and over the tour he had 75 points. Both tallies were points records for Scots on tour.

Such high-scoring games created obvious doubts about the tour's value to the Scots. An international between Canada and Scotland would have heightened the appeal, even if the tourists had not awarded Caps. That was not possible as Canada went off on tour to Australia while the Scots were in Alberta.

A year later Scotland took on a far more demanding tour with four matches in France after a 39–17 win over Spain in Cornella, near Barcelona. The only win in France was in the final game, when the Scots beat a Tarn Select 26–7 in Graulhet. Defeats by Côte Basque (40–19) and the French Barbarians (32–19) sandwiched a creditable draw (16–16) with a French XV in Tarbes.

By any measure the defeat in Bayonne was crushing. On their day Côte Basque are one of the strongest representative non-international rugby teams in the world, rivalling even Auckland. They would not have disgraced the national XV, though they had only a few Caps such as Patrice Lagisquet, Marc Sallefranque, Jean Condom, Francis Haget and Laurent Rodriguez. After only 13 minutes the French led 18–0, and at half-time the score was 28–3. It was to the Scots' credit that, refusing to succumb to a French Flodden, they worked back the try count to 7–3.

In all but name the match against a French XV in Tarbes was an international. The posters around the town described it so, and on a balmy night the atmosphere, though scaled down, was worse than Parc des Princes. Horns hooted, firecrackers blasted and the crowd bayed, but the Scots put the Bayonne defeat behind them. Scotland's breakaways, John Jeffrey, John Beattie, and Derek Turnbull, worked wonders. Beattie and Jeffrey scored the tries, and when Peter Dods converted the second the Scots led 13–6. It was, however, not enough of a cushion against a typical try by Patrick Esteve and two penalty goals by Jean-Patrick Lescarboura, he of the big boot and the Desperate Dan chin.

As in 1980, the French Barbarians fielded a team too strong for the Scots. Serge Blanco was in their number. So were Jean-Baptiste Lafond, Laurent Pardo, Jean-Pierre Garuet, Jean-Luc Joinel and Alain Carminati, who was to find infamy four years later by being sent off in a Murrayfield international. In the dust of a boiling Agen day the Scots started well, leading 13–6 after 25 minutes, but they could not maintain their pace and pressure. The French scored four tries in the next 25 minutes.

John Beattie maintained his ever-present record at number eight when the Scots played at Graulhet. Two other breakaway forwards, Derek White and Iain Paxton, had to be paired at lock because of injuries to Alan Tomes and Alistair Campbell, and Tarn, augmented by three outsiders, worried the Scots in a hard-fought match, sometimes nasty. Only in the last four minutes did the Scots find the control that had been missing from their game. In that time Douglas Wyllie scored two tries, adding to White's early one.

A year later the Scots were abroad again, this time in New Zealand for the inaugural World Cup. A draw with France was an early handicap, and though comfortable wins followed over Zimbabwe and Romania, the Scots finished only second in their group because they had scored fewer tries in their opening match. The consequence was a quarter-final with New Zealand and a 30–3 defeat. Gavin Hastings scored an international world record of 27 points in the 55–28 win over Romania at Carisbrook, Dunedin, but it lasted only a couple of hours. Didier Camberabero surpassed it with 30 for France against Zimbabwe the same day.

In 1988 Scotland won all five matches in Zimbabwe, only the third time they had had a 100% record on tour. Yet they did not play the game they had planned. The opening match in Harare was enough to convince the coaches, Richie Dixon and David Johnston, that the Scottish forwards would have to switch their second-phase base from ruck to maul. The hard grounds were more conducive to mauling, but, just as demanding, the Zimbabwean referees did not allow rucking at all. To say the least, some of the other interpretations, too, were weird.

It was so nearly disastrous off the field. The day after the uneasy opening win over Mashonaland by 16–12 the Scots were not even out of Harare when their bus was hit by a runaway cement truck. Miraculously, no injury was serious. A couple of faces had minor cuts that were soon cleaned, and the journey to Mutare resumed in a bus with a choking engine. Jock Steven, the tour manager, suggested that, as a farmer, if he had a tractor making that noise he would be tempted to scrap it.

In the 48–6 win over the Goshawks in Mutare, a township close to the frontier with Mozambique, David Leckie, the Edinburgh Academicals number eight, equalled the record of five tries by Keith Bearne and Sandy Hinshelwood 24 years earlier in Canada. On the morning of that match Leckie tuned up for his memorable afternoon by playing his bagpipes; the hotel staff could only stop and listen in amazement. A week later, after a one-night visit to Victoria Falls – where the team's hotel boasted riverside notices warning of crocodiles – Leckie scored three more tries in the 53–6 win over Mashonaland Country Districts at Kadoma. He finished as third top points scorer on the tour behind Peter Dods, the tour captain who had 42 in three games, and Ian Ramsey, the Melrose full-back who had 34 from two games.

That Kadoma match was sandwiched by Test victories in Bulawayo and back in Harare, Greig Oliver, the Hawick scrum-half, scored three tries in the first Test, a match in which the Scots could not maintain their initial impetus in Bulawayo's broiling heat. They still won comfortably by 31–10, and the second Test's margin was even wider (34–7).

Scotland, however, had no bigger win than their next tour match, a year later, opening their visit to Japan with a 91–8 win at the Prince Chichibu Memorial Rugby Ground, Tokyo. The victims were East Japan. Cameron Glasgow contributed 39 points by scoring two of the 15 tries, converting all but one of them, and kicking a penalty goal.

Three days later the Scots beat Kyushu 45–0 in Fukuoka, and given that the wet conditions were far from amenable, it was not far short of being as comprehensive a victory as the opening win. Harder games were to follow and when the Scots visited Osaka the Japan Under-23 team gave the tourists a taste of what was to come in the Test, though the margin was substantial enough at 51–25. The Scots were leading 36–9 in sticky, humid weather when they ran into rugby's equivalent of the marathon runner's wall. The home youngsters pulled the Scots back to 36–25 with three tries inside five minutes, but the tourists stuck to their game and won through, with Glasgow converting all seven tries as well as scoring one and kicking three penalty goals.

In two games Glasgow had scored 66 points, kicking all but one of the 22 conversions he attempted. He was only nine points short of the record Peter Dods had set in North America four years earlier, but he had a disaster of an afternoon when the Scots returned to the Chichibu ground for the Test.

After a 39–12 win over West Japan in Nagoya, the only floodlit match on the tour, they were confident of becoming only the third Scottish team to win all their games on tour, but on another sultry afternoon they were denied this by a team of contrasts. Japan's rugby at its best was gloriously exciting, typical of the national mien. At its worst it was cynically defensive. Japan went into the match determined to deny the Scots by fair means or foul. The home players were prepared to risk limbs, if not their lives, in killing ball on the ground. Twice Les Peard, the Welsh referee, warned home forwards for repeatedly going over the top of the ball, but all that happened was that, like the Hydra's head, another would appear to thwart the Scots. Peard awarded 23 penalties against Japan and only eight against the Scots, but the tourists could not profit. Glasgow had lost his kicking touch. He missed five penalties before Greig Oliver took over, pulling the Scots back to within two points at 18–20. Other Scots were out of sorts, and Japan, exploiting the escape from penalty, ran in four tries to the tourists' one in winning 28–24.

Almost as soon as that tour was over other Scots were on their way across the world with the Lions to New Zealand. Finlay Calder, the unexpected choice as Scotland's Championship captain that year, led the Lions, Ian McGeechan was coach, and with them were eight fellow Scots – Gavin and Scott Hastings, Peter Dods, Craig Chalmers, Gary Armstrong, John Jeffrey, Derek White and David Sole.

After the loss of the first Test the Lions came back to win the series. McGeechan was hailed as an outstanding coach, Calder justified the initial confidence in his leadership despite the criticisms fired his way after the first Test, and Sole took command in wins over New South Wales and, more significantly, against the Anzac XV, mainly Australians with a smattering of New Zealanders.

The following season at home Sole led Scotland to six successive victories, equalling the country's longest winning run in international rugby, and that culminated in the Grand Slam. So the scene was set for Scotland's 1990 tour to New Zealand – the duel between the World Cup holders and Europe's Grand Slam champions. For that reason alone, it was the most demanding tour Scotland had undertaken, and in terms of results, despite defeats in the two Tests, it was the most successful. The Scots were unbeaten in their provincial matches – five wins and a draw. No Scottish team had previously done that on an extended visit to a major rugby-playing country.

Gisborne, so far east it sees the first light of every day, was as pleasant as any place to open a tour. It had a homely, laid-back air, amenable for a whole week's preparation, and yet when match day came the Scots had no doubt where they were. The atmosphere before a tour game in New Zealand, even in small townships, is unparalleled.

John Beattie . . . a powerful number eight forward

Settling in, the Scots won comfortably against an East Coast/Poverty Bay XV, accelerating away from 15–0 at half-time to 45–0, but three days later, 400 miles to the south, it was a different game. Wellington, among the powers in the land, were the opposition, and the Scots only sneaked a 16–all draw. The home team scored three tries to one by John Allan, but the tourists let slip chances, twice losing the ball over the goal-line. It was a lesson remembered thereafter as the Scots beat Nelson Bays/Marlborough by 23–6, Canterbury 21–12 and Southland 45–12.

Early optimism, however, was not realised in the first Test even though the Scots led twice in the first half. Ian Jones, the new, lanky All Black who had toured Scotland with the New Zealand youth team two years earlier, dominated the line-out, and as even more of a handicap the Scots were denied a scrummage put-in for nearly 30 minutes in the second half. Strapped for possession, the tourists lost 16–31.

Three days later the reserve string had that satisfying 19–4 win in the bruising match at Palmerston North, and despite the Dunedin Test defeat the Scots returned to Auckland still with confidence for the second match of the series. It was not misplaced, especially after two huge penalty goals by Gavin Hastings. Throughout the first half, with the benefit of a stiff breeze, Scotland carried the game to New Zealand, and with tries by Tony Stanger and Alex Moore, the latter in his debut international, the tourists led 18–12 at the interval. It was not enough, however, as Grant Fox kicked the All Blacks back with three penalty goals. Two long shots by Gavin Hastings hung up in the wind.

So it was that Scotland ended three decades of touring with only one international win – on that memorable Brisbane day in 1982.

To Coach or Not to Coach?

Scotland's Adviser to the Captain

By DEREK DOUGLAS

TO COACH OR NOT TO COACH? That was the question. Twenty years on the answer would appear to be so obvious that the question seems ridiculously irrelevant. But this serves only to underline how dramatic have been the changes in attitudes and perceptions which the game has undergone in the past two decades.

When Bill Dickinson, PE lecturer and successful mentor to the Jordanhill and Glasgow XVs, was appointed to direct the fortunes of the Scotland XV at the start of the 1971 Five Nations campaign there was a powerful body within the game's hierarchy which considered that Murrayfield had entered into a compact with Beelzebub himself — and maybe they would have been happier at that! Such was the strength of feeling against the appointment that officialdom could not even bring itself to utter the detested word 'coach'. When Dickinson was appointed to the post, the title he was given was charmingly idiosyncratic, and almost feudal: 'adviser to the captain'.

But Scotland had not been alone in its wrestling with the dilemma of whether to coach or not. Those opposed to the appointment of coaches at senior and international level adopted their stance because of a conviction that coaches would make the game more professional (with a small 'p'), that coaching would in some way render the game unacceptably serious, and that it would detract from the standing and contribution of the players, in particular that of the captain. The coaching trail had been blazed in France and in the Antipodes. While the Home Unions continued with their 'will we, won't we' stance, world rugby moved on and southern hemisphere teams set the standard.

In the mid-Sixties Wales seized the initiative and a WRU working party was set up to settle the issue, in the Principality at least. Its terms of reference were as follows: 'Having regard to all the circumstances, particularly our experiences during recent tours and the implications of the amendments to the laws, to examine the state of rugby football within the Union and its constituent clubs and to recommend to the coaching committee what steps, if any, should be taken to improve standards of play.'

By the beginning of season 1964—65 the Working Party had concluded that the standard of play did indeed require to be raised, that coaching had a vital role to play in achieving this aim and that steps

Bill Dickinson with some of
his Scotland charges, Nairn
MacEwan, Roger Arneil,
Sandy Carmichael and the
captain to whom he was
'adviser', P. C. Brown

Getting the message across
. . . Bill Dickinson, Scotland's
first coach – or as he was
known at the time, adviser
to the captain

should be taken without delay to implement a fully comprehensive coaching scheme. The WRU adopted its Working Party Report with alacrity. Within a matter of weeks over 130 of the Welsh Union's 150 senior clubs had appointed coaches and a plan for a series of national conferences and training sessions was set in motion.

The WRU declared that modern rugby was a game of wits and intelligence and that no one could play it without thinking it. Rugby, said the WRU, was a team game in which each player was an essential part of the team and each player had to play a full part in it. This could only be achieved if a player was very fit, had mastered all the skills of the game, and was alive to modern tactics. The 15 players were no longer to be considered separate entities as forwards and backs – a player had to subordinate himself to the disciplines that team tactics demanded and therefore had to obey the instructions of the person responsible for those tactics whether he was the team captain or the coach. The old orthodox method of forwards automatically retailing the ball to the backs as the only method of attack had been proved to be outdated. To be successful now, the Welsh visionaries declared, a team working as a unit had to develop a series of continuous attacks in order to break down set defences. Only when these defences had been engaged and committed would it be possible to exploit fully the situations thus created. The WRU stated in a message to supporters in the programme for the Wales v Scotland match at Cardiff Arms Park on 5 February 1966, that it was sure its embracing of the possibilities afforded by coaching had been an unqualified success. 'We are confident that when the natural talent and instinct for the game which exists in the Principality is fully harnessed, the enjoyment of players and spectators will be increased, and the place of Wales among the leaders of world rugby will be assured.' Such confidence was not misplaced as the glory days of Welsh rugby, Edwards, John, Bennett, JPR, Faulkner, Windsor and Price *et al* was but half a decade distant.

The Welsh experience is worth quoting at length because it points to the revolution which was taking place in world rugby in terms of the care and thought being devoted to tactics and on-field organisation. And organisation was what coaches at international level were bringing to the game. Five years later, the match between Scotland and Wales at Murrayfield on 6 February 1971, is recalled most often for the last-minute, corner-flag conversion by the bearded and Afro-coiffured Welshman John Taylor. The flanker's left-footed kick (the greatest conversion since St Paul, it was called in some quarters) secured for Wales a 19–18 win. But in the development of Scottish rugby this exciting game between the coaching pacesetters Wales and Scotland was crucially significant in that it was the first in which a Scottish XV prepared by a coach, even if he was called adviser to the captain, had taken the field.

Dickinson recalls: 'Adam Robson and I had taken the teams for the international trial that year. I took the Blues and Adam took the Whites. Then the team went to France and were beaten 13–8. Neither of us had anything to do with that team. Then I was asked by the convener of selectors, Lex Govan, if I would take on the Scotland XV. He was really

Cigar-smoking Nairn MacEwan succeeded Dickinson as coach to the national team. The tension shows as he watches from the Murrayfield stand

the man who was behind the appointment. You'll remember that there was great controversy at the time over whether we should have anything to do with coaching. There was no real lobbying so far as I was aware but Lex must have persuaded his committee. He wanted somebody to organise. Lex realised that it was necessary to move forward. In Scotland, at national level, we still had this concept of the captain as a kind of sacrosanct figure and that was why they called me adviser to the captain initially.'

The Scottish Rugby Union had set up a coaching advisory panel towards the end of the Sixties and Dickinson, coach to the unofficial championship-winning Jordanhill side in 1969, had been one of those appointed to it. An advisory coaching booklet called *Raising the Standard* had also been published but Scottish rugby was still split on the question of a coach for the national side.

'One of the things that some of them at the top of the rugby tree might have been afraid of was this supremo, this organiser that the focus would be on. They were afraid that the spotlight would be on an individual rather than the team. It was understandable, I suppose. You have to remember that in football in the same era Jock Stein was a huge figure. He was referred to as the supremo. Even in club rugby there weren't many coaches about. It really was in its infancy. We would have single-day courses for coaches at Murrayfield and then weekends at Riccarton but it really was in its infancy. Schoolmasters were doing a lot of work but at club level there was next to nothing. You have to remember, too, that these were the days still of the closed clubs and they operated very much in the traditions of the closed clubs,' says Dickinson.

Dickinson, a player at Hillhead before the Second World War, was a

Three of the forwards who played key roles in Bill Dickinson's Scotland line-up – Ian McLauchlan, Sandy Carmichael and Nairn MacEwan

senior physical education lecturer at Jordanhill College in Glasgow and before his emergence on the national scene in Scotland had coached successfully at club and district levels. He had, too, been a pathfinder for Scotland at numerous rugby coaching courses, principally run under the auspices of the Irish Rugby Union at Mosney, near Dublin, to which the rugby élite from all over the world gravitated each summer. When he was approached by Govan to take over the Scotland team, it was his prime objective to bring organisation to the side. 'Everybody had to know exactly what they were going to do. Lots of the guys came to sessions and they all had their own ideas. They were doing good things within their clubs but my job was getting these guys together and getting the organisation right at international level. In other words it was my task to get them to play as efficiently as they possibly could.

'I was called in on the Thursday before that match against Wales to look after the team for the Saturday. I was feeling my way of course. I was listening to the back row and somebody said, "Who'll take the first man round the scrum?" Now my third team at Jordanhill College werenae very good but they damn well knew where to go and what to do in that kind of situation. We had to sit and talk all those things out. We didnae need to worry too much about the attacking patterns because we had such brilliant individuals as Jim Renwick, Andy Irvine and Ian McGeechan. What you had to do with these particular people was give them the reins. But, to give you an example of the kind of defensive situations that I'm talking

MacEwan's law . . . Nairn MacEwan leaves squad session participants in no doubt as to what he intends

The former Hawick and Scotland stand-off Colin Telfer was next to assume the coaching role

about, there was always great discussion about what we would do when the opposition full-back came into the line. I mean somebody like, say, JPR or Villepreux. The question was whether we would let them run and let the cover take them or whatever. At that time I decided we would do the kamikaze thing. The winger would come in and take the full-back, and the full-back would cover and get the cover defence across. I wanted the running man to be dead, you know, the man with the ball. It sounds simple now but these were the kind of defensive patterns that we had to get worked out.'

In Dickinson's first season that one point loss to Wales was followed by a 17–5 loss against the Irish at Lansdowne Road but two wins within a week over the Auld Enemy. At Twickenham, Scotland did to England what John Taylor and Wales had done to them earlier in the season and a P. C. Brown conversion gave Scotland a 16–15 victory with the last kick of the game. A week later at Murrayfield, in an extra game to mark the centenary of the first international match, victory was more emphatic, Scotland winning 26–6 with John Frame having scored a try within 12 seconds of the kick-off.

Dickinson was aware that there was still within Scottish rugby an influential body of opinion which wanted nothing to do with coaches and that he was under personal attack for adopting too technical an approach to the game. After a few years in the job certain sections of the Press were referring to his team as 'Dickinson's Daleks'. Twenty years later, though, he dismisses such criticism. 'There was no basis for it. How can you criticise a team that guarantees – guarantees, mind you – its own ball? In the scrummage we were guaranteed our own ball, good ball that the backs could make use of. That's the position we were in with Ian McLauchlan, Sandy Carmichael, Al McHarg, P. C. and Gordon Brown and these people. The scrummage was so good that psychologically it had an effect on other countries. Not just the scrummage, big Al McHarg was probably the most consistent line-out player I've ever seen. The back-row varied a lot and I think I had about six scrum-halves in as many seasons. I was never on selection but Lex Govan, and the others later on, would consult me as to what was what. Selectors are reasonable guys. I never got any players that couldn't do the job that you wanted to do with different players. I used to say, if any of them wanted a good kicking stand-off, I don't need a kicking stand-off now that you've given me Douglas Morgan at scrum-half. We just need a running stand-off.

'You see, we had Ian McGeechan who was, simply, a brilliant player. He and Colin Telfer, you know, were largely responsible on the international field for the development of Andy Irvine. When Andy came into the side he wanted to do everything. He wanted to be in every bloody move because he was in every move with Heriot's at Goldenacre.

'Consequently we called all the backs' moves Chatterbox One, Chatterbox Two, Chatterbox Three and so on. Andy was always talking. We made use of it. I used to say to whoever was at outside-half, "Look, they'll be planning to stop Irvine" – they had to, he was such a marvellous player – "if he comes up it doesn't matter. If it's not on don't give it to him." Andy learned from Colin Telfer and Ian McGeechan that they were in control of the situation at out-half. Andy learned a lot from these people, you know. He learned when and where not to use his tremendous powers.'

Throughout his term of office Dickinson was always aware that as the first Scotland coach he was setting the standard for those who would follow, and in the early days it wasn't absolutely certain that the post would be permanent at all. 'I was well aware that if I had made a mess of it or if I had been too flamboyant then that would put the whole concept back a while. I'll not mention the name of the SRU president concerned but after an international when we had won and won well, he came up to me and said, "Aye, quite good but I still don't hold with coaching." You really couldn't blame the old brigade. They had been successful in their days but some of their views on rugby football tended to be parochial. They

Jim Telfer, who was to coach Scotland to Grand Slam success in 1984, oversees a squad session before the Wales international in 1982

Jim Telfer was a rugged
captain and an equally
rugged coach

saw Scottish rugby well enough but they didn't see it in a world context
as it is now. They didn't see where the game was going. I was fortunate
enough to have been invited to coach in France and America and had
been to South Africa and Ireland. I could see where the game was going
so far as clubs and so on were concerned.'

Dickinson feels that the other Home Unions were always 18 months
to two years ahead of Scotland in those days. 'Wales and England had
appointed coaching administrators in Don Rutherford and Ray Williams.
Ireland and Scotland were quite a long way behind that. I think Ireland
had somebody just before us but if they did then there was very little in
it. In France there had been people coaching for a very long time. It was a
very prestigious appointment in France. When I went over there as Scottish
coach they thought I would be living like the French coach in a chateau
or something. If you were coach to an international side it was quite a
profitable sideline to have.'

He left the job at the end of the 1977 Five Nations Championship.
He reckons that including provincial games on the 1975 tour to New
Zealand he prepared the Scotland XV on about 40 occasions. The team's
away record wasn't anything to write home about but they proved almost
invincible at Murrayfield, losing only once in 14 games and that was to
New Zealand.

'We weren't so hot away from home. I think we had only one away
win. Ireland, I think. We had some really close things in Paris, though.
We were beaten 10–9 and the game ended with Andy Irvine hitting the
post with a penalty. And the great Welsh sides, whom we beat twice, full
of Lions in '73 and '75. We beat them at Murrayfield and we were beaten
at Cardiff 6–3.'

Did he fall or was he pushed from the Scotland job? 'I didn't go

Jim Telfer, circa 1966, at a
Scotland warm-up session at
Myreside. Following Telfer is
Hawick's Derrick Grant, who
would follow him, too, as
Scottish coach

voluntarily. I was relieved of the position. Scotland's fortunes had not been so good. We lost at Twickenham in what turned out to be my last season and there would be a new committee, you see. They probably thought it was time for a change. I had been doing the job for a long time.

'It was all done very pleasantly. I was told by phone by the chairman of selectors at that time, Tom Pearson. I knew Tom very well because we were in the same profession. I was aware that changes would come. Sometimes the Press are quite helpful in those ways. One or two members of the Press felt that Dickinson should go. I'd had a fair crack at it and nobody was depriving me of my livelihood. Of course nobody is ever happy to have to demit office when you feel you still have a contribution to make. When I stopped being the national coach I was a far better coach than I had been when I started. I had learned so much along the way.'

The identity of Dickinson's successor took many people by surprise. Jim Telfer, then still to make his name on the world stage as a coach, had been helping Dickinson at Scotland and Scotland 'B' level and it had been assumed in some quarters, not least by Dickinson, that when the man in possession went then Telfer would get the job.

'He had been with me two or three years and I thought he would automatically be the man who would follow me but he didn't. He wasn't invited. He stayed on to coach the "B" side. I don't know whether he expected to get the job or not. I've never discussed it with him. But I'm sure he must have been a bit disappointed.'

Nairn McEwan was the man appointed to succeed Dickinson. He had been an outstanding flanker and captain of the Scotland side but at that time (he has since gone on to become a coach of renown) he was short on coaching experience. Dickinson says: 'Nairn had been injured and his place in the national side became slightly like this and like that. He was in and out. Nairn went out to Japan on the 1977 tour as player-coach and that was certainly an indication that he and not Jim Telfer might be involved after me. I think the selection of Nairn as coach at that time was a mistake, if they had let Nairn take the "B" side for a few years that is one of the areas of apprenticeship. Nairn had done a lot with North and Midlands, both playing and coaching, and the logical progression could have been from that to the "B" side but my personal opinion is that he was pushed into the national job too soon. I don't care whether you're an international player or not, and I never was, there's a huge difference between being a player and international coach and you've got to serve your apprenticeship just as all the ex-internationals coaching now have had their experience as coaches in club or district. There is a recognised system now.'

After Scotland, Dickinson went back to coaching at Jordanhill, by this time a joint College and FP side. Thereafter he had spells at Selkirk, Heriot's FP and West of Scotland. At the time of writing, and approaching his mid-70s, Dickinson is still involved with the game, as coach to the Division Seven side, Irvine.

Derrick Grant, a tireless loose-forward for Hawick, Scotland and the British Lions, was built in the Jim Telfer mould and succeeded him as Scotland coach

But it is as Scotland's first national coach that Dickinson's place in rugby history is secure. 'When I was no longer required and Nairn McEwan followed me I wrote to Frank Coutts, the SRU president, saying that now that my term of office was over it would be far better if they called the new person coach instead of adviser to the captain. That was a term understood throughout the world. I was always very aware of being the first and, looking back, I'm very happy to know that I didn't do anything which detracted from the game and prevented coaching becoming an integral part of the system here in Scotland.'

A pensive Ian McGeechan. The Yorkshire-Scot, who had played with distinction as a threequarter with Scotland and the British Lions, coached Scotland to a 1990 Grand Slam which culminated in a winners-take-all victory over England at Murrayfield

Another time, another hairstyle. Ian McGeechan at a Scotland squad session in the Seventies

Sterling Stirling

The County Phenomenon

By DAVID STEELE

IT IS WHAT HAS BECOME KNOWN in Scottish rugby circles as the Stirling County phenomenon: how a junior club which began life in the lowest reaches of the game worked its way up through every level, with a visit to every league, to become not only an asset to the top flight but genuine Championship contenders and a model for the future development of the game in Scotland.

Not only has the club made a tremendous impact in its own right but players who have learned their trade at Bridgehaugh have helped in the revival of Glasgow district rugby. From being cannon fodder a few seasons ago the Glasgow side has moved on to become McEwan's Inter-District champions and runners-up in successive seasons.

There are those in the district who still cry foul, claiming that the main reason there is such an important county influence on the Glasgow side is because chairman of selectors Ken Crichton and coach Richie Dixon are both associated with the Bridgehaugh club. But detractors must stand accused of savouring the bitter taste of sour grapes – for these are honourable men and in recent seasons a genuine case for selecting another player before a Stirling man would be hard to find. It must also be remembered that players who have given such excellent service to club and district – Stewart Hamilton, Ian Jardine, George Graham and Kevin MacKenzie to name but a few – have gone on to represent their country at 'B' level. Yet there is more to this club than just the established 'stars' – they will blush at the sobriquet and doubtless be ribbed mercilessly – there is a tremendous team spirit which starts with the first day at mini-rugby and continues through to the painful moment when the boots are hung up.

No one waved a magic wand over Bridgehaugh. It took many years of hard work and dedication from a wide range of men and women before Stirling could be built up into the club which exists now and which continues to grow. Perhaps the most telling statistic amid the welter of fascinating facts which are made readily available to the visitor is that over half of the first team regulars started with the club as youngsters at either the mini- or midi-level. It is intriguing to be shown the team lists for the first three XVs and told that of these 45 players some 28 started at mini- or midi-rugby or joined the club at junior level.

It is perhaps in this aspect of the Stirling County phenomenon that we find not the entire answer but at least a strong indication why things have

Stirling stalwart Stewart
Hamilton has brought
experience and commitment
to Bridgehaugh

worked out as they have. There are still hundreds of youngsters, aged from eight to 16, who are being introduced to the game through the mini- and midi-sections at Stirling County. A host of volunteers give up their time to assist them in the basic skills and to develop particular promise which a fledgling player may have demonstrated. Most important of all is the fact that, all else being equal, players who make a start at Stirling tend to put down their roots there and not wander the country from club to club. It is also worthy of note that it is not just at senior level that honours are being won by representatives of the club – players have appeared at all junior levels for Scotland, several also have pulled on Glasgow jerseys at various levels.

The seemingly inexorable rise of Stirling County began in the early 1970s and, while Bridgehaugh folk are too modest to take individual credit for any revival in the club's fortunes, the name of Ken Crichton does keep cropping up. The ground work had been done by others such as John Henderson and Ralph McNaught but when Crichton came from Howe of Fife in season 1972–73 the club's fortunes began the upward spiral which continues today. He was appointed club coach and won the respect of players and supporters alike. As the club's brochure to celebrate 75 years puts it: 'Ken Crichton viewed the playing malaise with customary accuity and, on being appointed club coach, he literally took the playing side by the scruff of the neck, set long-term targets, exacted obedience, gained respect both for himself and his methods and really worked.

'Players' fitness, mental approach, turn-out, playing facilities, equipment, leisure amenities, choice of opposition, nothing escaped him in his search for perfection.'

Crichton arrived in Stirling through his surveying business and at first continued his rugby with the Howe as they were attracting better fixtures. What a change for the County now with a wide range of top-grade friendlies and the lowest first XV opposition being Perthshire who are traditional rivals.

In 1974 Crichton suffered serious ligament damage. His playing career was over and the invitation came – entirely out of the blue – to follow a line of successful club coaches. 'It is true to say that I set fairly exacting standards for the senior players which were not always popular. But when any player sees the success which follows hard work he does not find it quite so difficult.'

He is quick to praise the people who worked with the club in the Seventies when a shake-up of the committee structure left the management team leaner and more efficient. 'I reckoned then, and still do, that an efficient management leads to efficient performance in rugby as well as in business. We have tried to provide the best possible facilities and support for these players and I am glad to say that we have been rewarded on the field of play.'

He smiles when club coach Richie Dixon leans across and says: 'We need the junkies like Kenny in rugby, it may seem like an unfortunate word, but for me it sums up the hold the game has on some folk. It is them we need in greater and greater numbers.'

It has been some of those 'junkies' who down the years have helped build the Stirling rugby nursery – full of fine young performers in their own right and, as Richie Dixon alludes to later, young people being given a grounding in the game which is found at too few clubs. Ken Crichton recalls: 'When I came on the scene in 1974 there was a suggestion made that mini- and midi-rugby should be built up and encouraged. I went out that autumn to New Zealand and by the time I returned the numbers had grown to 80 or 90.

'I was astonished and impressed by the efforts of people like the late Ben Coull and Ian Nelson. They and others had written to every primary school in the area telling them what the plans were and asking if there was any interest. There was. We still have marvellous numbers at mini- and midi- and the rewards are being reaped.'

Stirling County was formed in 1946 by the amalgamation of Stirling High School FP and Bridge of Allan rugby clubs. In many ways it was the resurrection of an 'old' club as there are records of a Stirling Town and Stirling County playing rugby last century. It was also the kind of marriage of convenience which we are witnessing in the Nineties – two clubs close to each other competing for the same players to the detriment of one another and deciding to share their futures.

Then, as now, there were long and hard discussions over name, venue, finances and the like. Old rivalries died hard but those who attended that amalgamation meeting in the Golden Lion Hotel on 16 May 1946 should have the undying gratitude of everyone who has benefited from playing or watching County in modern times. The FP club had been affiliated to the then Scottish Football Union since 1904 and the SRU agreed that the new club should take that affiliation – hence the 75th anniversary celebrations

The Bridgehaugh boilerhouse . . . Stirling's sturdy and mobile pack is a match for any in the land. In particular the front-row of Brian Robertson, Kevin McKenzie and George Graham, now lost to Rugby League, combine technical expertise in the set piece with dynamic running in the loose

in 1979 and a centenary already being talked about although it is not for 13 years.

There are interesting comparisons between the Stirling club and clubs in the Borders. It may be surprising to some, perhaps even something of an insult to others, when the suggestion is put forward that County's humble surroundings and background are part of its strength. Yet that proposal comes with the best possible motives: if fielding sides devoid of the old school tie and sprinkled with working men, from field or factory, is good enough for the Border sides then it is good enough for Stirling.

Coach Richie Dixon – another of Stirling's bold and innovative moves was to attract the man who has been associated with Scotland 'B' and Glasgow for over 14 seasons – sees certain similarities. 'It is true that Stirling has a good share of farmers and men who work with their hands. That is the same as the Borders and is a positive bonus for a rugby player. There is also a tremendous county spirit around the area with people coming in from all around for shopping and activities. This is the focus for a huge area and that reflects in a wide range of areas players come from to play rugby.'

Richie Dixon in his days as a dynamic back-row player. Now he is an equally respected coach with Stirling, Glasgow and Scotland 'B'

Dixon has brought his own particular brand of enthusiasm to the club but freely admits that the spirit he encountered when he arrived quickly had him hooked. 'I said originally I would come down one night a week and help the people who were doing the coaching. Now I am at Bridgehaugh sometimes three times a week and either here or travelling on a Saturday. It has been that infectious.'

Dixon's philosophy is simple – set targets for players which are attainable and after that is done ask for a little more. He also wants players to bring out the best in themselves and accepts that there are some who will not go as far as others yet remain just as important to a team. 'I have found at Stirling that there is a pride in the club and that every player is happy to do his best for whatever team he finds himself in. Sure, everyone wants to be in the big team but that does not take away from their effort in the lower sides, merely adds to it.'

For that reason, and other reasons of club development, Dixon and the committee are examining an innovative scheme whereby an extra first XV would be raised in the club outwith the League side to honour fixtures at a higher level. 'You already see "2A" and "3A" teams at clubs so why not a "1A" which gives the players the experience of pulling on a first XV jersey yet allows the club to have its options open for the league matches?'

Dixon, the former Jordanhill and Scotland 'B' forward, now head-teacher at Currie High, has become a part of the scene at Stirling in just three seasons. He recalls: 'I came on an advisory basis and did not plan to be around as long as this. But I seemed to hit it off with the players and committee and was somewhat hoist by my own petard when on one occasion I said I would not be back unless they scored over 30 points against one team. I couldn't believe the effort which was put in to secure those last few points when they were under 30 up. Like in all games, even if Stirling are down, they will try right to the final whistle. I admire that tremendously in players.'

No pain, no gain . . .
hard work on the practice
paddock pays dividends on
Saturday match-days

Dixon adds: 'Patience has always been a virtue of mine and here, as in all coaching positions I have had, it has come in handy with some players and even some supporters. They may have not seen what it was I was trying to achieve right away or they were unwilling to put in the effort required to make it happen. That has changed now and I would like to think the club is reaping the rewards – not of my efforts but of theirs.'

He sees the coaching of a new set of players as being like building a jigsaw with none of the pieces making much sense in isolation but with the picture slowly building. 'The beauty of Stirling is that when a player comes to me and into the first team reckoning he has been grounded in the basics of rugby and no time has to be wasted on those aspects. For that we have to thank the hundreds of people who have put so much into teaching the youngsters here from as young as eight.'

Dixon is fulsome in his praise for those who built Stirling County from just another rugby club into one of the success stories of the game. Indeed the *Glasgow Herald*'s Bill McLaren received a call from colleagues in BBC Wales who wished to highlight the effect of leagues in Scotland and asked if Stirling County would make a worthy focus. He said they could do no better and added: 'Surely no club in Scotland can provide better evidence of the advantages of national league play than Stirling, and especially of the stepladder that the leagues provide for less fashionable clubs to show enterprise, initiative, ambition and planning by which they might aspire to joining the heavyweights at the top of the pile?'

Dixon adds his personal tribute, and again it carries weight despite his personal attachment. 'Over the years there has been tremendous vision in this club and there have been backroom people associated with this club who have worked harder and given more than many of their counterparts in so-called bigger clubs. That dedication and effort is beginning to bear fruit. We set meaningful goals and at the moment our goal is to get better week to week. We do not look towards Division One Championships or filling the cabinets with Caps and honours, we look forward to personal and team improvement. The rest can come with that.'

He is not a man who singles out players for special praise but when pressed will return to the 'B' Cap quintet of Hamilton, Graham, McKenzie, Robertson and Jardine. 'These guys have put a tremendous amount of work in and their success rubs off on other players perhaps less gifted than they are and spurs them on to greater effort.'

He also pauses to pay tribute to the mercurial Brian Ireland, the flanker who has done so much for Stirling County, for North and Midlands and latterly for Glasgow. 'He is a fantastic player and the greatest tribute ever paid to him comes from opposition forwards who say he is an annoying little b . . . . . . who is always hovering around the offside line – but we would love to have him on our side.' The fates dealt Ireland a cruel blow during a League game against Boroughmuir last season when he seriously damaged knee ligaments and had to undergo a series of operations. His long-term rugby future remains in the balance.

Ken Crichton remembers clearly the day when Stewart Hamilton met him for a pint to say that he wanted to move clubs. 'He was seeing it as the most difficult decision he would have to make in his playing career and we talked it over for a long time. Hammy said that he wanted a Cap and that if he did not at least get noticed with a better-known club then he would never know what might have been. We agreed that Heriot's would be the best bet and he went there – ultimately winning a Cap at 'B' level.'

Crichton was never in any doubt that Hamilton would return to Bridgehaugh and, despite the somewhat petty committee decision to take away his playing membership in favour of a social one during his sabbatical at Goldenacre, he did just that and is held in such esteem at club and district level that he was last season's Stirling County captain and stepped successfully into the Glasgow breach left by Shade Munro and earlier Alan Watt.

Hamilton, 35, who has now vacated the captaincy, expresses satisfaction with his last term as skipper which saw Stirling finish in the middle of the table with six wins, two draws and five defeats. Their points differential could not have been closer with 191 for and the same number against. The genial lock says: 'It was a good season and when I look back I remember many games which we could have won but at the same time others where we were a bit lucky. You make your own luck, though, and the atmosphere among the players and at the club is still excellent and we are all looking forward to another crack at Division One next season.'

The first-team camaraderie has been further forged with a tour of South-west France during which the highly rated teams of Dax and Biarritz were tackled by a full-strength Stirling County tour party. A measure of the humour abroad in the club came when Hamilton learned that Lourdes might well be within striking distance of the area in which the tour was being held and immediately suggested that the injured Brian Ireland should be taken along. He recalls: 'Fortunately it was not required as already Brian is out there doing some light training after an injury and operations which looked like bringing a great career to an early end.'

Hamilton retains one ambition as he continues to play rugby with as much enthusiasm as when he first laced a pair of boots. 'I have always wanted to play in the same team as my son Gregor. As he is only seven and playing away in the under-nine minis I may have a bit of a wait. I'm a patient sort of fellow, though, and I don't mind waiting until he is ready. I just hope that I'm still fit and get picked for many years to come.'

If there are a few lads like Gregor around who will play with the same zeal as the fathers and grandfathers who made Stirling County what it is today, then the future looks secure.

The Stirling County rise to the top flight began with appointment to Division Five (East) in the early stages of the National Leagues then a move, disappointingly for some at the club, to Division Seven.

Then came the real moves:
Season 1976–77 – Promotion to Division Six.
Season 1977–78 – Promotion to Division Five.
Season 1978–79 – Promotion to Division Four.
Season 1979–80 – Promotion to Division Three.
Season 1983–84 – Placed in reorganised Division Two.
Season 1988–89 – Promotion to Division One.

Colin Deans in typical pose.
His British Lions, captaincy
was awarded in unique
circumstances

Leaders of the Pack

Scots Captains of the British Lions

By DEREK DOUGLAS

FINLAY CALDER's captaincy of the British Lions during their victorious tour to Australia in 1989 meant that the name of the Stewart's-Melville FP player was added to an exclusive roll of Scots who have been similarly honoured. Scotsmen have assumed the role of Lions' 'captain for the day' on a number of occasions – most recently David Sole during the Calder-led tour and most memorably Jim Telfer and his 'dirty play' speech after the encounter with Canterbury during the 1966 outing to New Zealand.

However, only six Scots have achieved the ultimate distinction of becoming the Lions' tour captain, while one other was awarded the singular honour of captaining an official British Isles side which actually played a Test match in the British Isles – a trick sporting quiz question for future years if ever there was one.

W. E. MACLAGAN (Edinburgh Academicals and London Scottish)
South Africa, 1891

Played 19	Won 19	Lost 0	Drawn 0
Points for 224	Points against 1		

BILL MACLAGAN, a full-back or wing, won the first of his 26 Caps in a 0–0 draw against England in the last international match played at the Oval cricket ground in 1878, and he played, too, in the first encounter between the Auld Enemies for which the Calcutta Cup was at stake. This contest took place at Raeburn Place the following year, and it, too, ended in a pointless draw. This particular match was most notable for the action of one of the English backs who eschewed heroics in the face of a Scottish forward rush and carried over his own line to touch down. Such a prudent measure, though, did not find favour with the 10,000 spectators, who set up an unseemly hissing at such lack of moral fibre. A contemporary report noted that the crowd had given vent to its displeasure 'not because it lost a rare chance to Scotland but that it showed a want of pluck not normal with Britons'. Conversely, Maclagan was cheered to the echo as he showed how it should have been done and adventurously ran a ball from behind the Scottish posts.

The 1891 tour was spectacularly successful. The Lions powered their way through South Africa, winning all of their games and conceding just the single point, an arithmetical feat possible under the old scoring system.

Bill Maclagan's 1891 British Lions, although the second touring team to leave these shores, nevertheless blazed a trail in South Africa for future tourists and returned home with a spectacularly successful playing record
Courtesy of Scottish Rugby Union

At that time rugby in South Africa was in its infancy and largely based upon the scrummaging prowess of its raw-boned forwards. The sides which the tourists met experienced great difficulty in coming to terms with the speedy handling of the threequarters and the expert dribbling attacks of the forwards. Off the pitch, too, the tour was a great success – to such an extent that Maclagan's fellow Scottish international and tourist Paul Clauss was moved to observe that it had been a great adventure of champagne and travel.

The 1891 tour was notable, too, in that it bequeathed to South Africa the Currie Cup which is still played for annually by the country's provincial sides. The trophy was donated by the shipping-line magnate Sir Donald Currie with the intention that it should go to the side which provided the tourists with their sternest test. On that occasion it went to Griqualand West and since that time the Currie Cup competition has been South Africa's premier domestic competition and a proving ground for generations of Springboks.

Mark Morrison of Royal High School FP was one of Scotland's greatest forwards, and captained his country to a Triple Crown in 1901
Courtesy of Scottish Rugby Union

M. C. MORRISON (Royal High School FP)
South Africa, 1903

Played 22	Won 11	Lost 8	Drawn 3
Points for 231	Points against 138		

MARK MORRISON of Royal High School FP captained the fifth British Lions on the 1903 tour of South Africa, by which time he was already established not only as a world-class forward but also as captain of Scotland, an honour he was to experience on 15 occasions between 1899 and 1904. He gained the first of his 23 Caps as a teenager in a 6–0 defeat at Cardiff in 1896. He was a big man for his time and contemporary team photographs with him as captain show him as a square-jawed, powerfully serene and invariably hunched figure with the ball cradled in massive hands. Reports of the period declare him to have been an exceptionally strong forward but also pacey with a devastating tackle and finely honed handling skills.

He was a particularly effective captain of Scotland and was recalled by a colleague for the crisp directness of his team talks. Before one international match at Inverleith he told his fellow forwards: 'There are three things you must do today. The first is get the ball, the second is get the ball and the third is get the ball. If you don't know what to do when you've got it then you've no bloody right to be here!'

A farmer, he had played his first game for Royal High School FP against Edinburgh Wanderers in 1894. He played his last regular game for the side against Hawick in 1904 and during an eight-year international career missed only one match, that against England in 1903, because of injury. At the time of his Scottish captaincy RHSFP (one of Scotland's most venerable clubs) were well represented in the upper echelons of the game with J. W. Simpson a vice-president of the Scottish Football Union and J. Aikman Smith its redoubtable secretary.

The first Test, in Johannesburg, ended in a 10–10 draw, but it was notable for reasons other than the tied result. The captain of the Springboks that day was Alex Frew (Edinburgh University) who had been a member of Morrison's 1901 Triple Crown-winning Scotland XV, while the referee was W. P. 'Bill' Donaldson (West of Scotland & Oxford University) who had won six Caps in the Nineties and had played alongside Morrison in the 1896 team.

Against all the odds, the second Test, at Kimberley, was also drawn, the result this time being a 0–0 stalemate, and the series was decided in the Springboks' favour by virtue of an 8–0 win at Cape Town.

D. R. BEDELL-SIVRIGHT (Cambridge University, Fettesian-Lorrettians, West of Scotland, Edinburgh University)
Australia and New Zealand, 1904

Australia:	Played 14	Won 14	Lost 0	Drawn 0
Points for 265	Points against 51			
New Zealand:	Played 5	Won 2	Lost 2	Drawn 1
Points for 22	Points against 33			

DAVID 'DARKIE' BEDELL-SIVRIGHT had toured with Mark Morrison's Lions in South Africa in 1903, the only player to have taken part in both outings. He is generally reckoned to have been one of the roughest and toughest forwards of his era and his particular strengths were in the dribble and the cover-tackle which was of the 'no prisoners' variety. He was Capped 22 times between 1900 and 1908 at a time when the foot-rushes of the Scottish pack were a sight to behold – but not if one happened to be the unfortunate player who had to fall on a loose ball under the driving boot studs. It is now virtually impossible to say with certainty how Bedell-Sivright went about his work but from contemporary accounts it would probably be true to say that he was a pioneer of the voracious wing-forward style of today.

Bedell-Sivright was said by observers to be 'disregardless' and he himself, when chided about the robust nature of his play, declared: 'When I am on the field I only see the ball and wherever it goes I go. Should someone be in the road then that is his lookout.'

He had come to stay in Scotland when his parents returned from the West Indies. They set up home at Northcliff, North Queensferry, and Bedell-Sivright and his younger brother, who also played for Scotland, attended Fettes College in Edinburgh. He went on to Trinity College, Cambridge, and won four Blues between 1899–1902. He graduated BA from Cambridge and continued his learning at Edinburgh University where he studied medicine and captained the University team between 1906 and 1909.

On the 1904 tour, records show that Bedell-Sivright was 'indisposed' or 'injured' during the Australian leg and after captaining the Lions to a 17–0 win at Sydney the Test captaincy passed to the Welshman Teddy

D. R. 'Darkie' Bedell-Sivright was one of the toughest men ever to have played the game. After his retirement from rugby he became Scottish amateur heavyweight boxing champion. He died at Gallipoli during the Great War
Courtesy of Scottish Rugby Union

Morgan. The tourists won two further Tests in Australia but lost to New Zealand in a 9–3 match at Wellington.

Bedell-Sivright did not return home with the touring party but remained in Australia where he engaged in a spell of stock-rearing. However, he returned within the year, having written to a friend: 'At the end of a year's jackarooing I decided that what was I, with an average amount of brains and rather more money, doing prostituting one in order to increase the other, so I chucked it in in order to come home and study medicine.'

Once back in Scotland, Bedell-Sivright enrolled at Edinburgh University and resumed his international career. Newspaper reports of the period, virtually without exception, remark on the forthright nature of his play. While turning out for Cambridge in a game against Racing Club de France in Paris a French paper recorded: '*Il travaille avec vigueur, plaquant, chargeant, bousculant, carambolant sans lassitude.*' Meanwhile, a Welsh international who played against Bedell-Sivright confined himself to: 'He is very rough.'

When his international rugby career came to an end in 1908, Bedell-Sivright turned his attention to boxing and in 1909 became Scottish amateur heavyweight champion. A contemporary opponent confided that the only way to stand any chance of beating him was not to let him lay a hand on you. If he hit an opponent, even just once, then the chances were that the bout would end in a knock-out.

Sadly, Bedell-Sivright died in tragically ironic circumstances at Gallipoli during the Great War. He became a Royal Navy surgeon at the outbreak of war and in 1916 was sent with the Allied invasion force to the Dardanelles. As might be expected of one blessed with such a 'disregardless' nature he often told friends how frustrated he felt that as a medic he could not get in amongst the Turkish foe. Nevertheless, he was not short of work attending to the thousands of British and Anzac wounded. He spent many dangerous weeks at forward dressing stations among the trenches and killing grounds of the Allied beachhead.

In the book *Rugby Football Internationals' Roll of Honour*, written in 1919 by E. H. D. Sewell as a literary and lasting monument to those British rugby Caps who died in the Great War, a sizeable tract is devoted to Bedell-Sivright.

A friend is reported to have said that the last time he saw Darkie alive was when he and a few cronies gathered for dinner at Southsea. It was just before the start of the Dardanelles campaign and the friend wrote: 'Darkie was strangely silent. He seemed preoccupied and not at all like his old self.'

Another friend is reported as saying: 'I have seen a man who was with him nearly to the last. He tells me that Darkie had returned from a long spell in the trenches at an advanced dressing station and had come down properly fagged out. He had got bitten by some kind of insect and being in a weak condition, poisoning set in. He died two days later in the hospital ship.'

These were the days before antibiotics and Bedell-Sivright's system had been overwhelmed by a massive infection of the blood. Cruel irony. One of the toughest men ever to have played rugby for Scotland was done to death by an Aegean gnat. The date was 5 September 1915. He was just 34 years old.

A. R. SMITH (Cambridge University, Gosforth, Ebbw Vale, Edinburgh Wanderers)
South Africa, 1962

Played 24   Won 15   Lost 5   Drawn 4
Points for 351   Points against 208

Arthur Smith

ARTHUR SMITH's mercurial pace and devastating finishing were the answers to Scottish rugby's prayer when he won the first of his 33 Caps against Wales in 1955 and the team ended a 17-game drought with a 14–8 win. During his debut the new Flying Scot scored a try which was to typify his electrifying style of play. Adam Robson threw out a long pass to Smith, the young Cambridge University wing, who seemed to be well covered on the right touch-line. However, he took off like a graceful gazelle and had made all of 30 yards before kicking the ball over the head of the Welsh full-back, controlling it with a foot and plunging over at the corner flag for the first of many tries in a Scotland jersey.

At six feet and 12st 12lbs, Smith was ideally built for his role as a wing-threequarter and, in his days at Glasgow University had been a generally gifted athlete, winning the Scottish long-jump title in 1953. He was also academically bright, having gained a first in mathematics at Glasgow University before going on to Cambridge where he studied for a doctorate and won four rugby Blues between 1954 and 1957.

He was a member of the Lions' party which toured South Africa in 1955 when he had the misfortune to injure a hand in the opening match, thus greatly curtailing whatever contribution he might have made on the trip. Nevertheless, his enforced lay-off was put to good use as he worked assiduously on his goal-kicking and returned home as a goal-kicker of the front order.

Scotland took part in a trailblazing tour to South Africa in 1960 – the first major overseas tour by a Home Union country – and Smith scored seven of Scotland's points (with a goal and a conversion) during the 18–10 Test defeat at Port Elizabeth. He was, then, no stranger to South Africa when named as captain for the British Isles tour two years later. He had already captained Scotland on 15 occasions (equalling Mark Morrison's record) when nominated for the post and was uniquely qualified for the role both as a gifted player and an intelligent and astute off-field ambassador.

Smith played in all three of the Tests. The Lions got off to an acceptable start in the series with a 3–3 draw at Johannesburg but then had the galling experience of losing by the narrowest of margins, 3–0 at Durban,

Arthur Smith, who led the 1962 British Lions to South Africa, was an elegant wing-threequarter and an accurate kicker of the ball. He died tragically young of cancer

before succumbing in the third and final Test at Cape Town, by eight points to three.

After the 1962 tour Smith retired from the game and devoted his considerable energies to business. He had been a stockbroker in Edinburgh and was a director with an insurance company when he was struck down by cancer and died, in 1975, at the tragically early age of 42.

Mike Campbell-Lamerton

M. J. CAMPBELL-LAMERTON (Halifax, Army, London Scottish)
Australia and New Zealand, 1966

Australia:	Played 8	Won 7	Lost 0	Drawn 1
Points for 202	Points against 48			
New Zealand:	Played 25	Won 15	Lost 8	Drawn 2
Points for 300	Points against 281			

MIKE CAMPBELL-LAMERTON was already a seasoned Lions' tourist when he was named captain of the 1966 British Lions. The six-feet-four-inch, 17st 8lbs lock-forward had proved himself to be a great success in the preceding 1962 campaign in South Africa where he had played in a remarkable 20 of the 25 games and had turned out in the four Tests in the unaccustomed role of number eight. By the standards of the age Campbell-Lamerton was an extremely big man, a rugged scrummager but one who could also put himself about in the loose.

For the last game of the 1962 tour, against East Africa, Campbell-Lamerton – an Army captain – was made skipper for the day and it was a role which he resumed four years later when next the Lions ventured abroad.

Big Mike had captained Scotland on only two occasions, against Wales and Ireland in 1965, despite having gained 23 Caps between 1961 and 1968. He was, in some quarters, a surprise choice as leader for the 1966 party, many having felt that the honour would fall to the Welshman Alun Pask who had led his side to a Championship title the previous winter. During his term as Lions' captain in the Antipodes, Campbell-Lamerton was unable to recapture the form that he had displayed four years earlier against the Springboks and he, bravely, took the unprecedented decision to stand down from the Test side. David Watkins, the mercurial Welsh stand-off half, assumed the captaincy in Campbell-Lamerton's stead.

On the Australian leg of the trip Campbell-Lamerton's Lions recorded two Test victories (11–8 and 31–0) but the second, mammoth win, lulled the Lions into a false sense of security. Australia were not then in the first rank of world rugby and it was only when the Lions flew to New Zealand where they came up against an exceptionally strong All Blacks side that the true playing stature of the touring party began to emerge. The first Test in Dunedin was lost 20–3 and the touring party became the target for hostile media attention while there were also internal recriminations and accusations that the Welsh contingent, the largest, was stand-offish and arrogant. This was an accusation subsequently denied strenuously by Watkins who recalled in his autobiography how, after dinner one night in Wellington just a few days before the second Test, Campbell-Lamerton had taken him aside and announced that he was dropping himself from the Test XV. Watkins, who later went on to great success in Rugby League, became captain for that game but it, too, was lost, the only comfort being that at 14–16 the losing margin was more palatable.

Mike Campbell-Lamerton, seen here on the right offering line-out protection, was a big, strong, aggressive lock-forward who turned out at number eight on his first Lions tour but experienced problems with his form on the expedition he led to the Antipodes

Campbell-Lamerton was reinstated for the third Test at Christchurch but the All Blacks were well on top again and the tourists went down 19–6. Thereafter, with the tour by now in some disarray, Campbell-Lamerton dropped himself again for the fourth and final Test in Auckland but the Lions' fortunes were not restored and they lost 24–11.

By this time the tourists had been away from home for some five months and uppermost in the minds of many was simply the desire to get on a plane and touch down in the UK.

Despite his problems on the playing-field, Campbell-Lamerton continued with his extra-curricular captain's duties and he calculated on his return that he had made 267 tour speeches, given 80 radio interviews and appeared on television 36 times. Watkins put his skipper's loss of confidence down, in part, to this crucifying schedule.

Campbell-Lamerton's son Jeremy was a member of Scotland's 1987 World Cup squad during which he played against Zimbabwe and came on as a replacement in the Romanian match. In the Five Nations Championship the previous year, Jeremy had played against France.

C. T. DEANS (Hawick)
British Lions 7, Rest of the World XV 15
Cardiff Arms Park, 1986
A special game to mark the centenary of the International Board.

COLIN DEANS had captained every major team he had played for when he was nominated to lead the Lions in the celebratory match at Cardiff in April 1986. He had captained Hawick, the South of Scotland, the Barbarians and Scotland before reaching rugby's highest peak.

He went on to skipper Scotland in the inaugural World Cup in 1987 and to amass 52 Scottish Caps – still a record which he shares with clubmate Jim Renwick. At five feet ten inches and 13st 4lbs, Deans was comparatively small for a modern hooker but he more than compensated with his sizzling pace around the paddock. He had built on his natural speed during the summer months by donning spikes and joining the ranks of the professional sprinters at the many athletics events which take place during numerous Border Common-Ridings and festivals.

Deans had already toured Japan, New Zealand, Australia and Romania with Scotland before being selected as a member of the 1983 British Lions squad for New Zealand. It was not a happy tour for the Scotsman. The party was managed by Willie John McBride, captained by fellow Irishman Ciaran Fitzgerald and coached by Scotland's Jim Telfer. Fitzgerald, in Deans's position as hooker, struggled with his form throughout and there were many who felt that he should have emulated the course of action taken by Mike Campbell-Lamerton 17 years previously and dropped himself from the Test XV. In particular Fitzgerald was experiencing great difficulty with his throwing-in at the line-out and the story is often told of how on the morning of a midweek game he was seen practising in the hotel car park.

The Test matches were lost 4–0 and the Lions experienced only their second whitewash in almost 100 years of touring abroad. The tour had been a salutory experience, too, for Jim Telfer but he, and all the Scottish members of the party, more than made amends the following season when Scotland won only the second Grand Slam in their history.

Deans retired from the game after Scotland's 30–3 World Cup defeat by New Zealand. Scotland had held the All Blacks to 9–3 at the interval and the final scoreline flattered the New Zealanders. Many thought, though, that Scotland's 20–20 draw against France had been the game of the tournament. And it was a game which Deans's Scotland would probably have won had it not been for Serge Blanco's now famous 'sneak' try. The Scottish right-winger, Matt Duncan, had been injured and Deans was trying to attract the referee's attention in order that team physio David McLean could come on to treat the injured winger when Blanco took a quick tap penalty and ran in virtually unopposed for the try. The Scots fought back and levelled terms through a Duncan try but Gavin Hastings' conversion went just wide.

Thereafter, the Scottish captain penned his autobiography and retired from the game although, in subsequent years, he was heavily involved with Hawick Albion, an innovative Under-16 team attached to the Greens.

Colin Deans – a touch-line shot from the 1983 tour in New Zealand

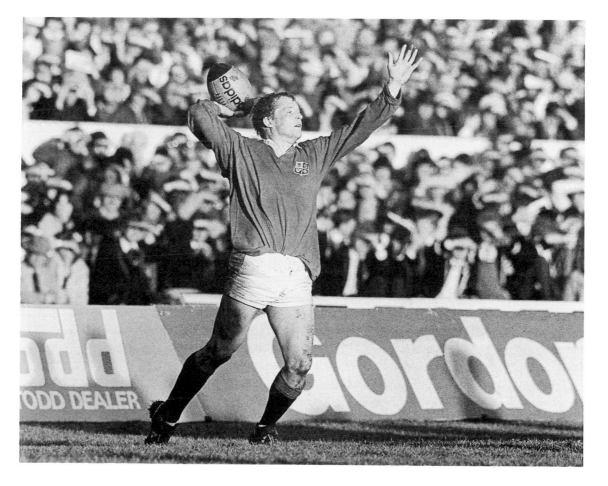

FINLAY CALDER (Stewart's-Melville FP)

Australia, 1989

Played 12	Won 11	Lost 1	Drawn 0
Points for 360	Points against 192		

FINLAY CALDER's leadership qualities were never more severely tested than after the morale-sapping 30–12 defeat in the opening Test at the Sydney Football Stadium. The series was to be decided over three Tests and to many it seemed that the Lions would never be able to regroup in time to get the tour back on the rails. The Lions, managed by Clive Rowlands and coached by Ian McGeechan and Roger Uttley, had gone into the Test with several key players injured but even allowing for this, such had been Australia's domination (reflected in a try-count of four to none) that it seemed the series was over almost before it had really begun.

After the game, a downcast yet still utterly determined Calder confided that never before had he been so depressed, dejected and disappointed. He added, though, that the Lions would never play so badly again. 'I can promise you it will be completely different next Saturday in Brisbane,' he declared.

Fin Calder . . . his defensive know-how and aggressive running with the ball in hand were the Stewart's-Melville flanker's trademark

Calder was as good as his word. Seven days later at Ballymore, Brisbane, in a ferociously contested second Test, the Lions came back off the ropes to record a 19–12 win. The game was played without quarter by both sides and following it the tourists were subjected to a barrage of criticism from sections of the Australian media, 'British Thugby Stars' being one of the kinder headlines. The tourists also came under psychological attack from the Australian Rugby Football Union when, on the eve of the third and deciding Test, the ARFU issued an intimidatory Press statement in which they condemned foul play and ordered a video recording of certain incidents in the second Test to be placed before the Home Unions' Committee. They also wished to pursue the possibility of video-taped evidence being admitted to the game's judicial structure.

In the third Test back at the Sydney Football Stadium the Lions played with rock-like determination to secure a 19–18 win and the first series victory for 15 years. The tourists saw a seven-point lead cut back to that slender one-point margin and the tackling during this period of the game, in which Calder led by example, was breathtaking in its clinical efficiency.

Calder had captained Scotland in the season prior to the Australian campaign but on his return to the side for the Five Nations' Championship the following year he had relinquished the role in favour of David Sole. This was, of course, Scotland's Grand Slam season during which Calder played some of the best rugby of his life and never more so than in the winners-take-all Calcutta Cup match at Murrayfield.

Two incidents involving Calder particularly stand out: his bone-jarring drive at the mighty English pack, from which Scotland secured the opening penalty goal, set the tone for the match while his shepherding of the distraught England hooker, Brian Moore, to the shelter of the stand at no-side was an object lesson in magnanimous victory. The Grand Slam match represented Calder's 26th and last international appearance for Scotland in the UK although he did turn out twice more, in the

Calder and the British Lions' management, plus tour mascot, hold a news conference during the Australian tour

summer tour of New Zealand, before announcing his retirement from the international game.

A dynamic flank forward who could be devastating with ball in hand, Calder followed his twin, Jim (a British Lion in 1983), into the Scottish XV to achieve a family double, with both having played in a Grand Slam-winning Scottish side, Jim scoring the 'turning point' try during the 1984 decider against France. Both brothers had the happy knack of invariably being in the right place at the right time although this blessed gift invariably had the effect of driving opposition supporters at club and country level to paroxysms of rage and frustration. A paeon of praise sung by the West of Scotland club as to the sterling qualities of one of their early forwards, J. E. Orr, who won 12 Caps in the 1880s and 1890s, might be appropriate: 'A dare-devil forward who knew no fear, nor when he was beaten, and who could play off-side, on-side or any side he liked so long as he thought he could do some good to his own side and upset the schemes of the opponents.'

Calder was always a much, much better player than he gave himself credit for and when he retired from the international arena his departure left a void which, even yet, has proved impossible to fill. That this was indeed the case was evidenced by the fact that Calder was prevailed upon to make himself available for Scotland's 1991 World Cup campaign, and that he played such a prominent part throughout.

Big cat, little cat . . . Finlay Calder captained the 1989 Lions to a historic Test series win in Australia, and this despite the morale-sapping blow of defeat in the opening Test

'Are Yer Lugs Loupin'?'

Reflections of a Rugby Writing Man

By BRIAN MEEK

IN 1971, ON A FLIGHT FROM LONDON TO GENEVA, the young man behind me tapped my shoulder and enquired: 'Hey yow, are ycr lugs loupin'?' The gentlcman asking the question was one James Menzies Renwick, and for those of you not of Hawick extraction he was wishing to know whether the pressure was making my ears pop.

Young Renwick had never been out of Scotland before – some said never out of the Borders – but we were on our way to the first-ever 'B' international against France at Oyannax in which the centre, although in a well-beaten side, was to make quite a mark. I saw his first 'B' Cap and his last full one, the 52nd, in Bucharest, Romania, 13 years later.

What pleasure Jim Renwick gave us over the piece. Mike Gibson of Ireland called him 'the most naturally gifted player I have ever seen. To be honest he does not know how good he is.' Those of us who travelled with him know how funny he could be – he could deliver a punch-line as well as a pass and even today he is still thoroughly involved in the game.

If you had asked Jim Renwick – a very talented swimmer as well – when he was a boy, whether he would travel the world playing rugby he might have given you one of his special withering glances. If you had told me I would spend over 20 years of my life writing about the game I would have been equally sceptical. But, the common thread was a Borders town . . .

In Hawick High Street there were, nailed to walls or shop doors, a number of small, wooden-framed, glass-encased notice-boards. On a Thursday evening a representative of each of the town's rugby clubs, the Greens themselves, the Trades, the YM, the Linden, the PSA, Wanderers and the Harlequins, would march solemnly towards them clutching the all-important sheet of paper which would bring joy, pride or disappointment to most young men of the locality. These were the teams selected for the Saturday. Quite often, in the run-up to a big match, a sizeable crowd would gather to await the deliberations of the selectors. Men would find that their dogs required exercise; a runner would be sent from the pubs with strict instructions to note down all the changes, then the discussions would begin. In Hawick, where I spent my early years, there were the woollen mills and the rugby; the mills were a hard, unhealthy graft; the rugby was the escape.

To pull that famous Green jersey over your head made one a Prince

'Hey yow, are yer lugs loupin'?' . . . a young James Menzies Renwick

of a town that called itself the Queen o' a' the Borders. I have to confess that such an honour never fell to me though my Uncle David was a winger for the club. Rugby was the all-pervading community activity: there were boys in Hawick who actually preferred football but they were considered to be in need of remedial education, tolerated right enough, but big Jessies just the same. To be a real Teri you had either to be on the field or the terraces at Mansfield Park, playing or officiating at the Volunteer, Wilton, or Burnfoot. It had been that way since the turn of the century.

Hawick is not unique; rugby still binds the whole of the Borders. In Melrose and Galashiels and Selkirk and Jedburgh and Kelso and Langholm this is the only game for real men, the sport they excel at, the activity which takes them to places they had only known as dots on a map, to represent their club, their district and their country all over the globe. Why rugby?

Historians far more knowledgeable than I will trace the sport from the town games, the Uppies and Doonies and the Wall Games, but rugby would not have flourished unless it had some special appeal. There is certainly the camaraderie, the crack, the feeling of being a member of a team, the exhilaration of proving yourself among the best. But it's more than that.

Strangely it was not a Borderer but the Scotland and Heriot's hooker, Kenny Milne, who, for me, best summed up the appeal of the oval ball game. 'It does not matter what size you are, what weight, there is a place for so many skills on a rugby field that everyone can find their own niche. The 18st prop forward [*who was he thinking of?*] is as much value to the team as the dashing full-back. The universal appeal of the game is that so many people can enjoy it.' Not bad for a member of the front row union!

Anyway by the time I left Hawick for school in Edinburgh the bug had bitten; my first appearance in a competitive match was at the age of seven; it soon became apparent that I was not going to be an internationalist but I was keen enough to play two games each Saturday for any Royal High side that would have me.

On leaving school I joined Lismore, on the advice of my Dad, who told me that at 9st 4lbs I was too light to go straight into the FP sphere. My first appearance for that club was against Hawick Harlequins at Volunteer Park. Having made the cardinal error of scoring an early try I was then given the full treatment by the home side and ended up having a leg gash treated by the local doctor. When I dropped my trousers he let out an almighty roar and I thought the end was nigh. 'X-fronts,' he bellowed, pointing to my underpants: 'How dare you come into Hawick wearing these?' The rival Y-fronts, it should be explained, were made in the town. Such was the start of a long and undistinguished playing career.

The Scottish Rugby Union ended it some 20 years later. To wit, I received a very polite letter from Mr John Law, the secretary, informing me that I had been declared a professional and was ordered to cease my playing activities 'forthwith'. The Lismore second XV were broken-hearted!

I had by that time been a journalist for several years, trained on *The Scotsman*, racing correspondent for the old *Evening Dispatch* and was, at this stage, a feature writer for the *Scottish Daily Express*. A couple of the features I had written were on the general state of rugby and the lack of foresight, as I saw it, of the SRU. That was enough to entitle me to a suspension *sine die* (when I was 42 the regulations were changed to permit full-time journalists to play but even the third XV didn't want me then!). John Law, whom I came to know as a real gentleman, was very apologetic about it all. 'Nothing personal,' he told me. Personal or not, the Union did me a favour they had not intended.

The rugby correspondent of the *Express* was the legendary Andrew 'Jock' Wemyss, a Scotland Cap before and after the First World War – having lost an eye in between – and not only a famous writer but a renowned broadcaster. Many of us were reared on Jock's commentaries as he roared 'Feet, Scotland, Feet!' over the airwaves. Being driven by Jock was a nerve-racking experience – he talked non-stop and often turned his good eye towards you to enforce his point. Passengers often shut both of theirs in panic.

As he was in his late 70s Jock was not averse to the editor's suggestion that he might take 'early retirement' from journalism. When I, the newly proclaimed professional, was offered his job I thought it was a joke. As for Mr Wemyss he never showed me anything but kindness and consideration and used to perch on my desk for hours recounting his favourite anecdotes.

It was an exciting time to become a rugby correspondent for great changes to the structure of the game were underway. The 'no kicking to touch on the fall outside the 25' regulation and the four-point try had already transformed most fixtures – the 0–0 draw was something out of the archives. More important, from Scotland's point of view, was the growing demand for a properly organised, fully competitive league structure to replace the unofficial championship. Leading the campaign, with the same consummate skill he had displayed on the playing field, was the former Scotland and British Lions captain, Arthur Smith.

I recall going with Arthur to a meeting to discuss the subject in the refectory of George Heriot's School. He put his case with all the passion of a missionary; indeed, an earlier Scottish winger Eric Liddell came to mind as he spoke. Sadly we were to lose Smith at almost as early an age as his predecessor but the effect Arthur had on the hearts and minds of those who would take the ultimate decision about a competitive structure cannot be underestimated.

Arthur Smith . . . leading the campaign for a fully competitive league structure in Scotland

The official championship was inaugurated in season 1973–74 and won, as it would be for the next five years, by Hawick. Before that I was 'bloodied' as an international correspondent with trips to Lansdowne Road and Cardiff Arms Park in 1970 and, in the following year, made my first and only visit to Colombes Stadium just outside Paris. This would turn out to be one for the scrapbook.

At the end of the match, which Scotland lost 13–9 – it would be a long time before I would witness them winning away from home – I was in a long queue of Pressmen waiting to send their copy. In those days you could not telephone directly from Paris to anywhere in the UK. You handed your number to a switchboard operator at the stadium, and you waited. I

The former Scottish Rugby Union secretary John Law . . . 'Are these people with you?'

hung on, it seemed, forever while every other correspondent filed his story. Then at last it was my turn and I sat at the phone in the open grandstand with my notes in hand. I had just read over the scoreline when every light in the stadium went out! There are those of you who may think we writers just make it up as we go along anyway but I can assure you that would be impossible in an international.

So, for the next half-hour, my friend and colleague Peter Donald, then of the *Daily Mail*, lit match after match then used up all the petrol in a cigarette lighter as I transcribed my piece. When I had finished we sat, shivering and quite alone, our relief soon tempered by the knowledge that we were locked in the stadium. The motion picture *Escape to Victory*, a story of POWs, was later filmed at Colombes; Peter and I would have been ideal for a part as we had to scale a barbed wire fence to make good our exit.

The French then switched their home games to Parc du Princes for which we were all grateful although I have yet to see Scotland win there.

When I started writing on rugby, relationships with the SRU were distant. The idea of interviewing a president or questioning a selector or even quoting a player was considered absolute heresy. There were no after-the-match Press conferences, there were no media people at the official dinners and there was a distinct distrust of all publicity that did not reflect directly upon the game. When Bill McMurtrie, Norman Mair and I travelled with the 'B' party to Oyannax in 1971 the passports of the team and officials were bound by one elastic band, those of the three Pressmen by another. 'Are these people with you?' a customs official asked John Law. 'With them but not of them,' quipped Norman.

Yet it was the 'B' trips which broke down many of the barriers; many, but not all. When we were travelling to such games in France it was impossible to impose complete segregation on a handful of Press writers. We had to be given a seat on the bus, a room in the same hotel and there was a discovery, on both sides, that nobody was a complete two-headed monster.

There were times when we saw Union officials letting their hair down; there were certainly occasions when the Press, although it is difficult in Norman Mair's case, did the same. Sometimes we discovered stories we could not print; after one defeat in France we learned that the Welsh referee had been ensconced in an hotel, and supplied with a local lady, for a week prior to the game. There were other stories, usually when Scotland were defeated, which irritated the authorities; in one small hotel, a chairman of the selectors and a journalist were at the point of exchanging more than insults.

But the relationship did change. Players could be, and were, interviewed; friendships between Press and Union men were struck; and, with the advent of coaching in a big way, there were new missionaries preaching the gospel. Bill Dickinson, Nairn MacEwan, Jim Telfer, Richie Dixon, Colin Telfer and Ian McGeechan were men with a message they wished to put across to a wider audience.

In the big thaw in relationships between the Press and the Union several people, apart from the coaches and players, deserve a mention. Presidents Wilson Shaw, Frank Coutts, Sir John Orr and Tom Pearson, selectors Iain MacGregor, Robin Charters, Bob Munro and Douglas Morgan have all gone the extra mile to make our job not only easier but more accurate. For that, on behalf of all my colleagues, they are to be thanked.

I was asked to speak on the role of the media at the SRU Coaching Conference, held at Heriot-Watt a couple of years ago. It has to be to report what we see, not what people want us to; we are paid to give opinions; these opinions will be better formed if we can talk to folk with an intimate knowledge of the game. I know of no player over the last 20 years whose career has been put in jeopardy by something he has said to the media; I know of several who have been protected. A fine forward who went on to win several more Caps informed me he was not prepared to play in the junior team in the final trial. I told him to think about it for 24 hours, after which I would publish, because if he took that line his international career was over. He thought and he played.

Mind you, I have, in the last two decades and more, made my own share of howlers. In an evening match at the same Poynder Park, Kelso, I was told the paper could only take one batch of copy midway through the second half – after that there was only room for the result. In my last paragraph the readers were informed that Bruce White, the Hawick wing, had gone off 'with what was obviously a recurrence of the leg injury which had made him doubtful for the game'. Imagine my chagrin when, minutes after I had come off the phone, White returned with his head bandaged!

More recently I was acting as a radio summariser for a district game between Glasgow and the North and Midlands. It was a bitterly cold day at Murrayfield with sweeping snow blowing into our commentary position. Authoritatively, I began to sum up the prospects for the second half and pointed out that the North and Midlands back row would play a key role. Just at that point a large blob of snow landed on my notes, completely obliterating the list of the teams. The third member of that blessed back row went straight out of my head and I mumbled incoherently while trying to dry the notes with one frozen mitt. We often make most of our mistakes in public.

But there are still flaws in the SRU's present system of providing information and there remain some officials who insist upon treating the Press as outcasts. Late in 1990, after the Scotland 'B' team had been beaten in Belfast, members of the Scottish Press corps asked if they could have a lift back to the hotel – it was a teeming wet day with no sign of taxis – in the team bus. 'You made your own way here, you can make your own way back,' they were told. That sounds just like the old days. Just for the record, the Irish offered seats on their bus.

I believe the SRU should have appointed a Press Relations Officer years ago. It is simply not adequate to expect secretary Bill Hogg to field queries about everything from the selection of the international team to how many pies are on sale at Murrayfield.

'Everyone can find their niche' . . . Heriot's FP and Scotland hooker, Kenny Milne

The Press facilities at our national stadium are the poorest of any ground used in the Five Nations' Championship. We enter through an ancient toilet, sit at the very back of the old stand and have our view obstructed by a television gantry. There are promises to alter this situation; a solution is long overdue.

As writers we too have to face up to our critics. Just before leagues were introduced I wrote a piece giving my views on the composition of the first two divisions. A week later on my way to the Press box at Kelso there was a storm of booing from the spectators. 'Who are they shouting at?' I asked. 'You,' came the reply, 'you put Kelso into Division II.'

That is all part of the game. This is a sport which thrives on discussion and argument, the 'crack' as the players call it, and one hopes that will never change. The great difference between rugby and many other major sporting activities is the social mixing of the players. And, it is to be hoped, the Press might continue to be included in that.

Many years after taking my pen to report on Scotland I was back with them in Dublin, 1984, with the Triple Crown in our grasp. Indeed, so confident of Scottish success were the Irish that you could buy Scottish Triple Crown ties at the airport on the Thursday before the match. But the prize still had to be won. No one in the Scottish Press Corps had ever seen their country clinch a Triple Crown before. As the final whistle blew we, impartial as ever, stood to applaud our team off the field. When we did so the Irish Press writers, to a man, came over to shake our hands. We felt we had played a small part in a marvellous occasion. I felt grateful to have been doused in the Hawick spirit, and to have been banned by the SRU.

FOOTBALL MATCH
Scotland v England

This great football match was played yesterday on the Academy Cricket Ground, Edinburgh, with a result most gratifying for Scotland. The weather was fine and there was a very large turn-out of spectators. The competitors were dressed in appropriate costume, the English wearing a white jersey, ornamented by a red rose, and the Scotch a brown jersey with a thistle. Although the good wishes of the spectators went with the Scotch team yet it was considered that their chance was poor. The difference between the two teams was very marked, the English being of a much heavier and stronger build compared to their opponents. The game commenced shortly after three o'clock, the Scotch getting the kick off, and for some time neither side had any advantage. The Scotch, however, succeeded in driving the ball down to the English goal, and pushing splendidly forward, eventually put it into the opponents' quarters, who, however, prevented any harm accruing by smartly 'touching down'. This result warmed the Englishmen up to their work, and in spite of tremendous opposition they got near the Scotch goal, and kicked the ball past it, but as it was cleverly 'touched down' they got no advantage. This finished the first 50 minutes and the teams changed sides. For a considerable time after the change the ball was sent from side to side, and the 'backs' got more work to do. By some lucky runs, however, the Scotch got on to the borders of the English land and tried to force the ball past the goal. The English strenuously opposed this attempt, and for a time the struggle was terrible, ending in the Scotch 'touching down' in their opponents' ground, and becoming entitled to a 'try'. This result was received with cheers which were more heartily renewed when Cross, to whom the 'kick off' was entrusted, made a beautiful goal. This defeat only stirred up the English to fresh efforts, and driving the ball across the field, they managed also to secure a 'try', but unfortunately the man who got the 'kick off' did not allow sufficient windage, and the ball fell short. After this the Scotch became more cautious and playing well together secured after several attempts a second 'try', but good luck did not attend the 'kick off', and the goal was lost. Time being then declared up the game ceased, the Scotch winning by a goal and a 'try'.

From the Glasgow Herald *of Tuesday 28 March 1871. The report was carried on page 5 on the day following the world's first international rugby match. It was sandwiched between a column devoted to commercial news and an item on 'Coursing'.*

William Webb Who?

The Early Years

By DEREK DOUGLAS

THE ORIGINS OF THE GAME we now call rugby football are obscure in the extreme. Of one thing, though, we can be absolutely certain. Despite all the brouhaha and received wisdom to the contrary, it most certainly wasn't invented at Rugby School in 1823 by William Webb Ellis.

Just why the credit for conception of the handling code should have gone to an otherwise undistinguished pupil at an English public school remains one of sporting life's great unsolved mysteries. After school, William Webb Ellis became a churchman and his last resting place is to be found in the South of France. However, it is for something he did not do that he is most remembered.

Although by all accounts Rugby School does not press the claim to have been the cradle from which the handling code took its first, faltering steps, there is a commemorative plaque on the precincts declaring that W. W. Ellis had, indeed, been the progenitor of a game now played all the world over.

THIS STONE
COMMEMORATES THE EXPLOIT OF WILLIAM WEBB ELLIS
WHO WITH A FINE DISREGARD FOR THE RULES OF FOOTBALL
AS PLAYED IN HIS TIME
FIRST TOOK THE BALL IN HIS ARMS AND RAN WITH IT
THUS ORIGINATING THE DISTINCTIVE FEATURE OF
THE RUGBY GAME
AD 1823

Perhaps the wording of the commemorative script gives the game away. There is no doubt, from well-documented sources, that the handling game was widely practised prior to young Master Ellis's exploit. However, perhaps at Rugby School the preference up until then had been for the kicking game. This would give credence to the opinion of a schoolboy contemporary of Ellis that he had been an 'admirable cricketer, but was generally inclined to take unfair advantage at football'!

So, if the claim of Rugby School to have been the birthplace of the great game cannot be sustained then how did its eponymous legacy come about? Simple. On 28 August 1845, the rules of the game as played at the school were committed to paper. Significantly, it had taken 22 years for

The Scotland XX who took on England at Edinburgh Academicals' Raeburn Place ground on Monday, 27 March 1871. Scotland won the rugby code's first international match by the margin of a goal and a try to a single try by England *BACK ROW*: R. Munro (St Andrews University), J. S. Thomson (Glasgow Academicals), T. Chalmers (Glasgow Academicals) *MIDDLE ROW*: A. Buchanan (Royal High School FP), A. B. Colville (Merchistonians), J. Forsyth (Edinburgh University), J. A. W. Mein (Edinburgh Academicals), R. W. Irvine (Edinburgh Academicals), J. W. Arthur (Glasgow Academicals), W. D. Brown (Glasgow Academicals), A. Drew (Glasgow Academicals), W. Cross (Merchistonians), J. F. Finlay (Edinburgh Academicals), The Hon. F. J. Moncreiff (Capt., Edinburgh Academicals), G. Ritchie (Merchistonians) *FRONT ROW*: B. Ross (St Andrews University), W. J. C. Lyall (Edinburgh Academicals), T. R. Marshall (Edinburgh Academicals), J. L. H. MacFarlane (Edinburgh University), A. H. Robertson (West of Scotland) *Courtesy of the Scottish Rugby Union*

the Rugby masters to have come to the conclusion that young Ellis might have been on to something after all. But by this time in Scotland the public schools in Edinburgh were already well on the way to developing their own versions of the handling code, while in the Borders, and elsewhere, great no-holds-barred ball games involving whole communities – Uppies v Doonies – had been enjoyed since time immemorial.

In local and national archives, in Scotland as elsewhere throughout Great Britain, there is entry after entry showing how the authorities, regal and magisterial, had frowned upon the playing of ball games. The general feeling was that such pastimes kept the common folk from their work or from martial sessions known in Scotland as 'wapingschawings' when all good men and true were supposed to be at practice with lance, axe, sword and bow.

Throughout the 19th century there are numerous references to games of 'hand ba'' in towns and villages throughout Scotland and elsewhere, while in 1815 on the Duke of Buccleuch's estate at Carterhaugh, outside Selkirk, Sir Walter Scott organised a well-documented game between shepherds and townsfolk of which contemporary accounts leave one in no doubt that handling was indeed permitted. In the great Scottish schools and universities, too, there was a tradition of playing a handling code of football and some evidence to suggest that in the Royal High School of Edinburgh, for instance, there existed a 'carrying game' nearer the beginning of the 19th century. In fact, one of Scotland's earliest international players, Harry J. Stevenson, an Edinburgh lawyer who gained 15 Caps between 1888 and 1893, incurred the displeasure of some English internationalist counterparts when he related the Royal High School experience during the 'centenary' celebrations of the handling game at Rugby School in 1923.

Subsequently, Stevenson declared: 'Many years ago, when I had occasion to hunt for the origins of rugby, I discovered that the High School played a carrying game around about 1810. This fact I mentioned to some of my old English football friends and others when we gathered at Rugby in 1923 as representatives of the carrying game to help to celebrate the centenary – so-called. When told that they had given the name "Rugby" to the game, but that they certainly did not invent it as it had been played in Scotland for unknown years before 1823 and by the High School about 1810, some of them were very annoyed. I am not an old High School boy and in fact was one of her "enemies" in the football world and only wish I could claim that my old school [*Edinburgh Academy*] was as close to the origin of rugby as was the High School.'

By 1858 Stevenson's *alma mater* had committed its version of the 'rugby' rules to print, while Merchiston, Loretto, Royal High, Glenalmond and other outposts throughout the country were all displaying an embryonic interest in the handling code.

One of the moving forces behind the development of the game in Scotland was Dr Hely-Hutchinson Almond, headmaster of Loretto School, Musselburgh (of whom more later), and it was following a suggestion of his that the so-called *Green Book* was prepared, in order to 'prevent

Ned Haig, the Melrose butcher whose concept of an abbreviated version of the game, intended merely as a fund-raising ploy for the Greenyard club, has spawned the seven-a-side game now popular all over the world
Courtesy of Scottish Rugby Union

confusion and disputes in future matches'. The clubs involved in drawing up the new rules were Edinburgh Academicals FC, Loretto, Merchiston and West of Scotland. When the new regulations had finally been agreed upon they were printed in the form of *The Laws of Football as played by the Principal Clubs of Scotland*.

By the end of the 1860s there were sufficient clubs actively participating in the handling code for fixture lists to be drawn up. The game was still, though, very much the preserve of the professional classes and the old-school-tie. The late Sandy Thorburn, official archivist and historian of the Scottish Rugby Union, during his fastidious researches, identified a large number of clubs active in the game as the decade drew to a close including school sides such as Edinburgh Academy, Merchiston, Royal High, Loretto, Craigmount, Blairlodge, Madras College and Glasgow Academy. Former Pupils' clubs encompassed Edinburgh Academicals, Merchistonians, Glasgow Academicals and Royal High School FP. Glasgow, Edinburgh and St Andrews Universities were also prominent and among the 'open' clubs regularly competing were Edinburgh Wanderers, West of Scotland, Blairgowrie, Kilmarnock, Ayr, Dollar, Alloa, Perth and Roland's Rooms (an Edinburgh fencing academy and gymnasium).

The legendary Scottish Rugby Union secretary J. Aikman Smith. His stern but beneficial stewardship of the SRU's affairs set the Union on the road to success. He disliked change, and when asked why the Scottish XV did not wear numbers on their jerseys is reputed to have replied: 'This, sir, is a rugby match, not a cattle auction!'
Courtesy of Scottish Rugby Union

That there was still much confusion as to the rules, however, is underlined by the fact that three years after publication of the *Green Book* in Scotland the Rugby Football Union, operating under the Rugby School rules, was formed in England and that a number of Scottish clubs applied for membership. West of Scotland, Glasgow Academicals and Edinburgh University signed on with the Rugby Union in 1871, followed the next year by Edinburgh Academicals, Royal High School FP and Edinburgh Wanderers. The RFU's first accounts depict the West of Scotland club as having been admitted to membership with its subscription having been paid on 4 October 1871.

Disagreements as to the laws of the game were over such basic matters as to whether matches should be played 20-a-side or 15-a-side (not finally settled until 1892) and whether or not, in the event of the teams being tied on goals at the close of play, the winner should be decided by the number of tries scored. At the time, a 'run-in' or 'try', as the latter term suggests, merely gave the scoring side an opportunity to 'try' a kick at goal and 'tries' were even considered to be subsidiary to 'field goals' which were, one supposes, the equivalent of the modern drop-goal. In the light of such scoring ambiguities it comes as no surprise to learn that in contemporary newspaper accounts of those early matches it was not uncommon for the scribe to conclude his report with the words 'the match ended in dispute'.

The handling code's first international match — between Scotland and England at the Edinburgh Academical ground, Raeburn Place, on Monday, 27 March 1871 — had its genesis in just such a dispute involving the handling and non-handling or Association codes. Similarly, the outcome of the game itself became the subject of hot debate involving an umpiring decision by the aforementioned Dr Almond. The Loretto

OFFICIAL PROGRAMME 10p

Artist's impression of the 1871 game

SCOTLAND V ENGLAND

MURRAYFIELD 27 MARCH 1971

The special programme
for the celebratory match
played at Murrayfield on
27 March 1971, to mark the
centenary of the world's first
Rugby Union international
– that between Scotland and
England at Raeburn Place
in Edinburgh on Monday,
27 March 1871. Exactly 100
years to the day later, history
repeated itself and Scotland
were once again victorious,
the score on this occasion
being 26–6 in favour of
the Scots

headmaster, said by contemporaries to be a great apostle of the muscular brand of Christianity, had taught at Merchiston before moving on to the Musselburgh school and was a great advocate of the handling code who regularly coached, umpired and played in his school sides.

In March 1870, under the auspices of the Football Association, an international match involving England and Scotland had been played at the Oval cricket ground in London. Later that same year, the FA decided to hold a second match and the Association's secretary, C. W. Alcock, wrote to the Scottish Press inviting Scottish-based 'Association code' clubs to put forward candidates for the second game. There were only a handful of clubs in Scotland operating under the Football Association rules and the feeling in Scotland was that ten home-based Scots should be despatched to London where they would meet up with ten exiles for the purpose of taking on England in a 20-a-side game. Alcock replied that under his Association's rules 11 was the maximum number of players permissible. 'More than 11 we do not care to play as with greater numbers it is our opinion that the game becomes less scientific and more a trial of charging and brute force,' he declared.

This prompted Dr Almond, under a pseudonym, to write to the Scottish Press declaring: 'Mr Alcock is a very leading supporter of what is called the "Association" game which is to Rugby Football, or whatever its detractors may please to call it, as is moonlight unto sunlight and as water unto wine.' Months elapsed before, on 8 December 1870, the Scottish clubs resolved the matter by issuing a challenge to their English counterparts through the correspondence columns of *Bell's Life* magazine in London and *The Scotsman* newspaper in Edinburgh.

The signatories of that historic letter were A. H. Robertson, West of Scotland FC; F. Moncreiff, Edinburgh Academical FC; B. Hall Blyth, Merchistonian FC; J. W. Arthur, Glasgow Academical FC; and J. H. Oatts, St Salvator FC, St Andrews:

> Sir
> There is a pretty general feeling among Scotch football players that the football power of the old country was not properly represented in the late so-called International Football match. Not that we think the play of the gentlemen who represented Scotland otherwise than very good – but that we consider the Association rules, in accordance with which the late game was played, not such as to bring together the best team Scotland could turn out. Almost all the leading clubs play by the Rugby code, and have no opportunity of practising the Association game, even if willing to do so. We therefore feel that a match played in accordance with any rules other than those in general use in Scotland, as was the case in the last match, is not one that would meet with support generally from her players. For our satisfaction, therefore, and with a view of really testing what Scotland can do against an English team we, as representing the football interests of Scotland, hereby challenge any team selected from the whole of England, to play us a match, twenty-a-side, Rugby Rules, either in Edinburgh or

Glasgow on any day during the present season that might be found suitable to the English players. Let this count as the return to the match played in London on 19th November, or, if preferred, let it be a separate match. If it be entered into we can promise England a hearty welcome and a first-rate match. Any communication addressed to any one of us will be attended to.

Not surprisingly, this public challenge elicited no response from Mr Alcock and the Football Association. It was, though, taken up by the rugby-playing clubs and officially responded to by B. H. Burns, Esq, secretary of the Blackheath club. In Scotland a committee was formed to take care of the arrangements.

A crowd of about 4,000 witnessed the match, played 20-a-side on a pitch 120 yards long and 55 yards wide. Scotland won by the margin of a goal and a try to a try, and it was the circumstance relating to Scotland's first try which provoked heated dispute and a judgment from umpire Almond with which today's referees will find great affinity.

One of the England players, A. G. Guillemard, later to become secretary, treasurer and president of the RFU, takes up the story: 'The game was very keenly contested until half-time, after which the combination of the Scots, who knew each other's play thoroughly, and their superior training began to tell, after a maul just outside the English goal-line Dr H. H. Almond, the famous Headmaster of Loretto, who was one of the umpires [*the other was A. Ward, England*] ordered the ball to be put down in a scrummage five yards outside the line. The Scottish forwards, instead of putting the ball down, held it up off the ground and pushed our men bodily over the line and secured the touch. We admitted the try because they assured us it was a fair try according to Scottish rules. At any rate, the honour of scoring it belonged to the whole Scottish front rank though it was Buchanan [*Angus Buchanan, Royal High School FP*] who actually grounded the ball and so had the distinction of being the first player to score in an international. W. Cross kicked the goal and in those days a goal was the vital score.

'Our first, and only, try in the match, was scored by R. H. Birkett. We pinned the Scots near their own line for some time before Birkett ran in close to the corner flag. Stokes, our captain, failed with a long, difficult place-kick in the cross wind.

'The second Scottish try was also got in a peculiar and, in our view, an illegal way. A long throw-in from touch by a Scot went past our forwards and one of theirs literally fisted the ball over our line and W. Cross, racing after it from behind, touched it down but his place-kick was unsuccessful.'

Some years later Dr Almond, who had also taught at Merchiston School in Edinburgh, recalled the events of the Raeburn Place match and had this to say about the contested opening try and his part in declaring it to be valid. From his explanation of what had occurred and that of England's Guillemard it is apparent that even years afterwards there was no accord as to what the dispute had been about. Dr Almond writes:

A selection of the oldest
Scottish international Caps
in existence. They now form
part of the Scottish Rugby
Union collection housed
in the SRU museum at
Murrayfield

'The ball had certainly been scrummaged over the line by Scotland and touched down first by a Scotchman. The try was vociferously disputed by the English team but on what ground I was then unable to discover.

'Had the good rule of the *Green Book* been kept, viz. that no one except the captain should speak in any dispute unless appealed to, I should have understood that the point raised was that the ball had never been fairly grounded in the scrummage but had got mixed up among Scottish feet or legs. This I only learned afterwards. Indeed, when the game was played 20-a-side, the ball, at the beginning of a scrummage, was quite invisible to anyone outside, nor do I know how I could have decided the point had I known what it was.'

Almond adds: 'I must say, however, that when an umpire is in doubt, I think he is justified in deciding against the side which makes the most noise. They are probably in the wrong.'

Two years after that first international, the game having become an annual event, the two teams met in a drawn match at the West of Scotland ground, Hamilton Crescent in Glasgow. Immediately at the close of play representatives of the foremost clubs in Scotland met in the old Glasgow Academy, Elmbank Street, for the express purpose of forming a Scottish Union. A committee was formed and charged with the tasks of formulating a set of bye-laws which would be placed before a general meeting during the close season. The captain and one other member from Merchistonians, Royal High School FP, West of Scotland, Glasgow Academicals, Edinburgh Academicals, Edinburgh University, Glasgow University and St Andrews University were responsible for drawing up the bye-laws which were submitted to the first AGM held in Edinburgh on 9 October 1873. In addition to the original eight member clubs, the meeting agreed to admit Edinburgh Wanderers and Warriston FC.

Over the next decade the game continued to expand and in particular to take hold outside Edinburgh and Glasgow. In 1889 the Northern and Southern Districts became entitled to representation on the Union committee alongside their counterparts from the East and West and by 1894 the South had succeeded in increasing its representation from one to two, while simultaneously reducing that of the West to two. The game took off in a big way in the Borders where its very robustness particularly appealed and, as in Wales and the North of England, it became the preferred game of the working man.

Throughout the 1870s the Border towns were forming their own clubs. Langholm, Hawick, Gala, Melrose, Kelso and Earlston were all early on the scene while in 1885 the Jed-Forest club was formed in Jedburgh. There was still a deal of resentment in the Borders as to the 'old school tie' nature of the ruling hierarchy and in season 1901–02 (apparently against the wishes of officialdom) Gala, Hawick, Jed-Forest, Langholm and Melrose decided to protect their regional identity and guarantee competitive matches by inaugurating an annual league, the outcome of which would be decided by a series of matches played on a home and away basis. Kelso and Selkirk were admitted to the Border League in 1912 and the stage was set for the world's most enduring league competition, which now co-exists with the national competition, itself an example of Scottish rugby foresight.

On the international scene the game continued to expand and relations were opened first with Ireland, the Scotland side scoring a handsome four-goal, two drop-goal, two-try to nil win in Belfast in 1877; then Wales, with a three goals to one win at Raeburn Place in 1883; and France, with a 27–0 victory at Inverleith in 1910. But relations between the international partners were not always cordial and it was a profound disagreement between the Scots and the English which led to the cancellation of the 1885 fixture between the two countries and, as a by-product, the formation of the International Board.

The disagreement had stemmed from a disputed try scored in the 1884 meeting between the two countries. England had won by the margin of a goal to a try but the English try, by R. S. Kindersley (Exeter), was contested by the Scots on the basis that a Scottish player had previously 'knocked back' the ball and that as this was against the rules as they understood them, most of the Scottish players, and not a few of the English, had ceased playing in anticipation of the referee ruling that an infringement had occurred. No such ruling had been forthcoming from the referee and Kindersley ran in to score an easy touchdown. At the time there was no such thing as an 'advantage' law and the Scots felt they were within their rights to dispute the try which had given the English the kick at goal which won for them the match. The Unions of Scotland and England were unable to agree on interpretation of the rules and the Rugby Union would not agree that the matter should go to arbitration, so the 1885 fixture between the two countries became a victim of the impasse. The Rugby Union, which obviously viewed itself as the guardian of the laws of the game, was unwilling to agree to an Irish proposal that an International Board should be formed to pronounce on such disputes and declined to become involved when Scotland, Ireland and Wales set up the first International Board in 1886. England persevered in glorious isolation and played no further matches until the end of the decade when, in 1890, a form of words was formulated as to the rules of the game which met with the Rugby Union's approval. In addition, England secured six places on the Board in sharp contrast to the two apiece from the other Home Unions.

Before the turn of the century Scottish, and more particularly Borders rugby, had initiated an event which has had a lasting, and still developing, effect on the game worldwide. At the end of the 1883 season the Melrose club were examining various means of enhancing club funds. A local butcher, Ned Haig by name, hit upon the novel idea of staging an athletics sports meeting, one of whose attractions would be a knock-out rugby competition. So that the contest could be concluded in the course of a single afternoon, ties were played over a 15-minute duration and teams were restricted to seven players apiece. Initially the playing line-up was four forwards, two quarter-backs and one full-back. In time, though, one forward was withdrawn from the scrum to become a centre and to form the configuration we know today.

A splendid example of Scottish thrift, or parsimony depending on your viewpoint . . . the ball used in both of Scotland's home matches during the 1910 Championship. It was used initially in the inaugural match against France when the Scots won 27–0 and then saw service in the game against England when the Sassenachs were the victors and won their first Championship since 1892. The ball is now on display at Murrayfield in the SRU museum

As a moneyspinner, a family day out and as a spectacle, Haig's abbreviated game concept was a big hit and in short order Gala, Hawick, Jed-Forest and Langholm were following suit with their own spring 'sports', as the sevens tourneys were, and still are, known in the Borders. It was an idea whose time had come. Selkirk and Kelso decided to stage their own tournaments in the autumn, at the start of the season, and soon the city clubs were getting in on the act too. In 1926, in England, the Middlesex tournament was held for the first time at Twickenham and in 1973, as part of the SRU centenary celebrations, an international sevens tournament was held for the first time at Murrayfield.

Now the Borders sevens circuit, although not as popular with city sides as it once was, continues to provide a source of entertainment and finance, while on the international stage the event held annually in Hong Kong is a highlight of the rugby calendar. In 1993 the inaugural World Sevens tournament, with rugby talent from a' the airts, will be held at Murrayfield, and thereafter in a different country every two years. Ned Haig's nice little Melrose earner has indeed become big business on a global scale.

Foresight, Good Sense and Obstinacy

The Border League

By DAVID STEELE

IT WAS STARTED with a sprinkling of foresight, a smidgeon of good sense and a couple of pinches of old-fashioned obstinacy.

The Border League, rugby's oldest and most established competitive league, is also considered by many to be its most fiercely contested. What is for sure is that its durability can never be questioned and the fact that it is so jealously guarded, merely admired.

The Border League was formed in season 1901–02 as the number and stature of clubs in the Borders of Scotland grew. Then, as now, they were keen to protect their identity and foster the rivalries between towns and their teams. Sides from Glasgow and Edinburgh, established in this relatively new game of rugby, were keen to test their mettle against the Borderers and while they were made welcome, there was still a touch of the 'wha's like us' abroad in the South.

Sadly the records of those early days of the League have been lost and it is not possible to record precisely why the established Border sides chose to 'go it alone' and set the pace in competitive rugby which the rest of Scotland, and indeed the world, would take over 70 years to catch up with. There are, though, many who have their opinions on why this League was formed. All share a great respect for the audacity of the founding fathers who cocked a snook at the ruling body, in those days the old school tie brigade of the Scottish Football Union, who were just a bit set in their ways. The SFU was firmly against the League plans put forward at that time, being of the opinion that this kind of competition would be detrimental to the game and bad for the players. 'Cobblers', or whatever the preferred word of strong disagreement was back then, came the reply from the Borderers and they went ahead and formed their League anyway.

Bill McLaren laughs when he speaks of those days – from research rather than recollection, of course! 'It was kind of typical of Borderers that they put forward this idea which found no favour at all with the administrators of the game. They went ahead with the plans anyway. Then they had the cheek one year to invite the Union's formidable secretary J. Aikman Smith to come and present the Border League trophy.

'I, for one, am glad that they persevered as the Border League has given me a great deal of pleasure down the years and I hope it will continue to do so for many years to come,' says McLaren, a native of Hawick and a former wearer of the Green.

In those early days the League was made up of Gala, Hawick, Jed-Forest, Langholm and Melrose. It was not to be brought up to full complement – with the addition of Kelso and Selkirk – until 1912. Then, as now, the teams played each other on a home and away basis – an arrangement which the participants saw as guaranteeing them a good number of worthwhile fixtures each season.

Despite the disapproval of the powers-that-were over the League it prospered and Hawick were to be the first champions, passing over the crown to Jed-Forest for the next three seasons. It was not to be until later in the history of the League that the Greens would again dominate, although their record in Border, as in National, League rugby is formidable.

By the end of season 1989–90 the League had been contested 73 times with Hawick winning or sharing the title (play-off games being a fairly recent innovation) on 42 occasions. Their closest challengers over

Borderers on the charge . . . stopping Kelso's John Jeffrey and Eric Paxton is not a job for the faint of heart

the period are Jed-Forest and Melrose with nine each, followed by Gala on six, Kelso on five, Selkirk on three and Langholm with a single title.

One of those who holds an opinion on why the Border League began is Walter Thomson of Selkirk, aka 'Fly-Half' of the *Sunday Post*. As always, it is an opinion worth listening to. 'I believe that the Border sides could see the game growing at an alarming rate and while they wanted to be part of that growth they also wanted to preserve the heritage of Border rugby. It is also possible that in those days, before sponsors and the like, the only income for a club was at the gate. They had seen how sevens attracted the crowds and perhaps thought that could happen with the full game if a little spice was added.'

It appears that in the early days Border League meetings were held at two famous rugby 'howffs' – the King's Arms, Melrose, and the Dryburgh at Newtown St Boswells. As Walter Thomson discovered in his own research of the history of the League: 'The set-up then was very similar to what it is now with club presidents taking it in turn to preside over League meetings. The work was left to the secretary, though, who was also secretary of the South District Union and it is amusing to

Colin Telfer makes full use of the protection afforded by a Hawick pack of the Seventies to make good his clearance kick

Another Championship for a Border side . . . a bloody but unbowed Keith Robertson accepts the 1990 Scottish Championship trophy

think that he could not allow his left hand to know what his right was doing for fear of upsetting the Union bigwigs.

'The League and Union representatives would often be one and the same and would meet in the same place on the same night. Two minute books would be kept – one for the Union's eyes, the other for League business.' Thomson also learned of the practice, which now seems faintly ludicrous, of skirting round the subject of the League when a visiting dignitary was in town.

'They would go through the clubs congratulating them on their achievements but when it came to the Border League champions they would say well done but not for what.

'It is also an amusing tale, if perhaps apocryphal, that the clubhouse photographs of the Border League champions would be turned to the wall for fear of upsetting a visiting Union man.'

The twin duties of Border League and South District Union secretary exist to this day, with George Murray taking over from the late John Robertson. That most able and popular official, shortly before his death, told John Smail on his excellent Radio Borders series tracing the story of Border rugby, of how fierce independence continued even into the early Seventies when National Leagues were being mooted for Scotland.

He recalled: 'We had visits from at least two presidents of the Scottish Rugby Union and they spoke to the various clubs. Eventually they agreed they would go into the National Leagues, the Border League members agreed, on condition that the National Leagues did not interfere with the Sevens and did not interfere with the Border League.

'These conditions are, in fact, recorded in the minutes of the AGM of the SRU which was held at the time, in the early Seventies.'

It was John Robertson who finally brought the Borders into the National League flock after the whole thing had been held up while they decided, something for which we must all be eternally grateful — even if some of those who have tasted defeat in the Borders may disagree. He and others who shaped the oldest League for rugby in the world must have laughed up their sleeves when the sport began to clamour nationally for what had been set up against the odds over 72 years before.

What is in no doubt is that Border clubs, perhaps due in no small measure to the honing of their competitive skills in their own League, have dominated the national stage. From the introduction of league rugby in Scotland in season 1973–74 until the end of season 1990–91, only two clubs from outwith the Borders – Heriot's FP from Edinburgh in season 1978–79 and Boroughmuir from the same city in 1990–91 – have won the Division One title. The figures tell their own story. Division One winners – Hawick on ten occasions, Gala thrice, Kelso in successive seasons and Melrose once.

For Robertson's successor, George Murray, working for the good of rugby in his area is something of a labour of love. He says: 'Rugby has always given me a tremendous amount of pleasure and much of that pleasure has been in watching and refereeing Border matches.' Murray is firmly of the opinion that, despite attempts down the years to kill it off, the Border League is alive and well and continuing to prosper, especially with the welcome financial support of £50,000 over three years which has come from the Bank of Scotland.

'I believe that the Border League is as strong as it has ever been; there is a bond between the seven senior clubs in the Borders and it would take a lot to break that.' He views with doubt, but does not dismiss entirely, the suggestion that there may be clubs like Peebles who pass, for example, Langholm in the National Leagues and who may feel that they have a case for inclusion in the Border League.

John Rutherford of Selkirk matured into one of Scotland's greatest ever stand-off halves

'It has always been the seven clubs since 1912, with nothing in the rules to cover relegation or exclusion. Some clubs have asked in the past to become members but none of them has been successful.'

On the League's current state of health Walter Thomson is in accord with Murray. 'I believe it is stronger now than it has ever been in its history. The National Leagues have added a new dimension to rugby but in the Borders it remains just as important, if not more so, to land a Border League title.

'I can remember one season in the Thirties when Hawick won the unofficial Championship, they lost only two games. Both were to Gala and it meant that Gala won the Border League title.

'You would have thought they would have been delighted at Mansfield Park but the loss of their local League hurt them quite a

Colin Deans . . . skipper of Hawick, the South, Scotland and a special British Lions XV

bit.' Colin Deans of Hawick, Scotland and the British Lions, in his autobiography, *You're a Hooker, Then*, sums up his feelings towards this institution: 'Where I play my club rugby we have a unique set-up known as the Border League. I can assure you that it's just as hard and competitive as the National League which brings with it the title of National Champions.'

David Bell, now Selkirk coach, holds a different view. 'I believe that the National Leagues have taken over in recent years. There is a feeling that the Border League has become a bit stale playing the same teams all the time. The players and the supporters want variety and they get that with the National Leagues.' The affable Bell admits, however: 'Perhaps my feelings towards the League are coloured by the fact that we used to get stuffed in those days by just about everybody.'

His fellow coach, celebrated Scotland and British Lions' stand-off John Rutherford, disagrees. 'I feel that the Border League keeps the players sharp from an early stage in the season and if all the games have not been played it means that 15-a-side rugby can still be enjoyed later in the season. Too often the big forwards or backs who are not interested in sevens drift off towards the end of the season. I have tremendous memories of the Border League and when I pulled on the Selkirk jersey for the first time I felt that it was not just representing a club but a town. That feeling, I am sure, is the same for every Borderer when he takes the field for a match against local rivals.'

George Murray describes a Border League Saturday thus: 'There is a buzz of expectation around the town. The crowd will be just that bit bigger if the game is against local opposition. People following one club will want to see old friends and old rivals on the field and in the clubhouse. The people who support the other lot will not have far to travel and will happily make the journey for a Border League fixture. Well and good if it is a double header with the National Leagues but I feel that in the Borders local rivalries and the possibility of a League title outweigh the lure of a national crown.'

He adds: 'I often hear the word bitter used for the rivalries between Border rugby clubs and the towns where they are situated. I would never see it as bitter, strong it certainly is, but any bitterness which is there is soon forgotten over a beer or two in the club rooms as that day's game and many more before it are discussed.'

Bill McLaren says: 'The rivalries have been there since time began and now they can be seen on the rugby field instead of the battlefield. Mind you, looking at some games over the years it was sometimes hard to tell the difference!'

Border terriers . . .
Roy Laidlaw and Gary Armstrong, both products of Jed-Forest, are the latest in a distinguished line of Border scrum-halves who have graced the game at international level

More sevens' silverware for the Mansfield Park trophy cupboard . . . a 1984 vintage Jim Renwick. The Borders sevens circuit has weathered the disinterest of city clubs and remains a popular feature of the Scottish rugby calendar

He would be the very last to admit it, but before his retirement, Bill McLaren of the *Glasgow Herald* and the BBC, did more than most to nurture young talent in his 'day job' role as a games master in Hawick

Jed-Forest's Gary Armstrong
in the thick of the
international action

Goldenacre Full-Back Factory

The Great Eight

By BRIAN MEEK

A SPECTATOR ONCE SHOUTED AT DAN DRYSDALE: 'I don't like your play, you are a lucky full-back, the ball always comes to you.' The great man took it as one of the finest compliments ever paid to him for it underlined the supreme rugby skill which made him the first of eight Heriot full-backs to play for their country – anticipation.

The 'lucky' Drysdale would win 26 successive Scottish Caps; he would be 18 times on the winning side; he would captain his country on 13 occasions; he would play in four Tests in South Africa for the British Lions; he would be selected for the Barbarians and he would be the founder of the full-back dynasty.

On 6 January 1975, at the Assembly Rooms in Edinburgh, the Heriot's Former Pupils Rugby Club staged a magnificent tribute dinner for the octet who had brought such honour and distinction to their school and community. Alec Bateman, a notable orator, toasted the first four, Drysdale, Jimmy Kerr, Tommy Gray and Ian Thomson. Alex Stepney, another who could captivate an audience with consummate ease, proposed the health of Ken Scotland, Colin Blaikie, who had travelled from South Africa, Ian Smith, who had come back from Hong Kong, and Andy Irvine. Those present, and I was fortunate enough to be one of them, will never forget the occasion.

And yet, what were we all celebrating? A coincidence, surely. The Heriot Club had not set out to produce international full-backs. Indeed most of the men being honoured had started their playing careers in other positions; one of them, Tommy Gray, was far more often seen at fly-half. Jimmy Kerr smiled when I put that point to him: 'In part it must be coincidence. But is it just possible that the club brought to the full-back position some special enterprise? Could it have been the way we played the game?'

I don't know. What is unchallengeable is that the Herioters and their guests had gathered to honour eight exceptional men, all with tales to tell that have delighted and fascinated me. I hope you enjoy sharing them.

'Those of you who believe in birth control,' quipped Alec Bateman, 'might like to know that Dan Drysdale was the 11th of a family of 12.'

Opposite:
Colin Blaikie . . . always in the right place at the right time

Dan Drysdale . . . neat and tidy in all he did and an immense influence on the game

Jimmy Kerr . . . never let the ball bounce, a fine piece of advice

Sadly, Dan was the only one of the group I could not interview – he passed on a couple of years ago. But his influence on Scottish rugby was immense. 'He was the hero figure always held up to us as schoolboys,' recalled Ken Scotland. 'I actually did some business with him,' Andy Irvine told me, 'and he gave me great encouragement.'

Dan Drysdale, neat and tidy in all he did, was a member of the 1925 Grand Slam side: he kicked a conversion against France, a dropped goal and a conversion in the Welsh match, a conversion against Ireland and another one against England. In that final encounter with the English, won 14–11, it was his tackle on the flying winger A. M. Smallwood which saved the day. Dan finished the match concussed from a kick on the head but there was no question of him leaving the field.

From 1923 to 1929 he reigned supreme. After retiring he worked for the Dunlop Rubber Company in Malaya for a spell but, on his return, threw himself into the administrative side of the game. Soon he was a selector, then chairman of the selectors and finally the first Herioter to become president of the Scottish Rugby Union. By this time he was also managing director of one of the country's largest timber companies.

Drysdale would touch the lives of two of the other full-backs but more of that later. Thanks to the kindness of Ian Thomson, who lent me the tape of the 1975 dinner, we can savour some of his thoughts on the game.

'The ideal in rugby,' he told that gathering, 'is and always has been to do the simple and basic things well. Giving a pass at the right time remains the most important factor.

'I am concerned about obsessive kicking: I am also worried about excessive coaching of backs which is likely to lead to a stalemate in many games [*how right he was*!] and it depresses me that so many matches are won by penalty kicks. When, I wonder, will the differential penalty be introduced?' When indeed, Dan?

Sir John Orr, another Heriot international, and one who saw all the full-backs in action, said simply of Drysdale: 'He was one of the game's gentlemen.'

The same accolade will certainly be applied to the next in line – Dr Jimmy Kerr, who, at 82, received me in his Liberton home and told of his five-Cap career between 1935 and 1937. Throughout his School career he operated at fly-half, but when he left for University he didn't play at all. There was a special reason for that: Jimmy came from a staunchly Christian family of five children, all of whom became graduates. His father was a postman and Jimmy, the youngest, went to Edinburgh on a Carnegie Scholarship. 'I felt it was incumbent on me to gain my medical qualification as quickly as possible. In the circumstances I could not afford to be injured and I was concerned about my hands.'

So it was not until his final year of medicine that he was persuaded to give it 'a canter' at full-back. John Orr says of him: 'He was immaculate in all he did. He was a great trapper of a ball and a very safe fielder.'

Actually, Jimmy told me it was his brother Christopher who had given him the best piece of advice. 'Never let the ball bounce.'

Kerr had the most daunting of debuts, against the All Blacks at Murrayfield. Scotland played well but went down 18–8 and Jimmy, at 10st 12lbs, recalls that they had several big tough guys, one of whom gave him a clout on the back of the head for good measure.

His next match, against Ireland at home, resulted in another loss, 10–4, and there was agony at Twickenham when Scotland went down by a point. In February 1937, at Swansea, Jimmy at last savoured the sweet taste of victory, and played a vital role. Fielding a kick, Kerr roared up the left wing and into the Welsh 25. It was at that point he heard the command 'Pass, Jim' and Wilson Shaw came up to take the ball for a vital try in the 13–6 success. Scotland's full-back, it should be noted, had been working in hospital up until the team had left.

There was some fun on the way home. Duncan Macrae, the St Andrews University centre, was a man who, Dr Kerr will tell you, 'liked his dinners'. When the team alighted from the town at Edinburgh's Caledonian Station Kerr noticed that Macrae was 'walking like a robot'. Enquiries as to what was wrong with him brought the response: 'I'm not sure. It could have been an injury I picked up in the game or maybe I fell down after the dinner.' Dr Kerr made a cursory examination and came to a swift diagnosis. He removed from Macrae's jacket a lavatory chain which had been inserted, by friends, down each of his arms and round his shoulder, complete with handle.

Jimmy's last game was against Ireland in Dublin. As he trained on the Friday a local man came up to him and asked if it was true the Scottish full-back could do 100 yards in just over ten seconds. 'Oh yes,' came the reply from a player not noted for his blistering pace. 'But I never told him how much over.'

He is a delightful man with a distinguished medical career which started as Assistant T.B. Officer for Edinburgh and ended as Medical Superintendent of Edinburgh Southern Hospitals with RAF service in between. Jimmy does not go to many games now but he was, with two following generations of his family, at the Grand Slam decider in 1990. 'We had a wonderful day. In fact I have had a wonderful life.'

Tommy Gray gazed out of the hotel window on to the Old Course. He has retired to St Andrews and still manages a game of golf at Crail. His left foot still hurts as well.

There are three remarkable aspects to this man's international career – he was basically a fly-half, he was 33 years old when he won his first Cap and he had survived a war wound which made walking, never mind playing rugby, a considerable achievement. Before the war he had been a member of a successful school side which, in 1934–35, had finished unbeaten without a try conceded.

Sir John Orr remembers: 'Tommy played at fly-half or centre and had terrific acceleration. He particularly excelled at sevens.'

Gray was working for the Northern Assurance Company (Motor Branch) when he made his debut in the FPs and he was beginning to interest the district selectors when war was declared. He became a Lieutenant in the King's Own Scottish Borderers and was posted to the

Tommy Gray . . . 'one of my boots had gone and so had part of a foot!'

Ian Thomson . . . a determined wee bugger!

Ken Scotland . . . beautiful balance, pace and the ability to read a game to perfection

42nd Mountain Division who were preparing for an assault on Norway. In the event the unit did not see action until November 1944 and were then posted to 'mountainous' Holland. Tommy, meantime, had been busy playing in five war-time internationals and in Army games alongside the great Hadyn Tanner of Wales and Gus Risman, later a Rugby League star, who said of Gray: 'I have never seen a better fly-half.'

Having advanced from Holland into Germany, Tommy led his men in a dawn attack on enemy tank positions. 'Six days earlier I had been given a beautiful pair of U.S. boots by a friendly American, and I was wearing them that morning. To this day I don't know if it was a mine I stepped on or a bullet which hit me. There was a flash as I tried to get into a trench. When I looked down one of the boots had gone completely: so had part of my foot.'

The war had only three months to run but Tommy spent a year in the Princess Margaret Rose Hospital, Edinburgh, where there were many operations. Yet he resumed playing in 1947 when he was an inspector with an insurance company. 'Ironically in that first season back, I hurt my other leg.'

Marriage took him to Northampton where he joined his father-in-law in a company which supplied chemicals to the shoe and leather trade. One of his customers, the Northampton Boot Company, offered to design a special boot to protect Tommy's foot.

By now he was playing for the local club and, early in 1950, he received word that Dan Drysdale, now chairman of the selectors, was coming to see him. To Gray's surprise the Scotland team required not a fly-half but a full-back and he was selected for his first Cap against England at Murrayfield on 18 March. It was quite a debut.

'The weather was dreadful, sleet and rain, but we were leading 8–3 at half-time. England kicked a penalty and converted a try to go in front 11–8.

'Right in the last minute Angus Cameron put up a huge kick which was collected by our centre Donald Sloan who just made it to the line.'

The scores were tied, Tommy Gray had to kick the conversion for victory, and he did: 'I was very nervous before a big game and would always be first into the dressing-room. But as soon as I came out of the tunnel I was fine. I thought I would kick that goal.'

He made only two other international appearances. Against France at Colombes in 1951 Scotland lost 14–12 and Gray still believes they were robbed. 'One of my penalty attempts hit a post and then went over the bar. The French judge signalled no goal and Wilson Shaw – of all people – went along with him.'

Ken Scotland

The next month there was more drama with three Heriot full-backs involved. On the day before that Welsh match Gray went down with flu and the following morning Dan Drysdale summoned 20-year-old Ian Thomson. 'I was at my mother's because, in those days, if you had an Edinburgh address you were not put up in the hotel.'

Thomson took the call at about 11 o'clock and reported to the North British at noon, stopping only to buy a pair of new laces. Mr Drysdale gave him his only instructions. 'You will take the short penalties.' That was it.

The Welsh were such hot favourites, no one would quote odds on them. They had 13 British Lions in their ranks and brought with them a travelling support of 20,000. But, in the game that will ever be famous for Peter Kininmonth's dropped goal, Scotland romped to an astonishing 19–0 victory, with young Thomson contributing a penalty and a conversion. Ian went to the dinner that night in the Royal Arch restaurant in Queen Street, then quietly made his way to meet his fiancée Margaret. They are now grandparents and live in Fairmilehead, Ian having recently retired from a post of deputy personnel manager with Standard Life.

'Thomson was one of the most solid and dependable full-backs in the business,' says John Orr. 'He had great shoulder strength, a perfect temperament and above all he was a determined wee bugger.' He still is, as anyone who takes him on at golf will tell you. Ian was also an excellent cricketer.

He gained seven Caps but was never again in a winning side. Mind you, he did manage to miss the South African debacle of 1951 when Scotland lost 44–0, which shows fine judgement. And, this will surprise those who know him well, he was once arrested in Paris along with some of his team-mates. 'On the way home from the dinner we were clowning around with a bottle which was smashed. The next thing we knew the gendarmes had us locked up in a cell and we didn't get out until an official came to vouch for us.'

Ian Thomson retired from playing at only 27. 'I don't know the real reason why – it just felt like the right time.' He went off to play golf and was not seen for many years at Goldenacre. Today he has returned and is the most faithful of supporters.

'It was Andy Irvine who brought me back. I think he was in a class of his own and he created excitement whenever he touched the ball.' (Andy was pleased to see Ian, he was even happier when 'Thompo' offered to tend his garden!)

Dan Drysdale was still the King but in the late Fifties another pretender came to challenge his throne. K. J. F. Scotland had arrived and with him a revolution in the style of full-back play. Defence was to be turned into attack.

There had been running full-backs before – Drysdale himself could shift. But it was normally on the counter-attack. The last line of defence did not join in set-piece threequarter movements. They did now.

Ken Scotland could, and did, play in most positions in the back division. A deceptively frail-looking figure, he had cricketer's hands, beautiful balance, enough pace to make a break and could read a game to perfection. It was the time of National Service and he was enlisted in the Royal Signals at Catterick.

'They had a first-class fixture list in these days and I was into the team at fly-half. I went on a Combined Services tour and played for the Army in my first season.

'The idea of using the full-back as an extra attacker was developed at Catterick because we had a Welshman, called Evans would you believe, who was also a good fly-half. When we put him to full-back we developed a number of ploys, sometimes using him as a decoy.

'Later, at Cambridge, when I was the full-back I used to come in between the outside centre and the wing. Eventually a defence was organised to cope with this but in the early days the move worked very effectively.'

Ken burst on to the international scene in January 1957. On his debut against France he dropped a goal and kicked a penalty to ensure a Scottish victory at Colombes. Indeed he scored in all four internationals that season, two of which were won. The following year he was in rugby's wilderness.

'I had left the Army to go up to Cambridge and played in a University trial, which was one of the most disastrous experiences of my life. Nothing went right and I wound up as the Varsity third choice full-back.'

He was recalled to Scotland colours only for the last game of 1958, the drawn game with England at Murrayfield. Yet Ken was to amass 27 Caps, pipping the Drysdale figure, was to captain his country and give distinguished service to the British Lions.

Perhaps because of his quiet demeanour and because he was a bit of a nomad – he played for Ballymena, Leicester and Aberdeenshire as well – Ken Scotland did not receive the adulation he deserved. He was, nonetheless, a pioneer and truly outstanding all-rounder. Of him John Orr commented: 'He was a class act. Ken had the hands of a wicket-keeper and he had the ability to ghost past people. His positional sense was acute.'

Ken Scotland, who is now a director of a charitable trust geared to restoring a stately country house at Paxton, near Berwick, played twice as fly-half for his country in 1963. And by then there was another Heriot international full-back.

It was a filthy foggy day in Edinburgh when I rang Colin Blaikie at his office in Rondebosch, Cape Province, South Africa. 'Lovely afternoon here,' he chirped. 'I was playing golf yesterday and the sun was beating down.'

He has been away from these shores for 20 years now and runs his own building business but Blaikie will always be remembered . . . though not always for the best of reasons. In his second Cap at Twickenham in 1963 Colin was sold an outrageous dummy by Richard Sharp, en route to a most spectacular match-winning try.

'He had already wrong-footed three people by the time he reached me,' Blaikie recalls, 'but they kept showing the clip on TV of him passing me for years afterwards. In fact there's a friend of mine out here who still has a video of the incident.' Some pal!

In fact Colin Blaikie, who won eight Caps in all, was a most accomplished footballer; that is what he set out to be, a soccer player, and he might have become a professional inside-forward. Instead the camaraderie of rugby captured him and he was a Goldenacre favourite in the Sixties.

Sir John Orr's verdict: 'A very steady player with excellent defensive qualities. Good kicker and, even if he wasn't the fastest chap in the world, he contrived to be in the right place at the right time.'

'Sid' Smith . . . international
rugby a great honour but
terrifying too

Blaikie was in and out of the Scotland side – 'More out than in' – over a six-year period but he was on the winning side four times. 'Maybe I was Capped a little early, I hadn't even played in a trial, but the experience was unforgettable.'

Colin has no doubt who he rates as the number one of the Heriot tribe. 'Ken Scotland was the most complete player of the lot.'

I asked him how he viewed modern rugby. 'Brutal,' he replied. 'The game is much more physical than when we played. I came across for last year's Grand Slam match and one has to applaud the commitment of today's players. But I am disappointed that the ball is not moved as much as it once was.'

Blaikie is ideally placed to speculate on the effect of a South African return to the world scene. 'They will be a force all right. I have seen some of their promising lads and they are monsters, I can tell you that.' He also believes the sport must face up to the challenge of professionalism. 'I have no hang up about paying players. With all the cash that is coming in they are entitled to their share. I just want it done openly and not under the counter.'

Ian Sidney Gibson Smith first came into my view when he was a teenager attending Scottish Schoolboys Club camps at Dalguise. By the time he was 25, and winning his first of eight Caps, he had filled out considerably but he had retained a precocious air and an independent spirit.

Everyone agrees on one point: 'Sid' Smith was not Allan Wells. 'He was slower than Bruce Hay,' quips Irvine, 'and that's saying something.' 'No, he wasn't fast but I think he was underrated,' says Sir John Orr. 'He must have had wonderful tuning. After all he scored two international tries which is more than I did,' Ken Scotland opines.

There is a view, held by the player himself, that Smith was never quite accepted by the Goldenacre cognoscenti. 'I played three years in the school first XV. When I looked at the FP set-up Colin Blaikie was the first choice full-back and Ken Scotland's brother Ronnie, a very fine player, was the reserve. I didn't fancy the thirds too much.' So he decided to play for Edinburgh University. 'Some people never forgave me for that.' It was a fine student side including John Frame, Ray Newton and Erle Mitchell, and Smith benefited from the class around him.

A dental surgeon, he then joined the Army and after a spell in Germany was posted back to England where he joined London Scottish. There was a problem there too – the exiles had a full-back, Gordon Macdonald, who had gained a Cap as a replacement, coming on with only two minutes remaining in the Ireland match of February 1969. The pair were to face each other later that year when a Scottish XV containing Macdonald faced a Combined Services side with Smith in tow. 'Sid' totally outshone his club-mate and was selected for the match against South Africa at Murrayfield that December.

It was, in many ways, a most wretched occasion. The Springboks had been harassed by anti-apartheid demonstrators throughout their tour and only 25,000 spectators, penned into two areas, saw the game.

Opposite:
Andy Irvine . . . the dashing
cavalier who sometimes
added to the drama by doing
daft things

Smith was the match-winner. He kicked a penalty to counter an earlier goal by the visitors, then, five minutes from time and fed by Frame, he galloped away for the deciding try. Smith gained his second try in the next match, against France at Murrayfield, though the Scots were pipped 11–9.

'John Frame supplied that pass too. He was quite the most unselfish man I ever played alongside.' Smith enjoyed the victory over England that season but, after three losses in 1971, he made way for Gala's Arthur Brown for the historic win at Twickenham.

I. S. G. Smith made a decision at that point, of which he has not spoken before. 'I asked the Army for an overseas posting and went to Hong Kong. Playing international rugby had been a great honour but every time I did so I was absolutely terrified. My stomach would give out days before the match and I had difficulty sleeping. I had had my time.'

He played for Hong Kong, at fly-half, and is today out of the services and running his own practice in King's Lynn. 'Sid' may not have been everyone's idea of the ideal athlete but he had the last laugh on his detractors.

If you ever doubt that sport can inflict its own cruelty, consider this: while Scotland were completing their Grand Slam in 1984, the finest player of his generation was warming up as a possible replacement at the back of the Murrayfield stand. Andrew Robertson Irvine never got on to the field.

He is worth a book to himself and, typically, he wrote it. From 1973 to 1982 Andy was the ignition of the Scottish team, the top try scorer, the top points scorer, the sometime captain; 51 times Capped, he was famous throughout the rugby world because of his Lions exploits; he was the dashing cavalier.

Sir John Orr told me: 'There used to be a Hearts goalkeeper called Jimmy Brown who would roar to his defence "Ma Ba'". Andy was exactly like that. He was the most exciting full-back I ever saw and he had this fantastic desire to play. Sure, he sometimes did daft things but that just added to the drama.'

Ken Scotland took a different angle. 'One of the reasons I admire Andy most is because he was an outstanding club captain. That is one of the most difficult roles in the game.'

The recipient of all this praise is today as successful in his chosen career, as a partner in one of the country's largest firms of chartered survey-ors, as he was on the field. The Irvine clobber does not come off the peg.

Yet he remains the ultra-enthusiast and a conversation with him always lights up your day. 'I didn't play full-back at school but, at centre, I couldn't get enough of the ball. No, I wasn't aware of creating history and I'm sure the Heriot record is a coincidence although Charlie Broadwood, who coached most of us, would have been an influence.

'As a kid I was more interested in going to Tynecastle so I didn't see much of my predecessors. Ken Scotland had to be great because he wasn't a flying machine; I respect him enormously – he was chairman of the selectors when we won the Championship.

'Colin Blaikie I played with in my first season with the FPs. Somebody gave me a bit of a duffing at Trinity and Colin came across and smacked the guy in the mouth. Great bloke.

'There could have been another Heriot international full-back. Peter Steven, who was Capped on the wing, could have made it. He had the essential speed. But I would not like to predict when the next one will come along.'

For some of us there will be one game that is forever Irvine and that was the encounter with France in February 1980. Scotland had gone 13 games without a win and at 14–4 down into the second half the omens were not promising. Andy had failed to convert John Rutherford's try and had missed a series of penalty attempts, one in front of the posts. 'Playing like a donkey,' he said afterwards. Then, after a brilliant handling move, Irvine crashed over at the corner. Of course he converted this one. Five minutes later there was another sweeping surge and Irvine once more grabbed the touchdown. A little out of puff, he allowed Jim Renwick to take the conversion. But Andy rounded off the day with two more penalty goals and Scotland had won 22–14.

As I walked through the car park after the game a man said to me: 'That Irvine is one of the luckiest players in Scottish rugby.' Sure he was, just like Dan Drysdale, and the other six.

Working with players at
international squad sessions
has dramatically increased
fitness and skill levels

Fit, Fit, Fit

Three Scots at the Fitness Sharp End

By DAVID STEELE

THREE SCOTS, two exiled from their homeland and one firmly established in Scotland, have played, and are playing still, an important part in the new approach to fitness in rugby football.

In just a few years the rules have changed beyond recognition. No longer does a prop forward train with a few light jogs, a quick visit to the weights room and a jug of beer. Similarly the speed merchants are no longer just on the wing. There is many a back-row forward who is as fleet of foot as his colleague who wears a higher number on the jersey.

These three Scots – David McLean in Scotland, Tom McNab in England and Jim Blair in New Zealand – have worked with others to improve the general fitness, and above all change the attitude towards training, among their national rugby squads.

A couple of seasons ago the work that David McLean had been doing for the Scottish international squad was given formal backing and the Fife-born physiotherapist was appointed fitness adviser to the squad. Since then history has been made with the Grand Slam of 1990 and a growth of interest in rugby in Scotland which is without precedent. It would be daft to suggest that McLean has turned around the fortunes of the international squad – and rugby further down the ladder – on his own. He is an unassuming man and would be quick to discount such a suggestion. Yet his contribution to the fitness of the 30 or so players who form the nucleus of the squad, and carry with them the hopes and aspirations of a nation now gripped by rugby, cannot be underestimated. During the Grand Slam season of 1989–90 there were serious injuries to just two of the players who played a large part in that memorable season's successes – Peter Dods fractured a cheekbone in a match between internationals and Derek White's leg injury forced him to retire from the crunch encounter with England at Murrayfield in March.

McLean says it was 'just one of those things' and points mainly to good fortune as the reason for such important continuity, but perhaps his modesty is again playing a part in that summary. Much of the work he has done in recent seasons has been in training to avoid injuries and in making players aware of how the knocks can be kept to a minimum. This has involved an enormous amount of work over a lengthy period by the coaching team and the players themselves. McLean explains: 'We had to get across to players that their fitness was as important in avoiding injuries

David McLean . . . 'we prepared a fitter, stronger and more balanced squad than had ever left Scotland before.'

as it is in playing the game itself. There was also a part to be played in the game plan and general tactics, for if a player becomes isolated he is more likely to get hurt.'

McLean has always followed the principle that prevention is better than cure in his particular field of sports fitness and injury. 'For too long people looked on me, and on other physiotherapists, as the man who worked some sort of magic when a player was hurt pursuing his or her sport. It has taken some time to get across the message that prevention is always better than cure. If a player reaches a high level of fitness and is trained for the particular requirements of a game then he is less likely to be injured.'

He is not, though, suggesting that players should avoid playing at full tilt in order to avoid knocks. 'What I am saying is that a fit, well-prepared and aware participant in any sport stands a better chance of avoiding injury. That, although it has taken some time, is now being accepted by coaches and sports people the world over.'

One of the best examples of specific preparation came in 1982 when Scotland toured in Australia. McLean recalls: 'We knew that the grounds would be hard so the players were advised to step up their road running to get used to solid surfaces. They would be falling on less yielding surfaces so their upper bodies, in particular their shoulder girdles, had to be well developed to take the knocks. In conjunction with the coaches, tactics and game plans were worked out in order to avoid players becoming isolated from the support. It is far easier to get hurt when there is no one to support you than when there is. I believe that with all the work that went in that year we prepared a fitter, stronger and more balanced squad than had left Scotland to tour ever before.'

McLean came to rugby late in life after a career in juvenile and junior football (the Association kind of which he is all but cured!), which came to an end because of a series of injuries to his ironically 'suspect knees'. Since then he has worked with Tommy Boyle, coach to world-class middle distance runner Tom McKean, on fitness programmes designed again to maximise performance while minimising risk.

It doubtless hurts a patriotic Scot like McLean to admit it but he looks to England for the main impetus in fitness training in recent times. 'The England rugby squad has been well served for fitness advice from people like Tom McNab and Rex Hazeldine and the club set-up at places like Bath is superb. It will not happen overnight but we must have the message of fitness and correct preparation spread far and wide if the success of rugby at international level in Scotland is to be reflected at club and district level.' Of his thoughts for the future, more later.

Things not happening overnight is a recurring theme when discussing the changes in approach with David McLean. He says there was no sudden happening or sea change in the approach and that for a time his message did not get through. 'In all walks of life, be it business or sport, it takes time for approaches to alter, for perspectives to change. It was like that when I was putting forward specific fitness programmes for the squad and the players in it,' he says.

Particularly in recent times, however, he has had powerful allies in Ian McGeechan and Jim Telfer who see the value of a fit squad with which to work and further their coaching ideas. 'Both these men, and Derrick Grant as well, were good athletes in their playing days and also trained assiduously. They appreciate the value of fitness and the message is getting across to players.'

He discloses, perhaps to the surprise of the millions who revelled in the Grand Slam triumph, that the squad at the time was 'not as fit as it should have been'. He adds: 'They won the Grand Slam through wonderful commitment allied to excellent tactical play. I am not for a moment taking anything away from those superb victories but in the season just gone the players were fitter after working hard on the programmes they had been given.'

McLean does not have the luxury enjoyed by Jim Blair during his stint with the All Blacks of having time to spend with individual players in the laboratory and the gym. Nor does the man, who pays tribute to his employers at Queen's College in Glasgow for allowing him the time he spends on rugby, think that is necessary.

'We have worked for quite some time on a squad basis and what I have tried to do is work on training programmes which can be geared by the players themselves to their own particular needs. It may appear that they are doing the same training but they are all doing it at different pace and for varied effect. A prop is not expected to break sprinting records and a winger is unlikely to need the kind of strength required for front row business but each must be as fit as the other in his own way.'

That philosophy fits perfectly into the overall approach taken to the game by McGeechan – that every player regardless of his number must be able to run, handle, stay on his feet to protect the ball and win possession when the need arises.

A second surprise comes from this man who says that the dangers of 'overtraining' cannot be emphasised enough. This is not to say that things should be taken easy when it comes to getting fit, merely that a player can have too much of what may on the surface appear a good thing. 'In the early days of my involvement with Scottish rugby there were those who did not appreciate the point I was trying to get over which was that too much training of the wrong kind will do more harm than good. There was a time when I felt as though I was trying to put out a fire while round the corner there were people pouring petrol on it. Slowly the message got through and relations have never been better.'

He also puts forward the laudable notion that fitness in rugby is not everything and that a team which has superior skills and tactical awareness will triumph over one which lacks these qualities yet is super fit. The one concession to his crusade for fitter players, however, is that if the skills are about even then the fitter side should come out on top.

He has to be pressed to name names when it comes to his work with the international squad but cites Chris Gray as a shining example of what can be done with a proper fitness régime. 'Chris came in as a bit of a

Tom McNab . . . author, journalist, broadcaster and fitness consultant

Expatriate Scot Jim Blair, fitness guru to the All Blacks, spent time passing on his expertise in Scotland as the guest of the Scottish Rugby Union

stop-gap for his early Caps and was not in shape for top-level rugby. But within a season he had shed over half a stone and by the end of the New Zealand tour last year was in great form and was voted best forward by such perceptive judges as the New Zealanders themselves.'

McLean sees the role of the international squad and the SRU as allowing ideas to 'trickle down' to the lower reaches of the game. 'We have to get it right at the top and then let coaches and players see what can be done with a professional – in the best possible way of course – approach to the game. That is starting to happen but there is a long way to go.'

Changes do not come overnight in rugby but we have all seen the huge steps taken in the last ten years through improved fitness and there may well be a strong case for a rugby fitness adviser working nationally under the aegis of the SRU. That case was supported as long ago as 1988 by the great Scotland half-backs Roy Laidlaw and John Rutherford. Laidlaw wrote in their autobiography *Rugby Partnership* about the contribution made to the All Blacks' fitness by Jim Blair and added: 'We have a ready-made Jim Blair in our physiotherapist Dave McLean, but I am afraid the SRU would have to swallow hard and draw a deep breath before enlisting the services of a paid trainer. Yet such a man could have much to offer at every level of the game, particularly if he were as steeped in his craft and as enthusiastic as McLean. John and I both consider that such an appointment has to come but fear that it may not be for many a day.'

Tom McNab, author, broadcaster and fitness coach for a wide range of sportsmen and women is in the unique position of having coached and advised teams at top level in three sports which could not be more widely varied – bobsleigh, athletics and now rugby football. When England began their preparations for the 1987 World Cup they had in their backroom staff this well-known Scotsman who was to help build them into one of the fittest and quickest squads on the world rugby stage. He is as enthusiastic about sport now as he was between 1952 and 1963 when he became Scottish triple-jump champion and was a member of his country's national athletics team. No one works harder at getting the fitness message across to those rugby men who aspire to wear the red rose than Tom McNab.

Yet it was not always that easy to have his ideas accepted for, as experienced by David McLean with the Scots in the early days, there were those Luddites in the camp who saw little point in all this fitness testing and preparation training nonsense. That has all changed now and as McNab puts it, with affection rather than admonition: 'Even the front row forwards are total converts to the idea of personal fitness, setting targets and improving on them all the time.'

He and colleague Rex Hazeldine of Loughborough University have taken rugby fitness on to a new plateau in the United Kingdom and there are few in the Scottish Rugby Union who would argue that the giant leaps taken north of the border in that department were encouraged by what happened in the English set-up.

It is not just that the English squad flew to the sun of Lanzarote in the depths of winter to prepare for the Five Nations Championships and World Cup, jolly good idea though that was, which shows how far things have come. It is more what went on while they were there – fitness testing using the most modern electronic methods, individual training programmes designed for players to make the best use of what they have got, and work schedules geared for the specific requirements of the opening match against the Welsh in Cardiff.

McNab says: 'We worked on the line-out in particular because of the importance of that area, concentrated on rucking and mauling and on keeping the ball alive to give the backs a run. Our part in all of this was to work on a bit of sprint training – for everyone – and to monitor the fitness and endurance of the entire squad.'

He reveals that it was on endurance – or runability as the catchword has it – that some of the players fell down and that decisions in some positions may have gone a certain player's way because of his performance in that aspect of training. 'If one player records 3.8 seconds for a 30-metre sprint and another clocks 3.75 then we don't have much to worry about but if the difference on our reckoning for endurance is, say 12.5 to 14.7, then the second guy has problems. We use a system developed by the Sports Institute and the players have to run between cones in time with the bleeps which get steadily faster. When he can't keep up any more with the bleeps he drops out and that measure is recorded. It gives a fairly accurate measure of running endurance.'

In co-operation with Rex Hazeldine and the rest of the backroom staff, McNab has a wide remit regarding the fitness of the squad. 'It can range from discussion on diet, the issue of diet sheets which is very much

Don't ask! You will scan the coaching and fitness manuals in vain for any hint as to what Scotland coach Ian McGeechan is up to here

Rex's department in conjunction with nutritional experts, right through to personal advice on a wide range of matters,' he says.

McNab and the support team meet the players at least once a year on an individual basis to test their fitness and discuss any problems which may have sprung up since the last meeting. He adds: 'You would be amazed at what spills out at these meetings. Rugby players are supposed to preserve this macho image and often find it difficult, for fear of being a bit soft, to discuss personal problems. I hope that we can at least provide a friendly and confidential ear. They know we will try to help and not pass any of it to the rest of the team.'

The 57-year-old Scot is fitter than most men half his age, and still turns out regularly for Dunstable Rugby Club – or indeed any team in the area which will give him a game. 'I came to rugby late, not starting to play until I was about 27, but since then it has given me an enormous amount of pleasure. I had played football for Glasgow Schools but athletics became my life. Although I was not a natural athlete I reached a fairly high standard by working damn hard at what I did. For that reason I have a tremendous sympathy with people who have to work that bit harder to bring out the best in themselves.'

He continues: 'The most important job I see for the backroom staff in any sport is providing players with access to everything that they need, be it personal fitness advice, the most modern machinery and facilities available or even just support when they most need it. The difference in attitude of players to what I am trying to do for them is like chalk and cheese to what it was when I started with the rugby squad. It is well worthwhile and something I enjoy doing for the time being.'

McNab sounds a note of caution to the rugby authorities, however, when he says that the day of the full-time support team may be imminent – and must be seen as both necessary and welcome. 'I have an enormous number of commitments, many of them voluntary, and it is becoming more and more difficult to devote sufficient time to the rugby squad. I have two points to make, one that the present arrangement is not good for the backroom staff, the second that it does not benefit the players as much as I feel it could. Neither has enough time with the other and as rugby grows in popularity and importance it becomes ever more important that the players are as well prepared as they can be.'

McNab, as well as his coaching credentials, has made his name as an author, journalist and broadcaster, having worked as a consultant on the award-winning film *Chariots of Fire* and writing three successful novels based around running – *Flanagan's Run, Rings of Sand* and *The Fast Men*. He is also heavily involved with local sports clubs near his home in Hertfordshire and is vice-chairman of the British Institute of Sports Coaches.

And now for the third member of our Scots' fitness team. A less likely start for a man who was to become internationally regarded as a fitness guru could hardly be imagined. Jim Blair was born within sight of Celtic Park in the East End of Glasgow and was raised a Protestant in a mainly Roman Catholic area. 'It was a fairly interesting experience and perhaps that is what made me keen on helping people to run faster and longer,' he says with tongue firmly in cheek.

Like Tom McNab, Blair finds himself in great demand from a wide variety of sports including yachting with the New Zealand Admiral's Cup squad, cricket with both the Kiwi and Australian squads and hockey again at international level. His connection with rugby began when John Hart invited him to assist the mighty Auckland provincial team and through Hart he met Alex 'Grizz' Wyllie who was in charge at Canterbury, then holders of the prestigious Ranfurly Shield. He worked for these fierce rivals for a spell and remembers the sportsmanship which meant that he was never asked for details about one by the other and put on the spot.

The two men became New Zealand selectors and were so impressed with the results Blair had achieved with their sides that they asked him to take on a similar role with the All Blacks. 'It came as quite a surprise at the time that someone with the traditional ideas of Wyllie took so well to what at the time was my somewhat unorthodox approach to fitness,' he recalls.

It is interesting to note that what was in those days considered unorthodox is now commonplace in rugby at all levels. Blair has always made it clear that he wanted the schoolboy and the veteran to benefit from his ideas just as much as the international player. In his book *Jim Blair's Rugby Fitness*, written with New Zealand sports journalist Brian Humberstone, Blair puts together a wide range of his ideas in such a way that they can be followed by every player and coach. Like so much of his work it is a pleasing blend of science and common sense.

Blair left Glasgow in 1962 after his education at Shettleston Primary, Eastbank Academy and the renowned Scottish School of Physical Education.

Coaching and fitness . . . the dual-carriageway to rugby success. Colin Telfer and a 1980s Scotland squad session

Like David McLean, for whom he has the highest regard, Blair had a soccer background, playing for Glasgow Schools and having spells on the books of Queen's Park and Hamilton Academicals.

During a return to his homeland in 1990, a trip organised by SRU technical administrator John Roxburgh, Blair paid tribute to the work being done by McLean and the pair worked together at a rugby fitness weekend at Gleneagles Hotel. He recalls: 'I was not in Scotland to preach or to tell my countrymen that they should be doing it this way or that. Instead I wanted to make my ideas and advice available to anyone who wanted to listen. If they liked what they heard then I'm happy and if I have been able to help the fitness development of the international squad and Scottish rugby in general then I am even happier.'

Blair always talks with coaches in whatever sport and finds out their requirements from each player or group of players. He can then assess what level they are at and work out specific programmes to help them achieve first their aims – and then perhaps a little more. The basic approach for Blair, one which is becoming more favoured as the gospel spreads, is that fitness programmes must be as efficient as possible so that maximum results can be obtained in minimum time.

He is of the firm opinion that training sessions should be shorter and more concentrated as players of whatever calibre can lose interest after 90 minutes or so. The other message on training is that it should be designed to be enjoyable and not a slog up and down a wet, muddy pitch. Amen to that, say the generations of rugby players who have slogged up and down muddy pitches.

Blair has studied closely, both for his rugby work and his wider remit as director of the Institute of Sport and Corporate Health in Auckland, the requirements of energy and muscular development not just for different activities but for individual positions. He says, 'I found eventually that rugby players could be broken down into four groups within which the overall requirements would be similar.'

These groups — prop and lock; hooker, scrum-half, flanker and number eight; stand-off; wing, centre and full-back — are given the same start in any of Blair's fitness programmes but as they develop each player may require changes in his programme which he is encouraged to discuss with the coaches.

With this aim in mind there is an idea bubbling away at the SRU that as well as an international fitness adviser there may be a strong case for such advisers in every district.

For New Zealand rugby, the Jim Blair message began with two great provincial teams, spread first upwards to the mighty All Blacks and is now filtering back down through all of that rugby-mad country.

As David McLean points out when discussing the set-up in Scotland, there is more of a 'trickle down' from the top with the early concentration on the international squad and the rest of Scottish rugby learning from that. Maybe that trickle will become a flood and the benefit clearly felt by the All Blacks before and since the 1987 World Cup will be experienced in Scotland sooner rather than later.

Five Nations '91

A Season in the Shade

By BILL McMURTRIE

SCOTLAND's XV basked in bright limelight with the Grand Slam in 1990. But they slid into the shade a year later. The old Paris hoodoo struck first. Scotland have not won in Paris since the days of the old Colombes stadium in 1969. Young men have grown old since then.

Scotland lost by 9–15 in a Parc des Princes match they should have won, a contest that defined how fine is the boundary that separates success from failure. In the aftermath of defeat Duncan Paterson, convener of Scotland's international selection committee, summed up that dividing line: 'When you win the Grand Slam you're not as good as you think you are. When you lose a game like that you're not as bad as it seems.'

His words sounded all the more apposite two weeks later. Scotland recovered from the Paris setback and turned the screws on Wales in a 32–12 victory.

Here, we thought, was the glorious recovery. Paris was only a temporary lapse. Instead, however, the Murrayfield win against Wales was a high note in a low-key season. It was Wales who were poor as much as Scotland who were good.

Disappointment followed at Twickenham. England, clinically efficient, won 21–12, revenge for their defeat in the Grand Slam decider at Murrayfield in 1990, and even in victory against Ireland at Murrayfield in the season's final Championship match, Scotland failed to please Ian McGeechan. The margin was 28–25, though Ireland scored four tries to three, and Scotland's coach was adamant that the visitors deserved to win. Ireland played the positive rugby McGeechan would have expected of his own charges.

Even the most optimistic of Scots could hardly have expected another Grand Slam, which would have been the second in two years and the third in eight years, but apart from the Welsh match, Scotland's fall was hefty. The impetus of the 1990 Grand Slam decider against England was missing all too often. Even more disappointingly, however, the lessons had not been learned from the tour to New Zealand that followed the Grand Slam.

As Ian McGeechan wrote in a *Glasgow Herald* article, summarising the Championship campaign, 'there is a feeling of flatness about this season, both in players and spectators, and that is partly due to expectation. We all believe we should be doing well, and that is an important element in providing success.

Opposite:
Derek White

'Why should we go from winning to losing just because we had one particularly good year? The important thing for us to remember is how and why we achieved success. We must never become complacent, only more demanding . . .

'Winning away from home relies on making every opportunity count and in doing so puts pressure on the home side to respond. In both the away games this year our opponents were able to stay in control of the scoring and so did not have to make the pressure decisions to produce points. Winning away from home remains the key to winning Championships while winning at home produces credibility.'

Here was the psychology of the difference between a Grand Slam Championship and a break-even season. The change from one season to the next, however, had its physical reasons as well. Finlay Calder had gone after the New Zealand tour. His devil, determination and drive were much missed. John Jeffrey had to switch to take over Calder's boots: Derek Turnbull filled the gap. But the breakaway trio of Turnbull, Derek White and Jeffrey did not gel as Jeffrey, White and Calder had done, though their liaison showed highly promising signs against Wales and Ireland.

Yet that was not the only physical reason behind the defeats at Parc des Princes and Twickenham. The Scots lacked presence in the line-out. Damian Cronin answered the challenge only in the match against Wales, and even Chris Gray was subjugated by England. Paul Ackford outplayed the Nottingham lock who had earned the plaudits of New Zealanders eight months earlier.

Scotland were so lost for possession in the line-out at Twickenham that they had to resort to avoiding kicking for touch. The options for Scotland were drastically reduced. Too many cards were held by England.

In victory over Wales, and even in the disappointing win against Ireland, Scotland had one cementing asset. They had that unity born of consistency of team selection. Only 17 players were utilised for the Championship matches, one more than in the 1990 Grand Slam, and 13 of those played in every game. The exceptions were Alex Moore (who missed the final game because of illness), Iwan Tukalo (who returned against Ireland), and the duelling hookers, Kenneth Milne and John Allan.

Such a tight-knit community, inevitably, had camaraderie. Just as importantly, they had self-criticism. No one had to tell them they had not played well in beating Ireland. Their demeanor in the aftermath spoke for them, and they took no consolation in winning while playing short of their best.

As Ian McGeechan said more than once during the Championship season, the Scots set their own standards in the 1990 Grand Slam. They had their targets in 1991, and only against Wales did they satisfactorily attain them. They knew they had better rugby in them than they produced against France, England and Ireland.

FRANCE 15, SCOTLAND 9

SCOTLAND'S AFTERNOON AT PARC DES PRINCES started badly, and it did not improve. The band played the wrong tune instead of *Flower of Scotland*, and thereafter it was the French who were more on song, though the rhythm was rarely *vivace*.

Scotland thus fell at the first hurdle on their attempt to repeat the 1990 Grand Slam, and their dismal Paris record continued. Not since their 1969 visit to Colombes have they won in France. Ten times they have lost since the French moved their Championship internationals back to Parc des Princes.

France were deserved winners. It was not that they looked potential favourites for the World Cup in October and November. They were a team who made their advantages count. Olivier Roumat gave them consistency in the line-out, their game generally was tighter and tidier, and they took their chances, though with drop goals rather than tries. Didier Camberabero struck two and Serge Blanco one. Not since Scotland's 6–0 win in 1957 has a Paris match between the countries failed to produce a try.

Ian McGeechan took slight solace in the fact that Scotland did not concede a try. Defensively, the Scots were secure. Even on the rare occasions that Blanco and Patrice Lagisquet escaped, the Scottish cover was not wanting.

Lagisquet was as close as any to squeezing a try. His thrust and chip to the left corner drew a save from Scott Hastings in a photo-finish when a try then would have taken France to 13–3 after less than half an hour: it could have finished the Scots.

Roumat's line-out domination was the crucially positive factor in the game. The Dax lock effectively shut out Damian Cronin as well as securing his own ball as the principal target-man. John Jeffrey and Chris Gray picked off a little line-out possession, though nothing like enough to respond to Roumat. Kenneth Milne, indeed, was not quite the accurate thrower he was in the Grand Slam. Once, late on, his long throw-in found Laurent Cabannes spot-on instead of Jeffrey.

Scotland contributed to their own downfall with too much looseness elsewhere, not least when Chalmers struck a 22-metre drop-out straight to Blanco, who dropped a goal from more than 40 metres.

Also, Scotland's breakaway trio was not the unified force that marked the Grand Slam, for all that Jeffrey's game maintained its pitch throughout. Finlay Calder was much missed, and it was not to be for the only time in this Championship campaign. Derek White's scrummage pick-ups had not the drive that carried him to two tries against Ireland last year, and in other respects his liaison with Jeffrey and Derek Turnbull obviously needed fine-tuning. So did the whole pack in reviving their togetherness.

Gary Armstrong, like Jeffrey, played within the upper reaches of his ability, and both Scottish wings, Tony Stanger and Alex Moore, profited from limited scope. Moore once took on the opposition in a battling drive which, in another international, might have magnetised the forward support. It was, though, an instance too rare for natural reaction.

France were on their way with Camberabero's penalty goal from 48 metres after only three minutes, White offside at a ruck, but the Scottish response was swift. Jeffrey fired an assault off the line-out tail, David Sole characteristically drove off a free-kick, Armstrong chipped to the right corner, Gavin Hastings sallied off crash ball, and Chalmers, switching from right foot to left, dropped a goal from a scrum.

For barely a minute the scores were level. Roumat creamed line-out ball, Blanco intruded, Lagisquet kicked ahead, and though Armstrong was back to touch down, anticipating precisely, it was then that Chalmers struck his wild drop-out for Blanco's score. Camberabero's second long-range penalty goal followed in 19 minutes.

Scotland squandered too much in the second quarter. Scott Hastings kicked loosely ahead for Blanco to reply comfortably with a deep diagonal, the same centre's rousing break went too far before he sought support, and his brother, Gavin, missed two penalties, one from only 25 metres after Ed Morrison, the debutant international referee, had blown his whistle for half-time. He restarted the game as one of his touch judges, Fred Howard, had spotted obstruction on White.

It was the second time Howard had flagged a French infringement. Pascal Ondart's punch on Jeffrey also was indicated by the touch judge who, as referee, sent Alain Carminati off from last year's corresponding Murrayfield match.

Neither touch judge, however, saw why Blanco and Armstrong had a wrestling duel yards away from play, and we were left to wonder why Morrison penalised Scotland after he had called Pierre Berbizier aside for a long chat. If the French scrum-half's offence merited words from the referee then it ought to have been penalised.

Chalmers, taking over from Gavin Hastings, kicked the two penalty goals that drew the Scots back to 9–all after 53 minutes, and that opening quarter of an hour in the second half was also the visitors' best phase. Roumat was twice upset in the line-out, Jeffrey and Turnbull profited from long throw-ins, Armstrong disrupted Berbizier at the scrum base to release the 3 D's – White, Turnbull, and Sole – and Jeffrey exploded from a maul to carry more than half of the French pack into their own 22 as the prelude to the equalising score.

Again, the Scots were only briefly level. Camberabero dropped a goal after his own long pass had sparked a Blanco intrusion.

Blanco was engulfed under a Chalmers up-and-under into the home 22, but the chance was lost when Armstrong was penalised for going into the ruck with a boot. Yet Armstrong was only trying to release the ball from Blanco's illegal hold, though Howard suggested afterwards that the Scottish scrum-half had stamped too close to the French captain's head. Howard hinted, indeed, that he might have sent Armstrong off.

Morrison spoke sharply to Armstrong. Yet in such circumstances the referee must share blame for not penalising the ball-holder before an opponent has to try to do it his way. In the circumstances Howard's pronouncement was ludicrous.

Scotland lost another opportunity after Sole's tap-penalty charge released Jeffrey, Stanger and Milne up the right touch-line. Jeffrey, however, could not hold the hooker's awkward in-field pass, and after Camberabero had missed two penalties in quick succession he made certain with his second drop goal, struck to perfection on the turn.

FRANCE		SCOTLAND
S. Blanco (*Biarritz*) captain	15	A. G. Hastings (*Watsonians*)
J. B. Lafond (*Racing*)	14	A. G. Stanger (*Hawick*)
F. Mesnel (*Racing*)	13	S. Hastings (*Watsonians*)
D. Charvet (*Racing*)	12	S. R. P. Lineen (*Boroughmuir*)
P. Lagisquet (*Bayonne*)	11	A. Moore (*Edinburgh Academicals*)
D. Camberabero (*Beziers*)	10	C. M. Chalmers (*Melrose*)
P. Berbizier (*Agen*)	9	G. Armstrong (*Jed-Forest*)
G. Lascube (*Agen*)	1	D. M. B. Sole (*Edinburgh Acad'ls*) captain
P. Marocco (*Montferrand*)	2	K. S. Milne (*Heriot's FP*)
P. Ondarts (*Biarritz*)	3	A. P. Burnell (*London Scottish*)
M. Tachdijan (*Racing*)	4	C. A. Gray (*Nottingham*)
O. Roumat (*Dax*)	5	D. F. Cronin (*Bath*)
X. Blond (*Racing*)	6	D. J. Turnbull (*Hawick*)
M. Cecillon (*Bourgoin*)	8	D. B. White (*London Scottish*)
L. Cabannes (*Racing*)	7	J. Jeffrey (*Kelso*)

Referee: E. F. Morrison (*England*)

Penalty goals:	*Penalty goals:*
Camberabero (2)	Chalmers (2)
Drop-goals:	*Drop goal:*
Camberabero (2)	Chalmers
Blanco	

SCOTLAND 32, WALES 12

NEVER IN MODERN RUGBY have Scotland so dominated a match against Wales as they did at Murrayfield in February. Victory with four tries to one was no less than deserved.

Scotland's performance was leagues ahead of their fractured game in Paris two weeks earlier, and nowhere was the improvement more marked than in the forwards. The scrummaging grew in strength, the line-out game was more productive, and the unity in the loose, especially the breakaway forwards' liaison, was more akin to the coaches' ideal.

That was apparent from the kick-off by Neil Jenkins. Damian Cronin caught the ball, the rest of the pack swarmed to the landing point, and the driving machine clicked immediately into an upper gear.

Indeed, the final margin could have stretched beyond record limits if Scotland's overwhelming pressure in the first half hour could have been converted into more than the 13–6 lead they held at the interval. Craig Chalmers kicked only two goals from five attempts, and afterwards Ian McGeechan referred almost ruefully to 12 or more points that had escaped his team's grasp in that first half.

It was frustrating, too, that the Scots conceded penalty goals to Paul Thorburn immediately after two of their three first-half scores. The Welsh had six points in the bag before they had even ventured into the Scottish 22. Thorburn's penalties pierced tremors of unease in Scottish hearts, and when the Welsh captain added the goal to Steve Ford's try midway in the second half, cutting the margin to 20–12, the visitors more than hinted at revival. Scotland, however, ensured that the last quarter was emphatically theirs.

In purely statistical terms the try margin was less than the 5–1 in the 34–18 victory at Cardiff in 1982, a match which, as Scotland's first away win in seven years, signalled the opening of the era that was to produce two Grand Slams. Even in that match nine years ago, however, Scotland had not the forward dominance they exerted that Saturday.

Before the Murrayfield match McGeechan *et al* had expressed respect for Wales despite defeat by England two weeks earlier. The Welsh scrummaging was held in especially high regard. Yet it was in that art that Scotland, exploiting their weight advantage in half a stone a forward, asserted themselves so forcefully that three of their four tries were born in the scrum. Two were even off Welsh heels as Gary Armstrong, temporarily burying friendship, poached from Robert Jones.

Scotland's other try, their first, was won off a line-out ball which, though loose, was part of Cronin's restyled package. The Bath lock answered the criticisms that had been flying around about his touch-line game since the first Test against the All Blacks in June. What he lost in the Edinburgh of the southern hemisphere he regained in the original Dunedin. It helped Cronin's game, too, that the Scottish desire for flexibility eased him out of his standard role as mid-line-out jumper. He found new freedom in the less cluttered spaces at the tail, once notably to release the peeling Derek White on a storming drive as the prelude to Armstrong's try.

White, quite apart from his own two tries, was more on song than he had been in Paris, as were John Jeffrey and Derek Turnbull. The number eight's scrummage pick-ups in liaison with the flankers generated mini-mauls that fired one or other of the locks, and whether at close quarters or farther afield the Scottish breakaways, individually and together, were more influential than their opposites. Jeffrey, especially, had the penchant for being on the right spot to pick up to revive from the tackle. It spurred the flow. Continuity was the name of the game that was played on the feet instead of the ground. David Bishop, the New Zealand referee, let it be known that he did not approve of players going to ground beside the tackle. That suited the Scots.

Bishop was unhappy, too, about the terms of the scrummage duel between David Sole and Paul Knight. The Scottish captain was the first the referee accused of taking the scrum down, but thereafter Knight was penalised as the culprit, twice late on. By then, the Scottish scrummage, with Kenneth Milne hooking in place of the injured John Allan, was fearsomely dominant, and the home team were surging on to 12 points in the last ten minutes.

On their heels Armstrong was at his classic best – ever ready to probe the fringes, strike a testing kick, plunder the opposition, or, more especially, spark the outside-backs. It was not for the want of variety in the scrum-half's game that wave after wave of Scottish assaults, bar one, were denied in the first-half. Jones, Scott Gibbs, and Ieuan Evans were notably secure in the Welsh defence.

First, after only two minutes, the Welsh stifled Cronin's thrust into the 22, but the ensuing ruck induced offside. Chalmers kicked a penalty goal from only ten metres, but when Cronin gathered the restart kick the Scots were penalised for protective blocking, Thorburn striking the goal from 30 metres wide on the left.

Chalmers missed two penalties from the right, one rebounding away off the near post, before the Scottish pressure had its due reward after Armstrong had kicked into the right corner midway in the first-half. Thorburn fumbled before clearing for a line-out only two metres out, Cronin tapped down, Armstrong fed, Chalmers cut in for support as the only option, Allan surged on from the ruck, and when Glen George denied the hooker White charged over. Chalmers, though, missed the conversion.

Five minutes later, after White's thrust off Cronin's line-out tail deflection, Armstrong scored what he himself described as the easiest try he will ever have. Wales heeled under pressure on their own line, Jones stepped aside to allow Paul Arnold to pick up, and Armstrong struck like a cobra before the number eight could react.

Chalmers converted from tight on the left touch-line, but straight away Sole was penalised for a high tackle on Jones. Thorburn kicked the goal from close on 40 metres, and though he missed a longer one soon afterwards, a Mark Ring punt into the left corner prompted Wales into the Scottish 22 for the first time: 36 minutes had gone.

Scotland revived their eagerness after the interval. White peeled again off Cronin, Jeffrey drove from his pick-up at the tackle, Alex Moore had a go, a lateral run by Chalmers exploded Gavin Hastings on an intrusion run that magnetised a driving maul almost to the line, and when Milne took over as hooker the Scottish pack forced the Welsh scrum off a Jones put-in.

Scotland could not control the ball there, and the chance was lost. They settled, though, with a scrummage drop goal by Chalmers, and the stand-off completed his round of scores with a try in 53 minutes. Armstrong pillaged from Jones off a scrum just inside the Scottish half, releasing Turnbull and Jeffrey, and Chalmers finished off from 20 metres out, prising the final opening with feint and acceleration.

Gavin Hastings missed the conversion from well out on the right, and it was here that Wales had another ascendant phase, though brief. Brian Williams was held up over the Scottish line, with Armstrong under the ball, but Ford was not to be denied. Jenkins looped Ring, Thorburn intruded, Gibbs carried on, and Glen George and Alun Carter linked for the left-wing to score.

Thorburn's conversion cut the margin to only eight points, and Scotland needed a score to thwart the threatened Welsh comeback. Come the hour, came the man. Gavin Hastings stepped in with two penalty goals in five minutes – the first from 18 metres after Knight had collapsed a scrum, and the second from close on halfway out to the right after a thrust by Cronin, Jeffrey and Paul Burnell. The ball just sneaked over, raising to four figures the points scored in the 27 Royal Bank internationals at Murrayfield.

By then, Scotland were rolling again. Armstrong released Tony Stanger up the blind side, and when the wing was stopped, the scrum-half picked up to lead the forwards on yet another stirring drive almost to the line. White scored in a pushover there, with the Welsh pack disintegrating, and Gavin Hastings converted from the right with the last kick of the match.

SCOTLAND

A. G. Hastings (*Watsonians*)	15
A. G. Stanger (*Hawick*)	14
S. Hastings (*Watsonians*)	13
S. R. P. Lineen (*Boroughmuir*)	12
A. Moore (*Edinburgh Academicals*)	11
C. M. Chalmers (*Melrose*)	10
G. Armstrong (*Jed-Forest*)	9
D. M. B. Sole (*Edinburgh Acad'ls*) captain	1
J. Allan (*Edinburgh Academicals*)	2
A. P. Burnell (*London Scottish*)	3
C. A. Gray (*Nottingham*)	4
D. F. Cronin (*Bath*)	5
D. J. Turnbull *Hawick*	6
D. B. White (*London Scottish*)	8
J. Jeffrey (*Kelso*)	7

Replacement: K. S. Milne (*Heriot's*) for Allan (47 minutes)

WALES

P. H. Thorburn (*Neath*) captain	
I. C. Evans (*Llanelli*)	
M. G. Ring (*Cardiff*)	
I. S. Gibbs (*Neath*)	
S. P. Ford (*Cardiff*)	
N. R. Jenkins (*Pontypridd*)	
R. N. Jones (*Swansea*)	
B. R. Williams (*Neath*)	
K. H. Phillips (*Neath*)	
P. Knight (*Pontypridd*)	
Glyn Llewellyn (*Neath*)	
Gareth Llewellyn (*Neath*)	
A. J. Carter (*Newport*)	
P. Arnold (*Swansea*)	
G. M. George (*Newport*)	

Replacement: A. Clement (*Swansea*) for Thorburn (67 minutes)

Referee: D. J. Bishop (*New Zealand*)

Tries:
White (2), Chalmers, Armstrong

Try:
Ford

Conversions:
A. G. Hastings, Chalmers

Conversion:
Thorburn

Penalty goals:
A.G. Hastings (2), Chalmers

Penalty goals:
Thorburn (2)

Drop-goal:
Chalmers

ENGLAND 21, SCOTLAND 12

REVENGE IS SWEET. England savoured the succulent taste in beating Scotland at Twickenham, regaining the Calcutta Cup, going halfway to their Grand Slam aim, and atoning for their shattered dream at Murrayfield 11 months earlier.

Victory was efficiently clinical. England had neither airs nor graces in their rugby. They expanded their game only for one try, and they went on to beat Ireland and France by the same methods. They will not be remembered as a great team.

That did not matter to them. They wanted to be winners to justify the belief held in England and beyond, even on our side of the Border, that they were potentially the best side in the Championship.

England were a team with undoubted strengths, and they played to them in beating Scotland. The vital ingredients were a secure scrummage, an almost total domination of the line-out, forceful driving and tackling, a latterly masterful grasp of tactical punting by Rob Andrew, and mechanical goal-kicking by Simon Hodgkinson.

At times England played a type of game that approached the driving rugby which had so marked Scotland's performance in the corresponding match last year and again in victory over Wales at Murrayfield earlier this month. It was not so tight as the Scottish driving had been in sweeping the Welsh aside, but the English game, with Dean Richards and Mike Teague often at its heart, was enough to knock the visitors back, physically.

That aspect of the English game was effectively a backhanded compliment to Scotland. Roger Uttley, England's coach, had been at Murrayfield to see the Welsh game for himself, and the clear impression left on his mind was that that was where his forwards had to take the Scots on.

Uttley was satisfied with the performance and the result. He believed that, with his team playing to a winning plan, he was at last emerging from Ian McGeechan's shadow, the role into which he had been sketched since he was the Scot's assistant on the Lions' 1989 tour to Australia. The shade deepened at Murrayfield last March: it lightened greatly this Saturday.

To Scotland's credit, they refused to succumb even in the fractured type of match that did not suit their desire for continuity. They played with the belief that they could yet pluck enough from their meagre rations to snatch victory. The Scots hung in, drawing level with a brace of Craig Chalmers penalty goals for 6–all after 27 minutes and cutting back to 12–15 midway in the second half with two more such scores.

Almost without exception Gary Armstrong was the inspiration behind Scotland's resilience. The Jed-Forest scrum-half added to his credits even in defeat. In all-round ability he has no equal in the Championship. He is sharp in the essentials, he is strong in defence as he is on the probing thrust, and he has that vision to read danger and opportunity almost before they occur.

John Jeffrey was a willing lieutenant, and his fellow breakaways, Derek Turnbull and Derek White, also fulfilled their role in defence almost without fail. Briefly in the second half they threatened off the scrum base. They maintained their stature in the field of intense competition.

Even England's try was a compliment to the Scottish breakaways. The trio had to be tied in to dilute the defence. Paul Ackford won a two-man line-out close to the Scottish line, Richard Hill slipped through the gap between the locks, Teague worked off the ensuing maul, Richards drove to commit Turnbull, Peter Winterbottom did the same to check Jeffrey, and swift cross-field passing beat the ragged cover for Hodgkinson's long, precise pass to let Nigel Heslop in at the right corner. Hodgkinson's touchline conversion took England to 15–6 only four minutes into the second half.

England's scrummaging down the right through Jeff Probyn, the oldest player on the field at the age of 34, manifested itself, however illegally, when Kenneth Milne twice lost the strike on Gary Armstrong's feed. Only one counted: England were penalised on the other occasion.

It was, though, on the touch-line that England asserted themselves most firmly in set-piece control. Ackford was the supremo, whether on full or shortened line-outs. He almost completely cleaned out Chris Gray, and therein lay the heaviest disappointment in Scotland's defeat. Gray fell far from the heights he set himself on Scotland's tour to New Zealand last year.

In the first half Scotland won clean line-out ball only twice. Gray cleared the first, as prelude to the opening Chalmers penalty goal in 21 minutes, and Jeffrey had the other take.

So great was Scotland's handicap in the line-out that they latterly had to fall back on not kicking for touch. Gavin Hastings would thump long punts up-field for Hodgkinson to reply so that Scotland at least had the throw-in. The result of that ploy was that England had only four throw-ins in the whole of the second half. Scotland could have found it more profitable if those kicks had had more air and less depth. A garryowen or two would have stirred the charge.

For a short phase on either side of the hour Scotland gained slight profit from Gray, Turnbull, White and Jeffrey off Milne's throwing variety. Even that was too little, though Scotland came back in that time to 12–15. Jeffrey's line-out take preceded the third Chalmers penalty goal, and after a brave touchline run by Armstrong the half-backs cleared scrappy line-out possession for Sean Lineen and Gray to induce Teague to kill the ball, the infringement from which the Melrose stand-off kicked his fourth goal.

That phase of the game might have been even more meaningful but for inhibiting incidents immediately before and after the interval. First, within range of the posts, Damian Cronin rushed to take a tapped penalty. A goal then would have cut England back to 9-all at the interval, and when the second half was only in its infancy Andrew struck a cruel kick into Scotland's right corner. It was the overture for England's try as well as being what was to become the fly-half's signature tune.

ENGLAND		**SCOTLAND**
S. D. Hodgkinson (*Nottingham*)	15	A. G. Hastings (*Watsonians*)
N. J. Heslop (*Orrell*)	14	A. G. Stanger (*Hawick*)
W. D. C. Carling (*Harlequins*) captain	13	S. Hastings (*Watsonians*)
J. C. Guscott (*Bath*)	12	S. R. P. Lineen (*Boroughmuir*)
R. Underwood (*RAF and Leicester*)	11	A. Moore (*Edinburgh Academicals*)
C. R. Andrew (*Wasps*)	10	C. M. Chalmers (*Melrose*)
R. J. Hill (*Bath*)	9	G. Armstrong (*Jed-Forest*)
J. Leonard (*Harlequins*)	1	D. M. B. Sole (*Edinburgh Acad'ls*) captain
B. C. Moore (*Harlequins*)	2	K. S. Milne (*Heriot's FP*)
J. A. Probyn (*Wasps*)	3	A. P. Burnell (*London Scottish*)
P. J. Ackford (*Harlequins*)	4	C. A. Gray (*Nottingham*)
W. A. Dooley (*Preston Grasshoppers*)	5	D. F. Cronin (*Bath*)
M. C. Teague (*Gloucester*)	6	D. J. Turnbull (*Hawick*)
D. Richards (*Leicester*)	8	D. B. White (*London Scottish*)
P. J. Winterbottom (*Harlequins*)	7	J. Jeffrey (*Kelso*)

Referee: S. R. Hilditch (*Ireland*)

Try:
Heslop

Conversion:
Hodgkinson

Penalty goals:
Hodgkinson (5)

Penalty goals:
Chalmers (4)

SCOTLAND 28, IRELAND 25

NOT EVEN SCOTLAND'S HISTORIC VICTORY could please Ian McGeechan. Scotland's coach freely admitted that Ireland deserved to win the Murrayfield international. Theirs was the more positive rugby. Theirs was the rugby McGeechan would wish to see from his own charges. He took little satisfaction from a scoreline which showed Scotland winning by three points but hid the fact that Ireland had a 4–3 edge in tries.

Despite McGeechan's criticisms, Scotland wrote a new line in their record book. It was their ninth successive win at Murrayfield, and never before had they had so long a string of home victories.

As a spectacle, the match was overflowing with entertainment and excitement. The contest stirred the emotions. As a game of rugby, though, it left much to be desired in the minds of those who, like McGeechan, plan all-round efficiency. As McGeechan commented, Scotland 'hung in' and scored more points. Experience carried them through. They knew how to lift themselves when they were rocked back on their heels. It was a point that Ciaran Fitzgerald, Ireland's coach, acknowledged when he remarked that his team, much recast this season, will have to learn to consolidate when they go ahead. Scotland twice came from behind.

In terms of ability the crucial factor was that Scotland's worldly-wise breakaway trio exerted more influence on the game than their counterparts, for all that Brian Robinson scored a scrummage pick-up try out of Derek White's book. White's scrum-base control still allowed John Jeffrey to lie off a lot, Derek Turnbull did much notable chopping, and Jeffrey himself had that instinctive appreciation of being in the right place at the right time.

Jeffrey's support for Scott Hastings was vital in the latter's try. That score, though with bizarre origins, was the third of three by which Scotland turned a four-point deficit into a 28–19 lead in the space of nine minutes.

A succession of accidents preceded that try. Neil Francis won a line-out to release Brian Rigney, White robbed the Irishman, Craig Chalmers ran around in ever decreasing circles before punting ahead, Robinson failed to clear to touch, and Jeffrey threw a horrid pass to Gavin Hastings before the rugby regained its senses with a chip kick by Scott Hastings. Jeffrey toed the ball on, gathered from the kind bounce, and sent a precise reverse pass inside for Scott Hastings to run in.

Ireland could hardly have believed that the fates were so unkind. Yet that try was typical of the match, as was the produce from the line-out, an area of the game that Kerry FitzGerald left to the forwards to sort out for themselves. The referee even defined his own line-out rules to the two teams before the game.

Francis was the main force on the touch-line, but the vital line-out ball went mainly Scotland's way. Ken Reid, Ireland's team manager, even suggested that the result hinged on three line-outs.

First, as injury time was stretching on before the interval, after Robb Saunders had struck a 55-metre kick for a line-out close to Scotland's goal-line, Damian Cronin gathered two-handed and galloped up the left before kicking into the Irish 22. In the consequent pressure White, Gary Armstrong, David Sole, and Chris Gray each had a go for the line, and eventually a slanting run by Chalmers put Gavin Hastings over for a try by which the full-back became the first to pass 300 points for Scotland.

Gray won the second line-out on Reid's list, the lock firing a drive that magnetised support and surged fully 30 metres to cross the Irish goal-line. No try was awarded, though John Allan claimed afterwards that he had pulled Gray down in the maul to score, but a try immediately followed. White picked up from the five-metre scrum, Turnbull drove the number eight on, and White's flipped pass put Tony Stanger in for his tenth international try. In its conception, with the wing intruding off the narrow side, the score was similar to Stanger's try in the 1990 second Test against the All Blacks.

Chalmers converted for 21–19 after 48 minutes, and the third of Reid's line-outs soon followed. Phil Matthews was penalised for being offside in stealing Gray's tap-down, and Chalmers kicked the goal for a match haul of 13 points. The Scott Hastings try soon followed.

Reid could have cited also the Irish throw-ins stolen by Gray and White close to the Scottish goal-line. White's tail take helped to thwart Ireland's brave finale.

Even while the match was turning, Ireland mainly played the game that suited them. It was nearly always running at a hectic pace, helped greatly by sympathetic refereeing by Kerry FitzGerald. The Australian referee cut the penalties down to a minimum of 11, only four against Scotland, though to do so he opted out of the strictest demands of the line-out law.

Ireland, their team reshaped in this season's Championship, revelled in such a game. Saunders served swift and long, Brian Smith answered his critics with heady rugby, and always the Irish plan was to spread the game wide to Simon Geoghegan and Keith Crossan, with Jim Staples threatening on the intrusion, whether to handle or act only as decoy.

Three of their tries were with such delightful rugby. Crossan stamped the intentions midway in the first half, Geoghegan maintained his scoring run in his debut season, adding to his tries against Wales and England, and Brendan Mullin finished off by breaking an Irish record that had stood for 61 years. The centre's try was his 15th for Ireland, surpassing the 14 by George Stephenson between 1920 and 1930.

Two Chalmers penalty goals gave Scotland a 6–0 lead after 15 minutes, but Ireland quickly responded. Smith stepped inside Chalmers, and the Irish stand-off's lateral run, with Mullin as decoy, let Crossan cut in-field to score between the posts in 19 minutes.

Smith converted, and Ireland almost monopolised the remainder of the first half. Mullin went close to the posts, denied only by Scott Hastings inches from the goal-line, and though Smith missed two penalties he dropped a goal and converted Robinson's try, a score which exploited Scotland's numerical disadvantage before Peter Dods replaced Iwan Tukalo.

Gavin Hastings, however, replied to Smith's drop goal with a huge penalty goal from more than 40 metres, and after six minutes of added time Chalmers converted the full-back's try. Scotland could hardly believe their good fortune that they were level at the interval.

Ireland restored their lead early in the second half, Mullin's delightful lofted pass over Dods putting Geoghegan in, but Smith could not convert. It was his third missed goal, and Scotland came back with those 13 points in nine minutes. The gap was too much for Ireland to make up, though Dave Curtis put Mullin in at the left corner after Saunders and Geoghegan had stretched Scotland on the right. Smith converted from tight on the touch-line, but the stand-off was wide with a belated drop-kick that would have salvaged a draw, which would have been no less than Ireland deserved. History, though, does not remember or record brave losers.

SCOTLAND		IRELAND
A. G. Hastings (*Watsonians*)	15	J. E. Staples (*London Irish*)
A. G. Stanger (*Hawick*)	14	S. P. Geoghegan (*London Irish*)
S. Hastings (*Watsonians*)	13	B. J. Mullin (*Blackrock College*)
S. R. P. Lineen (*Boroughmuir*)	12	D. M. Curtis (*London Irish*)
I. Tukalo (*Selkirk*)	11	K. D. Crossan (*Instonians*)
C. M. Chalmers (*Melrose*)	10	B. A. Smith (*Leicester*)
G. Armstrong (*Jed-Forest*)	9	R. Saunders (*London Irish*) captain
D. M. B. Sole (*Edinburgh Acad'ls*) captain	1	J. J. Fitzgerald (*Young Munster*)
J. Allan (*Edinburgh Academicals*)	2	S. J. Smith (*Ballymena*)
A. P. Burnell (*London Scottish*)	3	D. C. Fitzgerald (*Lansdowne*)
C. A. Gray (*Nottingham*)	4	B. J. Rigney (*Greystones*)
D. F. Cronin (*Bath*)	5	N. P. J. Francis (*Blackrock College*)
D. J. Turnbull (*Hawick*)	6	P. M. Matthews (*Wanderers*)
D. B. White (*London Scottish*)	8	B. F. Robinson (*Ballymena*)
J. Jeffrey (*Kelso*)	7	G. F. Hamilton (*North of Ireland*)
Replacement: P. W. Dods (*Gala*) for Tukalo (32 minutes)		*Replacement*: K. J. Murphy (*Constitution*) for Staples (70)

Referee: K. V. J. FitzGerald (*Australia*)

Tries:	*Tries:*
A. G. Hastings, Stanger, S. Hastings	Geoghegan, Mullin, Crossan, Robinson
Conversions:	*Conversions:*
Chalmers (2)	Smith (2)
Penalty goals:	*Drop-goal:*
Chalmers (3), A. G. Hastings	Smith

Doddie Weir, the Melrose lock, towers over the Japanese at Murrayfield

John Jeffrey, playing in what he maintained was his swansong tournament, always posed a threat with ball in hand

World Cup '91

A View From Scotland

By BILL McMURTRIE

WHEN ROB ANDREW'S drop goal sailed between the posts at Murrayfield's ice-rink end about 3.50 p.m. on Saturday, 26 October, Scottish rugby was rudely awakened. The World Cup dream was over. England were ahead with only seven minutes left, and Scotland were heading out of the tournament.

England went on to the final but lost to Australia. The Wallabies had grown as favourites as the tournament progressed and their 12–6 victory amply proved that rating. So ended a jamboree of rugby that had begun with New Zealand's 18–12 win over England at Twickenham on 3 October.

It had been a month of memories. Canada and Western Samoa reached the last eight. The Samoans crucified Wales and captivated Scotland. Australia beat New Zealand's defending champions and won the support of the world outside England. Even New Zealanders were drawn to agree with Australian rugby rather than the English version. Scotland aspired and fell short against the old enemy. Ireland ran Australia so close that only Campese could rescue the Wallabies.

Players, like countries, left their marks. David Campese continued to tease opponents, as he has done on Australia's behalf since 1982. His worth has been recorded in his 46 international tries, six in this tournament, but expressed in memories. Hiroyuki Kajihara's try for Japan against Ireland will last as long in the memory as on videotape. So will Ivan Francescato's try for Italy against the United States, a score of individualism unsurpassed in the tournament. Gordon Hamilton's try for Ireland against Australia would have been the World Cup's *pièce de résistance*, taking his country to ecstasy at 16–15, had it not been trumped by Michael Lynagh's salvation score.

More important, rugby had a world stage. More than 70 countries took television coverage. The millions there could be left to decide on their own favourites – Australia the all-rounders, England the conservative, Scotland the brave, Ireland the almost team, Western Samoa and Canada the emerging nations who emerged.

Campese, the Australian genius, departed from international rugby with the final. Two Scottish flankers, Finlay Calder and John Jeffrey, went from the scene, too. Calder's departure was pre-planned: he had returned to Scotland's XV only for the finals. Jeffrey's retirement was a well-kept secret until he led the Scots on to Murrayfield for the semi-final against

Support from the Murrayfield crowd was a major factor in Scotland's progress during the competition

Finlay Calder and Gavin Hastings, a formidable sight in full flight

Treatment on the way for David Sole as the Scottish skipper gashed an ear after a clash of heads

England. Neither Calder nor Jeffrey would claim to be a magician like Campese, yet rugby is the poorer for the retirement of all three. Calder and Jeffrey were as much masters in their own ways.

Two days after the tournament's opening game Scotland's entry followed with a 49–9 win over Japan at Murrayfield. Then came Scottish wins against Zimbabwe by 51–12, Ireland by 24–15 and Western Samoa by 28–6, all played at Murrayfield. Before then, however, the Scots had a rocky road in preparation. As Ian McGeechan, Scotland's coach, remarked more than once, the match-practice before the tournament was effectively squeezing five months' work into five weeks. A visit to Bucharest was not an auspicious opening to the preliminaries, Romania beating Scotland 18–12. A week later Scotland drew 16–all with the Barbarians' star-studded team and, changing their guise, the Scots continued as the SRU President's XV, though with mixed fortune. They beat the Anglo-Scots' augmented XV 32–4, but then lost 13–19 to Edinburgh Borderers, led by Jeremy Richardson, who, by that result, had a small compensation for being the only member of Scotland's 1987 World Cup squad still uncapped. Within the Scottish squad, however, the belief was that all would come right on the day. Thoughts followed the theatrical line that the quality of the first night would be in inverse proportion to the standard of the dress rehearsal.

Yet even against Japan the Scots had an uneven first half. At the interval they led by only 17–9. The lively Orientals had proved a hot handful even though Doddie Weir, Chris Gray and Derek White were creaming the

Successful service from Gary
Armstrong. Doddie Weir,
David Sole and Finlay Calder
watch the ball on its way

ball off the line-out almost as they pleased. Early in the second half
Sean Lineen, Jeffrey and Stanger made the running before Calder surged
away towards the posts, the flanker stopped only by Yoshida's high tackle.
Gavin Hastings converted the penalty try and added two penalty goals for
29–9, one from near halfway. But it was the last quarter before Scotland
pulled out their best. Gray's long pass released the Hastings brothers for a
White try, Calder's long pass let Tukalo jink over, and Gary Armstrong's
run off a halfway scrum made one for Gavin Hastings. The full-back also
converted all three.

It was a victory not without cost. Chalmers took a knock on his throat,
and David Sole's right ear was cut when he collided with Jeffrey. Sole's
departure late on allowed David Milne to win his first Cap, joining his elder
and younger brothers, Iain and Kenneth, in the list of Heriot's international
players.

Eight changes were made for the next match, though the threequarter
line was kept intact and, when David Milne dropped out with a groin
muscle strain, Burnell switched to loose-head and Alan Watt was given his
first Cap. The Glasgow High/Kelvinside forward, weighing in at over 20 st,
was the first international player from Old Anniesland for 17 years, and
his promotion was vindication of those who had prompted his transition
from lock to prop.

Zimbabwe, like Japan, troubled Scotland early on and twice Adrian
Garvey, denying his role at prop, galloped away for tries. Brian Currin,
Zimbabwe's full-back and captain, converted both, the first equalising

after Tukalo's opening try and the second pulling Scotland back to 15–12 with six minutes left in the first half. Douglas Wyllie's garryowen made Scotland's opening try, Lineen sending Tukalo over. Lineen also had deft hands in the two other first-half tries, one by Derek Turnbull and the other by Scott Hastings. Peter Dods, captaining Scotland for the first time, converted all three as well as kicking a penalty goal, though his striking rate dropped in the second half. The full-back converted just two of the five tries, though he kicked a penalty goal from well over 40 metres. Tukalo had his second and third tries, and Stanger scored one, as did Weir and White.

With Chalmers and Sole fit, Scotland returned to their first-choice team for the match against Ireland. But as in the two previous games, the Scots were not at their best in the first half, and when Ralph Keyes kicked his fifth goal five minutes after the interval the visitors were 15–9 up. By then, too, Chalmers had retired with a bruised hip, injured in a tackle by Phil Matthews, and the Melrose stand-off's club colleague, Graham Shiel, took over for his first Cap at the age of 21. Armstrong nursed the try-scoring newcomer so well that Scotland came back to win despite the enforced change, though that was not the only strength in the scrum-half's game. He kicked positively even under pressure, his close-quarter defence was water-tight, and he found the ways and means for exemplary crossfield cover, as when he denied Simon Geoghegan on one of the rare instances that the electrifying wing was allowed a run. Ireland, well though they played, failed fatally to utilise the Geoghegan missile.

Scotland's win kept them at the top of their group and ensured that they would have a quarter-final at Murrayfield. Ireland, though runners-up, also had a home quarter-final.

Elsewhere, the six others in the last eight were slotted in, though with upsets to two seeds, Wales and Fiji. Western Samoa beat Wales 16–14 at Cardiff with a dubious try by To'o Vaega – Robert Jones appeared to get the first touch as the pair chased through on to the ball – and Canada, not so unexpectedly, defeated Fiji 13–3 in Bayonne. Canada did not surprise those who had seen them beat Scotland 24–19 five months earlier in St John, New Brunswick. Wales hung on to hope by beating Argentina 16–7 at Cardiff. But they then lost to Australia 3–38, also at Cardiff, and the last slender Welsh thread was cut when Western Samoa defeated Argentina 35–12 at Pontypridd. The valleys went into mourning, and Western Samoa, as group runners-up to Australia, flew to Edinburgh to play Scotland.

Scotland's victory over Ireland was costly. Not only was Chalmers injured but Lineen had taken a kick on the knee. The blow had jerked the kneecap out of place and Lineen said afterwards he had experienced pain the like of which he had never known. Fluid had to be drained from the joint the following day. Donald Macleod, the Scottish squad's physician, reckoned that both suffered what he called 'seven to ten day' injuries. The prospects were far from good that either player would be fit, but along came modern technology in the shape of a hyperbaric-oxygen chamber. Its recognised place was in the realms of deep-sea divers, but a regular course

The Pride of Scotland: Scotland's 1991 World Cup squad and officials. *BACK ROW*: Greig Oliver, Mark Moncrieff, John Allan, Douglas Wyllie, Alan Watt, Graham Marshall, Doddie Weir, Derek Turnbull, Tony Stanger, Ken Milne, David Milne, Paul Burnell, Graham Shiel *MIDDLE ROW*: SRU secretary Bill Hogg, assistant coach Derrick Grant, fitness adviser David McLean, Peter Dods, Sean Lineen, Chris Gray, Damian Cronin, Craig Chalmers, Gary Armstrong, baggage master Milton Floyd, assistant coach Douglas Morgan, liaison officer Charlie Ritchie *FRONT ROW*: Finlay Calder, medical officer Mr Donald Macleod, Derek White, coach Ian McGeechan, John Jeffrey, team manager Duncan Paterson, David Sole (c), SRU president Gordon Masson, Gavin Hastings, assistant coach Jim Telfer, Scott Hastings, physiotherapist Dr J. P. Robson, Iwan Tukalo *Courtesy of Scottish Rugby Union*

of high-pressure oxygen was known to speed recovery from injury. From the Tuesday onwards Chalmers and Lineen had regular sessions sitting in the monotony of the chamber for spells of an hour and half, as well as normal physiotherapy. The machine was taken from one base to another when the Scots moved from St Andrews to Dalmahoy. Chalmers recovered to play against Western Samoa, but Lineen had to wait for the semi-final against England. Instead, Shiel had his second Cap as Lineen's deputy at inside centre.

Western Samoa had caught the headlines not only with their win over Wales and their narrow defeat by Australia: their tackling was also fearsome, especially when it was aimed around chest and ribcage. They relished hard contact and, for all that the Samoans represented islands with a home population of about 167,000, they had players well experienced in the harsh realities of New Zealand provincial rugby.

Ian McGeechan and Jim Telfer knew that Scotland could not afford a start as low-key as they had in the pool matches against Japan, Zimbabwe and Ireland. The Scots had to stamp their mark on the game as early as possible, and twice in the opening minutes Gavin Hastings was released in storming runs at Samoa's close-quarter defence. It was a clear statement that Scotland were prepared to play as hard as the Samoans.

It was, however, John Jeffrey who marauded, plundered and ripped into the South Sea Islanders. Twice the Kelso flanker surged over for tries, and often he was at the heart of the Scottish forwards' driving game that carried his country through to the semi-finals. Jeffrey had by then scored 11 international tries — more than any other Scottish forward, a record he had lost to his back-row compatriot, Derek White, earlier in the tournament. Calder and White were worthy allies against the Samoans, Gray and John Allan had outstanding games in the loose, and Gary Armstrong, sharp on the forwards' heels, had another memorable match. The tackling of Scott Hastings gave the Samoans a taste of their own medicine. Nor was Shiel backward at going forward into the tackle in his first full international.

Scotland's game was designed to take the Samoans on in a frontal assault, not only by firing the forwards. Their aim was to turn the Samoans' offensive defence into pure defence. In addition, David Sole imposed self-inflicted pressure on his team when, winning the toss, he opted to play against the stiff northerly wind that cut downfield from the ice-rink end. It was a deliberate ploy to rouse the Scots into a sharper start than they had had against Ireland the previous week. It worked only in the respect that Scotland set their standard. Nearly half an hour had passed before they led for the first time with a Stanger try, and in doing so they came back from the loss of an early penalty goal to Matthew Vaea.

A 13–3 lead was a satisfying margin for Scotland to take into their wind-assisted second half, but it seemed to breed complacency. However slight, it was enough to spring the Samoans free of their shackles. For quarter of an hour the visitors threatened. Three times Timo Tagaloa escaped Stanger for threatening runs, drawing out saving tackles by Gavin Hastings and Armstrong. Steve Bachop, too, essayed a break from defence, beating Iwan Tukalo, and Sila Vaifale tested Jeffery's defensive powers.

Slack handling let the Samoans down, and when Scott Hastings tackled the intruding Aiolupo with the finality of a Samoan, Tukalo picked up to scamper over from halfway. The try was chalked off because Scott Hastings was judged to have been offside.

A Scottish score, however, was not long in coming. Armstrong attacked off Weir's line-out tap, the scrum-half turning on a sixpence to profit from loose possession, and when Samoa killed the ball at a ruck set up by Allan, Gavin Hastings kicked a simple penalty goal. Bachop immediately responded with a drop goal, but Gavin Hastings took Scotland 13 points clear again with a goal from a ball-killing penalty six metres inside his own half. It was downwind but still a huge kick and a hefty killer blow.

Jeffrey's second try was the icing on Scotland's tasty cake. Again Calder was in close attendance, and again Gavin Hastings kicked the conversion. His final penalty goal gave him 16 points in the game. He had six successful kicks out of seven on a windy day, on his way to 55 points in the tournament.

Western Samoa still had the last word, deservedly so, though it came after the match. They had given so much to not only to a memorable Murrayfield occasion but also to the tournament. They ran a spontaneous lap round the ground, and they danced a final *siva*. Almost as one, the crowd waited to praise them and thank them.

Later that afternoon Parc des Princes had a sharply contrasting quarter-final, England beating France 19–10 in a torrid match. It was tight until Will Carling's try near the end. The next day Australia and New Zealand

No prizes for guessing who they support

Lion rampant: the Scots' banner flies over the Murrayfield terraces

Derek White, John Jeffrey, David Sole and Doddie Weir contest line-out ball during Scotland's Murrayfield tussle with Ireland, World Cup 1991

followed through into the semi-finals, with respective wins over Ireland and Canada, though the Wallabies had a close run before edging a 19–18 victory. Waltzing Matilda drowned Mollie Malone.

England travelled to Edinburgh after their Paris win, but the Scots were confident not only because of the manner of their quarter-final victory over the Samoans. Memories did not have to be stretched too far to recall Murrayfield's 1990 Grand Slam decider in which Scotland beat England by 13–7. Scotland's dream, however, was shattered not only by England's 9–6 victory but also by the sterile manner of it. Their game was dull, limited and unimaginative. The talents of Jeremy Guscott and Rory Underwood were sacrificed for the sake of the one-track policy. Geoff Cooke and Roger Uttley, the architects of England's victory, were blinkered by the objective. The excitement of the day was generated only by the closeness of the game and the occasion itself.

Of course, as Cooke admitted earlier in the week, the supporters of both countries wanted to win. But I would like to think – indeed, I am certain – that Ian McGeechan, Scotland's coach, would have served rugby better if he had had the benefit of England's massive domination and the thumping power of their forwards in the loose.

England had the wherewithal to win by more than just two Jon Webb penalty goals and a Rob Andrew drop goal to two Gavin Hastings penalty goals, and I for one would not have been quite so deeply disappointed if the visitors' game had flowed enough for them to score even one try to emphasise their forward superiority. My heart was sad, almost as much for rugby as for Ian McGeechan, Jim Telfer, David Sole, and all those Scots who had given so much in their World Cup preparations and playing.

At the end of the match Scotland's world briefly stopped. The Scottish players stood or lay still for what seemed a long minute before they congratulated the victors. Moreover, the Scots returned to the field to applaud the support who had carried them through 13 successive international wins at Murrayfield. That, more than the moment of defeat, brought a lump to the throat.

The next day Australia inspired the tournament with the manner of their 16–6 victory over New Zealand. Theirs is an all-round game, even though they had to rely on that man Campese for their tries: he scored one with brilliant perception and deceptive acceleration, and he gave Tim Horan the other with a deft flip over his shoulder. So the Wallabies went to Twickenham for the final and the All Blacks, winners of the first World Cup in 1987, were sent to Cardiff to play Scotland for third place.

In that Cardiff match the Scots, courage personified, fought a rearguard action for 77 minutes, but, with only injury-time left, their resistance broke. Walter Little ran over for the only try of the play-off, and New Zealand secured the silver medals with their 13–6 win.

Calder and Jeffrey thus bowed out of international rugby without the consolation of Scotland's first win in 16 matches against New Zealand. Calder has tasted defeat in four of those games, Jeffrey in three. Some of us have seen more of the All Blacks' 14 wins as well as the two draws, but at the end of the Cardiff match the feeling was not of abject disappointment,

Line-out action from the Scotland v England semi-final at Murrayfield. The touchline battle proved to one of the crucial areas of the game

as it had been after Scotland's defeat by England on the Saturday. Partly it was resignation that Scotland are fated against New Zealand; partly it was that Scotland had bravely kept themselves in the contest.

Here was a rugby match, even if it was peppered with mistakes. The fervour of the competition on a sunny afternoon could not be denied. Neither team played as if for consolation. Even third place was a prize worth winning.

Before Little scored the try the margin was only 9–6. Jon Preston had kicked three penalty goals for New Zealand, Gavin Hastings had had two, and the Scots were threatening. The last quarter was Scotland's best spell, even though they lost the try in that time. Yet, based on set-piece possession alone, Scotland should not have been that close that late. Gary Whetton and Zinzan Brooke exerted heavy command on the line-out for an hour, and at times the New Zealand scrummage, if not always legal, wrecked the Scottish platform.

Scotland's outer game, however, was more productive. They occasionally sparked rucking close to New Zealand's old class, Gary Armstrong was a typical terrier on the forwards' heels, and the game that Calder and Jeffrey played was a heart-rending reminder of what Scotland would miss now that they have gone from international rugby. The flankers played with honour to the end.

It was a contest without rancour. Rugby was the object, and the one serious penalty was when Fred Howard, touch judge on the press-box side, spotted a severe kick on Armstrong by Richard Loe. Steve Hilditch,

Wade Dooley, the giant England lock, seems set to do Scott Hastings a grevious mischief. John Jeffrey comes in to support the Scottish centre

the Irish referee, spoke severely to the prop. Such incidents were as rare in the tournament as a whole as in this match.

When viewed in defensive terms, the Scots were magnificent. At least half a dozen tackles were memorable, each in its own right. Only Armstrong's retreating cover denied Terry Wright and Va'aiga Tuigamala in the first half, Scott Hastings twice thwarted Wright, Weir appeared from nowhere to haul Preston into touch at the left corner, and Jeffrey swept back to save from a John Kirwan kick up the right touchline. Scotland signalled their intentions when they stood up to the All Blacks' haka before the kick-off. Weir stared Tuigamala down so closely that the New Zealand wing almost bumped into the Scot on the final leap of the dance, and with only three minutes gone in the match the Scots had their sign on the scoreboard. Gavin Hastings kicked the opening penalty goal from 42 metres after New Zealand had strayed offside at a ruck induced by an Armstrong probe.

Gavin Hastings finished with a strike rate of two out of three, his second penalty goal pulling the All Blacks back to 9–6 in 73 minutes after the omnipresent Michael Jones had tackled Lineen high. That score was also reward for a stirring run by Scott Hastings out of his own 22, prompted by his brother and supported by Calder. Throughout the last quarter the Scots played their most forceful rugby. Tukalo, Armstrong and the Hastings brothers were the principals. Allan and Gray chipped in notable back-up liaison with the breakaway trio. Briefly, after Chalmers had trapped Wright in the New Zealand 22, the Scots camped on the All Black's goal-line.

Finlay Calder and John Jeffrey, who both maintained they were making their last Murrayfield appearances, get to grips with the English during the Auld Enemy semi-final. Derek White and David Sole are close by

White and the sniping Armstrong were held there. Most of the threats, however, were from longer range, and when the Scots tried once too often to run out of defence Armstrong was clobbered by Michael Jones. The loose ball eluded Chalmers, the All Blacks swept it away, and Wright put Little over on the left, though too far out for Preston to convert.

Twickenham's final was a contest worthy of the occasion, though the rugby did not quite attain the heights set in the 1987 equivalent. Four years previously the All Blacks played dominant rugby, stifled the French breakaways' threat and created three class tries, whereas here the Australians wrung victory out of minority possession.

Sceptics among us did not believe England would expand their game, even if they could. To their credit, they did move the ball wider than they had done in winning at Parc des Princes and Murrayfield, but they overdid it. Because of too little recent practice in a more open game England were loose. Their direction often was not right and their timing was wrong. They were not quite like headless chickens, but they did look as though they knew the slaughterman was just behind them, as when wide passes were thrown out to Rory Underwood. England's intention was to unleash Underwood to test Campese's defence early on, but the ploy went a-gley. Nor did Jeremy Guscott look confident when he was utilised as the midfield spearhead. His game ought to have been for finishing rather than setting up rucks, even with the close support especially of Peter Winterbottom.

Ackford was the line-out key, as he had been throughout England's Cup

Iwan Tukalo and Derek White close in on England's Simon Halliday

Chris Gray coming to grips
with New Zealand number
eight Zinzan Brooke during
the third-place play-off
in Cardiff

Finlay Calder, in his last
appearance on the world
stage, and Doddie Weir
form the horizontal layers
in a Cardiff pile-up. Gary
Armstrong and Derek White
are in close attendance during
the play-off game against the
All Blacks

campaign. Australians, even the potentially talented John Eales, were left clutching at straws as Derek Bevan, the Welsh referee, allowed the line-out mainly to sort itself out, as Steve Hilditch had done in the third-place play-off. Hilditch was at least consistent in that whereas Bevan was not. He turned to penalising Australia out of the line-out in the second half. Australia suffered from only one of those penalties, when Jon Webb kicked the goal that cut Australia to 9–3 on the hour. Lynagh, however, soon restored the 9-point margin when Mike Teague went over the ball off Australia's loose line-out possession. The final score of the match came when Webb kicked a second penalty.

Defence was an Australian strength throughout the tournament. They conceded only three tries over their six matches – two to Argentina and one by Gordon Hamilton which, though briefly, allowed Ireland to lead Australia before Lynagh salvaged that quarter-final. It was the last time in the tournament that Australia were flustered. They were competent and complete champions. They proved their competence in the final even if they could not expand as they had done in the semi-final against New Zealand.

To the victors the spoils: Australian skipper Nick Farr-Jones and player of the tournament David Campese with the Webb Ellis Cup after victory over England at Twickenham. The Wallabies' 12–6 win over England in a pulsating final represented Campese's 100th appearance in an Australian jersey

World Cup Results

Pool 1 – England 12, New Zealand 18 (at Twickenham); Italy 30, USA 9 (at Otley); New Zealand 46, USA 6 (at Gloucester); England 36, Italy 6 (at Twickenham); England 37, USA 9 (at Twickenham); New Zealand 31, Italy 21 (at Leicester)

Pool 2 – Scotland 47, Japan 9 (at Murrayfield); Ireland 55, Zimbabwe 11 (at Lansdowne Road); Ireland 32, Japan 16 (at Lansdowne Road); Scotland 51, Zimbabwe 12 (at Murrayfield); Scotland 24, Ireland 15 (at Murrayfield); Japan 52, Zimbabwe 8 (at Ravenhill, Belfast)

Pool 3 – Australia 32, Argentina 19 (at Llanelli); Wales 13, Western Samoa 16 (at Cardiff); Australia 9, Western Samoa 3 (at Pontypool); Wales 16, Argentina 7 (at Cardiff); Wales 3, Australia 38 (at Cardiff); Western Samoa 35, Argentina 12 (at Pontypridd)

Pool 4 – France 30, Romania 3 (at Béziers); Canada 13, Fiji 3 (at Bayonne); France 33, Fiji 9 (at Grenoble); Canada 19, Romania 11 (at Toulouse); Romania 17, Fiji 15 (at Brive); France 19, Canada 13 (at Agen)

Quarter-finals – Scotland 28, Western Samoa 6 (at Murrayfield); France 10, England 19 (at Parc des Princes); Ireland 18, Australia 19 (at Lansdowne Road); New Zealand 29, Canada 13 (at Lille)

Semi-finals – Scotland 6, England 9 (at Murrayfield); Australia 16, New Zealand 6 (at Lansdowne Road)

Third-place play-off – New Zealand 13, Scotland 6 (at Cardiff)

Final – England 6, Australia 12 (at Twickenham)

SCOTLAND'S WORLD CUP MATCHES

Scotland 47, Japan 9 (at Murrayfield on 5 October)

Scotland – A. G. Hastings; A. G. Stanger, S. Hastings, S. R. P. Lineen, I. Tukalo; C. M. Chalmers, G. Armstrong; D. M. B. Sole (captain), J. Allan, A. P. Burnell, C. A. Gray, G. W. Weir, J. Jeffrey, D. B. White, F. Calder *Replacements* – D. S. Wyllie for Chalmers (70 minutes), D. F. Milne (Heriot's FP) for Sole (75 minutes)
Tries: White, Tukalo, A. G. Hastings, S. Hastings, Stanger, Chalmers (penalty try)
Conversions: A. G. Hastings (5) *Penalty goals*: A. G. Hastings (2), Chalmers

Japan – T. Hosokawa; T. Masuho, E. Kutsuki, S. Hirao (captain), Y. Yoshida; K. Matsuo, W. Murata; O. Ota, M. Kunda, M. Takura, T. Hayashi, E. Tifaga, H. Kajihara, S. Latu, S. Nakashima
Try: Hosokawa *Conversion*: Hosokawa *Penalty goal*: Hosokawa

Referee – E. F. Morrison (England)

Scotland 51, Zimbabwe 12 (at Murrayfield on 9 October)

Scotland – P. W. Dods (captain); A. G. Stanger, S. Hastings, S. R. P. Lineen, I. Tukalo; D. S. Wyllie, G. H. Oliver; A. P. Burnell, K. S. Milne, A. G. J. Watt, D. F. Cronin, G. W. Weir, D. J. Turnbull, D. B. White, G. R. Marshall *Replacement* – C. M. Chalmers for Stanger (79 minutes)
Tries: Tukalo (3), Stanger, S. Hastings, White, Turnbull, Weir *Conversions*: Dods (5)
Penalty goals: Dods (2) *Dropped goal*: Wyllie

Zimbabwe – B. S. Currin (captain); W. H. Schultz, R. U. Tsimba, M. S. Letcher, D. A. Walters; C. Brown, E. A. McMillan; A. H. Nicholls, B. A. Beattie, A. C. Garvey, M. L. Martin, H. Nguruve, D. G. Muirhead, B. W. Catterall, B. N. Dawson *Replacements* – R. N. Hunter for Garvey (46 minutes), E. Chimbima for Walters (56 minutes), C. P. Roberts for Hunter (79 minutes)
Tries: Garvey (2) *Conversions*: Currin (2)

Referee – D. N. Reordan (USA)

Scotland 24, Ireland 15 (at Murrayfield on 12 October)

Scotland – A. G. Hastings; A. G. Stanger, S. Hastings, S. R. P. Lineen, I. Tukalo; C. M. Chalmers, G. Armstrong; D. M. B. Sole (captain), J. Allan, A. P. Burnell, C. A. Gray, G. W. Weir, J. Jeffrey, D. B. White, F. Calder *Replacements* – A. G. Shiel for Chalmers (42 minutes)
Tries: Armstrong, Shiel *Conversions*: A. G. Hastings (2) *Penalty goals*: A. G. Hastings (3) *Dropped goal*: Chalmers

Ireland – J. E. Staples; S. P. Geoghegan, B. J. Mullin, D. M. Curtis, K. D. Crossan; R. P. Keyes, R. Saunders; N. J. Popplewell, S. J. Smith, D. C. Fitzgerald, D. G. Lenihan, N. P. J. Francis, P. M. Matthews (captain), B. F. Robinson, G. F. Hamilton
Penalty goals: Keyes (4) *Dropped goal*: Keyes

Referee – F. A. Howard (England)

Scotland 28, Western Samoa 6 (quarter-final at Murrayfield on 19 October)

Scotland – A. G. Hastings; A. G. Stanger, S. Hastings, A. G. Shiel, I. Tukalo; C. M. Chalmers, G. Armstrong; D. M. B. Sole (captain), J. Allan, A. P. Burnell, C. A. Gray, G. W. Weir, J. Jeffrey, D. B. White, F. Calder
Tries: Jeffrey (2) Stanger *Conversions*: A. G. Hastings (2) *Penalty goals*: A. G. Hastings (4)

Western Samoa – A. A. Aiolupo; B. Lima, T. Vaega, F. E. Bunce, T. D. L. Tagaloa; S. J. Bachop, M. M. Vaea; P. Fatialofa (captain), S. To'omalatai, V. Alalatoa, M. L. Birtwhistle, E. Ioane, S. Vaifale, P. R. Lam, A. Perelini
Penalty goal: Vaea *Dropped goal*: Bachop

Referee – W. D. Bevan (Wales)

Scotland 6, England 9 (semi-final at Murrayfield on 26 October)

Scotland – A. G. Hastings; A. G. Stanger, S. Hastings, S. R. P. Lineen, I. Tukalo; C. M. Chalmers, G. Armstrong; D. M. B. Sole (captain), J. Allan, A. P. Burnell, C. A. Gray, G. W. Weir, J. Jeffrey, D. B. White, F. Calder
Penalty goals: A. G. Hastings (2)

England: – J. M. Webb; S. J. Halliday, W. D. C. Carling (captain), J. C. Guscott, R. Underwood; C. R. Andrew, R. J. Hill; J. Leonard, B. C. Moore, J. A. Probyn, P. J. Ackford, W. A. Dooley, M. G. Skinner, M. C. Teague, P. J. Winterbottom
Penalty goals: Webb (2) *Drop goal*: Andrew

Referee – K. V. J. Fitzgerald (Australia)

New Zealand 13, Scotland 6 (third-place play-off at Cardiff on 30 October)

New Zealand – T. J. Wright; J. J. Kirwan, C. R. Innes, W. K. Little, V. Tuigamala; J. Preston, G. T. M. Bachop; S. C. McDowell, S. B. T. Fitzpatrick, R. W. Loe, I. D. Jones, G. W. Whetton (captain), A. T. Earl, Z. V. Brooke, M. Jones *Replacement* – S. J. Philpott for Tuigamala (half-time)
Try: Little *Penalty goals*: Preston (3)

Scotland – A. G. Hastings; A. G. Stanger, S. Hastings, S. R. P. Lineen, I. Tukalo; C. M. Chalmers, G. Armstrong; D. M. B. Sole (captain), J. Allan, A. P. Burnell, C. A. Gray, G. W. Weir, J. Jeffrey, D. B. White, F. Calder *Replacement* – P. W. Dods for Stanger (47 minutes)
Penalty goals: A. G. Hastings (2)

Referee – S. R. Hilditch (Ireland)

Opposite:
Gavin Hastings in full flight against the Japanese, World Cup 1991

Chris Gray on the charge
against the Japanese, World
Cup 1991

Finlay Calder gathers in
Craig Chalmers' pass, World
Cup 1991

Scotland centre Sean Lineen
breaks clear against the
Japanese, World Cup 1991

Scott Hastings and
Derek Turnbull target
the Zimbabweans, World
Cup 1991

By Royal appointment: SRU patron, the Princess Royal, with the Scotland team prior to the Murrayfield semi-final against England, World Cup 1991

The Scots charge on against Ireland. John Jeffrey has the ball while Finlay Calder, Paul Burnell and Derek White move up in support, World Cup 1991

Scotland wing-threequarter
Tony Stanger samples the
effectiveness of the Western
Samoan defence, World
Cup 1991

Scotland skipper David
Sole attempts to breach the
Western Samoan line, World
Cup 1991

Doddie Weir and Chris Gray in line-out action against England. The touch-line battle was a crucial area for both sides, World Cup 1991

Gary Armstrong and Craig Chalmers are at the centre of the action against England at Murrayfield, World Cup 1991

David Sole eyes the skies
as Jeremy Guscott closes on
the Scotland skipper, World
Cup 1991

Hard landing: All Black full-back Terry Wright takes a nose-dive in the third place play-off match against Scotland at Cardiff Arms Park. Peter Dods, Finlay Calder and Gary Armstrong are in close attendance. Craig Chalmers attempts to keep out of harm's way, World Cup 1991

Gary Armstrong at full stretch as the Scotland scrum-half attempts to charge down All Black full-back Terry Wright's clearance kick during the third place play-off in Cardiff, World Cup 1991

High Grade and High Speed

A Post-war Scotland XV

By BILL McLAREN

IT STOOD TO REASON that when Derek Douglas and his *Glasgow Herald* disciples wanted someone to select the greatest-ever Scotland side from the post-war years, they would turn to the ageing geezer with the greying temples although, come to think of it, Brian Meek *looks* older than I do!

It is some task and it leaves one open to criticism from all those who naturally have their own favourites. Of course, it always seems a kind of fruitless exercise because, apart from quality of opposition and of pressure exerted at different periods of the game, the Rugby Union game has undergone such transformation over the years in the realm of laws, ploys, personnel, pressure, fitness, attitude, commitment and opportunity, that you have the feeling of never being able to compare like with like so that an element of unfairness is present. At the same time it is a pleasurable exercise, too, as the mind drifts back over the great occasions, the great feats and the great players of yesteryear and sets up comparisons with the outstanding performers of modern times.

In seeking the greatest Scottish XV of the post-war years some might be inclined not to stray far from the 1984 or 1990 sides that won Scotland their Grand Slams, because you have to be well off for personnel and following a very sensible tactical blueprint in order to achieve such eminence. After all, in the 84 years since France entered the international Championship, the Grand Slam has been achieved only 24 times. Clearly, too, those two well-balanced sides, that gave Scots everywhere marvellously unforgettable and emotional involvement and national pride, had forged a team spirit that any makeshift XV would find hard to match. The 1990 side was described by all those operating at the sharp end as having virtually a club spirit and rapport with everyone playing for everyone else. Yet although there have been different eras in the game in which styles and approaches have varied greatly, there have been players in each period who, because of their special gifts and aptitude, would have flourished whatever the circumstances of tactical and fitness requirements and, whatever laws under which the game was to be played.

Hugh McLeod . . . fire and commitment

Just as one example compare the relative merits as full-backs of, for instance, Keith Geddes (London Scottish), Stewart Wilson (London Scottish), Ken Scotland (Heriots FP), Andy Irvine (Heriot's FP), Peter Dods (Gala) and Gavin Hastings (Watsonians). I have no doubt that had Gavin Hastings played in the Fifties when full-backs tended to be basically full-backs, committed almost exclusively to orthodox chores of catch, punt, tackle and fall, he would have been outstanding. Had Keith Geddes played today he would have made his mark because, apart from having the fundamentals at his fingertips, he was one of the first attacking full-backs in the modern era with a flare for running out of defence, regarded by some in those post-war days as slightly eccentric. Ken Scotland was the complete footballer of silken running grace and attacking flair. Actually, Scotland the country has reason to claim the very first attacking full-back in H. J. Stevenson (Edinburgh Academicals) who just could not curb his desire to carry the ball forward when moved from centre to full-back in the Scottish sides of the 1890s. But to pick the best full-back of the past 45 years could cause quite an argument although, for myself, there isn't a problem — well, not much!

In seeking the cream XV I would look for a pack of set-piece ball winners that also had at their command collective mobility with pace allied to good hands for as much support broken play handling as could be created. A secure gel at half-back would include a scrum-half with lightning service and with an eye for a break that would create doubt in the minds of initial opposing defenders and a stand-off with vision, a big, educated boot but also with a desire to tilt his lance when the opportunity presented itself, and with very quick hands so that the outsides would receive the ball without delay. The other backs would be chosen for their gifts of elusiveness, quick acceleration and adventurism because I would want to see them have a go at beating people as often as their judgement suggested that was on offer, although, because of the modern game being tilted in favour of defenders, each back would require a hefty boot for clearing messy situations. One would hope that the collective adventurism of the backs would lead to far more handling out of defence than one sees at the top level nowadays. And everyone in the side would be geared to tackle commitment just like the 1990 Grand Slam squad.

Gavin Hastings is arguably the best all-round full-back Scotland has ever had and Peter Dods the most consistent goal-kicker, as well as being far more secure under the high ball than his slight physique would suggest. But I go for the one who once scored five tries from full-back for the British Lions against King Country–Whanganui and simply shocked New Zealanders with such audacity. Andy Irvine might create heart murmurs on those occasions when, waiting for the mortar bomb to drop, he let his mind wander to what he would do with the ball when he got it. Sometimes he didn't! But he was the full-back all opponents respected and feared and it was typical of his awesome gifts that, having taken quite a bit of flak from the terraces for missing several goals against France at Murrayfield in 1980, he then proceeded to score two amazing tries, two penalty goals and a conversion to turn a 4–14 deficit into incredible victory by 22–14.

George Stevenson . . .
eccentric but gifted

Opposite:
Iain Laughland . . . versatile
and quick

Peter Brown . . . number eight with a unique goal-kicking style

My wings would be Keith Robertson (Melrose) and George Stevenson (Hawick), both subject to moments of eccentricity, both thoroughly gifted footballers and both capable of leaving opponents cross-eyed with jink, dummy or pace change. There would be one rule that 'Stevie' must observe – no attempted drop goals – although one has to admit that whenever 'Stevie' tried a drop goal, the result usually was touch or a try at the corner flag! Jim Renwick would be the inside centre, for here is the complete footballer with big match temperament and sharp tactical awareness, as when he noticed a defect in Welsh alignment at Murrayfield, and suggested that Keith Robertson should take a short pass with specific angle of run to exploit the Welsh positioning. The result – a Scottish try. With Robertson, Stevenson and Renwick together there would be some adventurism and fun as well as sleight of hand and trickery. There are so many other splendid candidates for the other centre berth – Russell Bruce (Glasgow Academicals), Iain Laughland (London Scottish), Jock Turner (Gala), Chris Rea (West of Scotland), John Frame (Gala), David Johnston (Watsonians), Scott Hastings (Watsonians) and Sean Lineen (Boroughmuir). My choice would be Laughland, wonderfully versatile, scaldingly quick, a determined tackler and good enough to have played for Scotland eight times at stand-off and with five different partners and 23 times as a centre. He also was one of the finest sevens players of all time.

Scotland has had a number of effective club partnerships at half-back since the war – Norman Davidson and Kelso Fulton (Edinburgh University), Laughland and Tremayne Rodd (London Scottish), David Chisholm and Alec Hastie (Melrose), Ian Robertson and Graham Young (Watsonians), Jock Turner and Duncan Paterson (Gala) and Ron Wilson and Alan Lawson (London Scottish). Robertson and Young once shared in Scotland creating a 9–0 lead over Wales at Cardiff in 1970, Robertson scoring a try and drop goal before Wales turned the tables and won 18–9. Wilson and Lawson were the slickest at getting ball to their threes, Lawson with a big pass and a powerful break. Perhaps the most successful were the Melrose pair, Chisholm and Hastie, whose first ten internationals together were marked by eight wins and two draws, their victories being over South Africa, Australia, England (two), Ireland (two), Wales and France. The Turner-Paterson alliance also figured in Scotland's first win at Twickenham for 33 years in 1971 and the very next Saturday at Murrayfield, their biggest margin over England, 26–6, until the 33–6 triumph in 1986. But what was virtually a club partnership has to be first choice, John Rutherford and Roy Laidlaw, who still hold the world record of 35 major international appearances as a half-back partnership and who provided such a secure link, not to mention scoring potential, in Scotland's 1984 Grand Slam.

No Scottish loose-head prop since the war played with more fire and commitment than Hawick's Hugh McLeod, with his fetish for fitness, his tactical awareness and total devotion to the Scottish cause. Even though no giant, McLeod would have been impressive in any era. Ian McLauchlan (Jordanhill College) brought a new dimension to scrummaging and was a hard little man out of Tarbolton and Jordanhill College. He also holds the Scottish record of having captained the national side in 19 Cap internationals. Jim Aitken (Gala) led the Grand Slam side of 1984 and shared in Gala's Championship years of 1980, 1981 and 1983. But David Sole (Edinburgh Academicals) seems to me to embody all the requisite qualities for a complete loose-head prop in the modern game, including the necessary ballast, impressive pace and very good hands. His hooker should be Colin Deans (Hawick), a superb thrower-in and the fastest hooker in my experience who could put sharp pressure round the front of the line-outs and often got to places where he was least expected. Frank Laidlaw (Melrose) was a lightning striker and Norman Bruce (London Scottish), a rugged all-rounder, but Deans was something special.

Tight-head prop would be between David Rollo (Howe of Fife), Sandy Carmichael (West of Scotland) and Iain Milne (Heriot's FP). Rollo the brave, a son of the soil, played most of his first international against England at Twickenham in 1959 with a broken nose, returning to the field in days when no replacements were allowed. Milne was perhaps the greatest Scottish scrummager, a massive corner stone, but my choice would be Carmichael, a tremendous force, quicker than he seemed, one of

Jim Renwick . . . the complete footballer

John Jeffrey . . . skill
and pace

Gordon Brown . . . a
forward's forward

Alastair McHarg . . . cunning
operator

Colin Deans . . . something
special

Gary Armstrong . . . the
Jed terrier

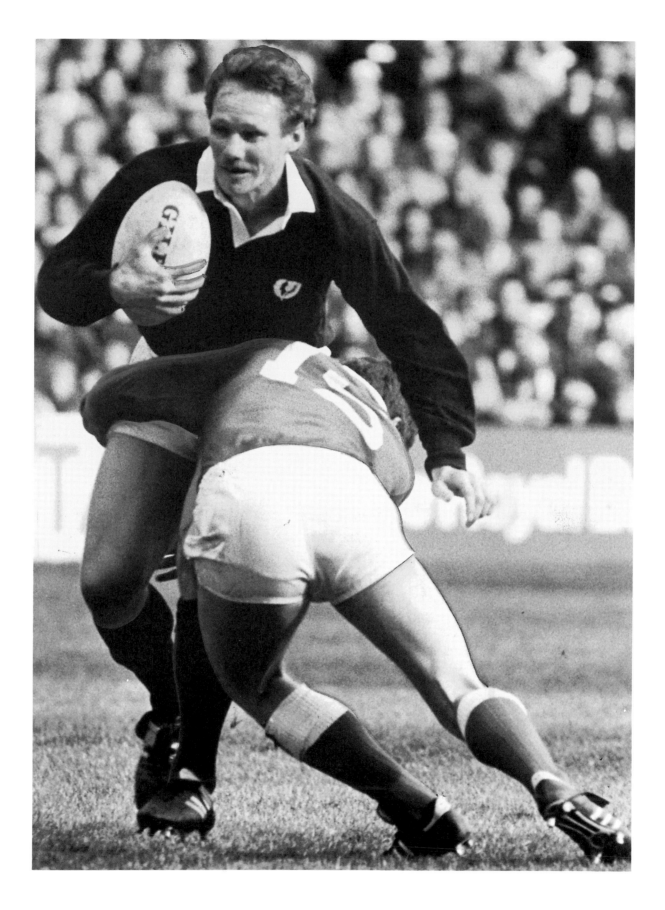

the great tackling props and, like Milne after him, one who did not need to resort to nastiness or brutality for his success.

Chris Gray (Nottingham) has made such an impressive advance since he first emerged in the Anglo-Scots side who beat the touring French in 1987 as to have been nominated the outstanding Scottish forward on the tour of New Zealand in May and June 1990 and, at his best, his partner, Damian Cronin (Bath), has had some great moments in the Scottish jersey. So indeed has Alan Tomes, Scotland's 'Grand Slam' lock of 1984 and their most Capped lock with 48, who played a prominent role in some of Scotland's most spectacular tries. But I go for the contrasting pair who formed the stoke-room in several tremendous Scottish packs of the late Sixties and early Seventies. Gordon Brown (West of Scotland) perhaps played his best rugby in the Lions jersey but he was in every sense a forward's forward for Scotland, tough, unceremonious and a scrummaging donkey. Alastair McHarg (London Scottish) wasn't everyone's cup of tea as a lock for he tended to pop up in places where locks were not supposed to be, but he was one of the most cunning line-out operators with an impressive standing jump and Scotland's scrummaging of that period proved that he shoved his weight. Brown and McHarg were lock partners for Scotland in 22 internationals if one includes Argentina, 1973, and Tonga, 1974, a spell during which Scotland beat all four of their Five Nations rivals, indeed, England (four times) and France (twice) and held New Zealand to 9–14.

Five number eight forwards in particular come to mind – Peter Kininmonth (Richmond), Peter Brown (Gala), Iain Paxton (Selkirk), John Beattie (Glasgow Academicals) and Derek White (Gala and London Scottish). Kininmonth had some great moments in the blue of Scotland, was good enough to play in three Tests against New Zealand for the 1950 British Lions and has gone down in rugby legend for his astonishing drop goal from the left touch-line that inspired Scotland to their historic 19–0 win over a Welsh side packed with Lions at Murrayfield on 3 February 1951. Kininmonth captained the side then, as he did on eight occasions between 1950 and 1952. Of Peter Brown's 27 Caps, 14 were at number eight and, though there was an ungainly touch to his running, he compensated with a keen positional and anticipatory sense and a high degree of all-round skill incorporating a somewhat eccentric place-kicking style. He placed the ball then turned his back on it to walk to his mark. Having tweaked his nose, he then advanced on the ball with that splay-footed run of his, for all the world, as P. G. Wodehouse would say, 'with the intention of catching the ball by surprise and with a painful blow'. Not all of his kicks travelled in a straight and true line. In fact part of the charm of his individual style was that several simply defied the science of ballistics. Yet he kicked some great goals and was a pain in the neck to the English. In five matches against England between 1969 and 1972, one as lock, four as number eight, he scored in every one for a total of seven penalty goals, three tries and three conversions for 37 points, keeping in mind that the try counted for four points only from 1972. At the height of his powers Iain Paxton, Capped 36 times, was virtually a complete number

Roy Laidlaw . . . a half-back world record

Opposite:
John Rutherford . . . scoring potential

Andy Irvine . . . awesome
gifts

Keith Robertson . . . leaves
opponents cross-eyed

eight and a superb support runner. He made the crucial contribution to the
Jim Calder try, started off by Roger Baird, that lit the torch to Scotland's
memorable display in beating Wales by 34–18 at Cardiff in 1982, and in
1985 at Murrayfield, Paxton scored two tries against Wales, one of them
a rip-roaring, hack-and-chase effort over three-quarters of the length of
the pitch. John Beattie was one of the quickest number eight forwards
fielded by Scotland, very abrasive especially in the tackle and a reliable
line-out provider.

In flank forwards, too, Scotland has spawned some splendid exponents. The raw-boned farmer, Douglas Elliot (Edinburgh Academicals),
was rated in every country as one of the greats in the immediate post-war
years. He and Kininmonth played together as wing-forward and number
eight on 20 occasions. Ian MacGregor (Hillhead FP) was a quick, hard
man and Adam Robson (Hawick) was no flying machine but one of the
fittest forwards ever to don a Scottish jersey. He just kept on running
and running. Robson and MacGregor formed with number eight Jim
Greenwood (Dunfermline and Perthshire Academicals) Scotland's back
row on eight occasions in 1955, 1956 and 1957. There were those two
rumbustious Kelso farmers, Ken Smith and Charlie Stewart, who were
together against Wales, 1960, and France, 1961. Smith went on to gain 18
Caps in all. Ron Glasgow (Dunfermline) struck varying degrees of appre-
hension into opposing stand-offs because he was so quick and aggressive
and a punishing tackler. Derrick Grant (Hawick) was in the same mould,
an all-action forward who stood on no ceremony and simply revelled in
putting opponents on the floor. Nairn MacEwan (Gala) proved one of
the most effective maulers, a genuine rip-and-tear merchant, who formed
the loose forward unit with Peter Brown and Roger Arneil (Leicester)
when Scotland beat England 16–15, 26–6 and 23–9 and France 20–9
in 1971 and 1972. Mike Biggar of London Scottish was another non-stop
campaigner, a dependable floor ball winner and one who performed the
unglamorous chores with relish. Jim Calder (Stewart's-Melville FP) was a
prolific poacher and predator, never far from the ball and with the good
hands of a skilled sevens forward. He scored one of the most thrilling
Scottish tries of all time at the end of a Roger Baird-Iain Paxton-Alan
Tomes thrust the length of the pitch against Wales in 1982. Jim Calder also
will always be remembered for the try that clinched the Grand Slam against
France at Murrayfield in 1984. David Leslie was perhaps the outstanding
50-50 ball winner, totally committed, an astute judge of what was possible
and, although no giant, his liaison with Colin Deans and his throwing-in
proving hugely influential in Scotland's 1984 Grand Slam.

One can dream up several very effective breakaway trios – Elliot,
Paxton and Leslie or Smith, Kininmonth and Finlay Calder or Glasgow,
Arneil and Peter Brown. But for a breakaway gel that offered virtually
the ideal balance and that especially had enviable overall pace, defensive
surety and superb skills, one cannot go beyond the 1990 threesome – John
Jeffrey (Kelso), Derek White (Gala and London Scottish) and Finlay Calder
(Stewart's-Melville FP). They would have been successful in any era of the
game and they left a huge imprint upon Scotland's memorable 1990 Slam

Sandy Carmichael . . . a
tremendous force

and especially in the greatest of great days when they beat hot favourites England in the decider on 17 March 1990.

So my top Scottish side from the post-war seasons is one guaranteed to provide high-grade spectacle at high speed, continuity of action and certainly a touch of the unorthodox and the eccentric.

BILL McLAREN'S POST-WAR SCOTTISH XV

ANDY IRVINE
(Heriot's FP)

KEITH ROBERTSON   GEORGE STEVENSON
(Melrose)   (Hawick)

JIM RENWICK   IAIN LAUGHLAND (c)
(Hawick)   (London Scottish)

JOHN RUTHERFORD
(Selkirk)

ROY LAIDLAW
(Jed-Forest)

DEREK WHITE
(London Scottish)

JOHN JEFFREY   FINLAY CALDER
(Kelso)   (Stewart's-Melville)

GORDON BROWN   ALASTAIR McHARG
(West of Scotland)   (London Scottish)

SANDY CARMICHAEL   COLIN DEANS   DAVID SOLE
(West of Scotland)   (Hawick)   (Edinburgh Academicals)

Replacements: GAVIN HASTINGS (Watsonians), SCOTT HASTINGS (Watsonians), GARY ARMSTRONG (Jed-Forest), HUGH McLEOD (Hawick), FRANK LAIDLAW (Melrose), PETER BROWN (Gala)

Opposite:
Derek White . . . successful
in any era

Frank Laidlaw . . . a
lightning striker

Gavin Hastings . . .
outstanding

David Sole . . . the complete
loose-head prop

Scott Hastings . . .
devastating tackler

Finlay Calder . . . balance
and pace in defence
and attack

Statistics

(Up to the end of the Five Nations Championship 1991)

INTERNATIONAL RESULTS
(Abbreviations: DG – Dropped Goal; G – Goal;
PG – Penalty Goal; T – Try; GM – Goal from a mark)

SCOTLAND v ENGLAND
Played 107 – Scotland 39, England 51, Drawn 17

1871 – Raeburn Place – Scotland 1G 1T to 1T
1872 – Kennington Oval – England 1G 1DG 2T to 1DG
1873 – Hamilton Crescent – Draw no scoring
1874 – Kennington Oval – England 1DG to 1T
1875 – Raeburn Place – Draw no scoring
1876 – Kennington Oval – England 1G 1T to 0
1877 – Raeburn Place – Scotland 1DG to 0
1878 – Kennington Oval – Draw no scoring
1879 – Raeburn Place – Draw Scotland 1DG England 1G
1880 – Whalley Range (Manchester) – England 2G 3T to 1G
1881 – Raeburn Place – Draw Scotland 1G 1T England 1DG 1T
1882 – Whalley Range (Manchester) – Scotland 2T to 0
1883 – Raeburn Place – England 2T to 1T
1884 – Blackheath – England 1G to 1T
1885 – No Match
1886 – Raeburn Place – Draw no scoring
1887 – Whalley Range (Manchester) – Draw 1T each
1888 – No Match
1889 – No Match
1890 – Raeburn Place – England 1G 1T (6) to 0
1891 – Richmond – Scotland 2G 1DG (11) to 1G (4)
1892 – Raeburn Place – England 1G (5) to 0
1893 – Headingley – Scotland 2DG (8) to 0
1894 – Raeburn Place – Scotland 2T (6) to 0
1895 – Richmond – Scotland 1PG 1T (6) to 1PG (3)
1896 – Hampden Park – Scotland 1G 2T (11) to 0
1897 – Fallowfield (Manchester) – England 1G 1DG (12) to 1T (3)
1898 – Powderhall (Edinburgh) – Draw 1T (3) each
1899 – Blackheath – Scotland 1G (5) to 0
1900 – Inverleith – Draw no scoring
1901 – Blackheath – Scotland 3G 1T (18) to 1T (3)
1902 – Inverleith – England 2T (6) to 1T (3)
1903 – Richmond – Scotland 1DG 2T (10) to 2T (6)
1904 – Inverleith – Scotland 2T (6) to 1T (3)
1905 – Richmond – Scotland 1G 1T (8) to 0
1906 – Inverleith – England 3T (9) to 1T (3)
1907 – Blackheath – Scotland 1G 1T (8) to 1T (3)
1908 – Inverleith – Scotland 1G 2DG 1T (16) to 2G (10)
1909 – Richmond – Scotland 3G 1T (18) to 1G 1T (8)
1910 – Inverleith – England 1G 3T (14) to 1G (5)
1911 – Twickenham – England 2G 1T (13) to 1G 1T (8)
1912 – Inverleith – Scotland 1G 1T (8) to 1T (3)
1913 – Twickenham – England 1T (3) to 0
1914 – Inverleith – England 2G 2T (16) to 1G 1DG 2T (15)
1920 – Twickenham – England 2G 1T (13) to 1DG (4)
1921 – Inverleith – England 3G 1T (18) to 0
1922 – Twickenham – England 1G 2T (11) to 1G (5)
1923 – Inverleith – England 1G 1T (8) to 2T (6)
1924 – Twickenham – England 3G 1DG (19) to 0
1925 – Murrayfield – Scotland 2G 1DG (14) to 1G 1PG 1T (11)
1926 – Twickenham – Scotland 2G 1DG 1T (17) to 3T (9)
1927 – Murrayfield – Scotland 1G 1DG 4T (21) to 2G 1PG (13)
1928 – Twickenham – England 2T (6) to 0
1929 – Murrayfield – Scotland 4T (12) to 2T (6)
1930 – Twickenham – Draw no scoring
1931 – Murrayfield – Scotland 5G 1T (28) to 2G 1PG 2T (19)

1932 – Twickenham – England 2G 2T (16) to 1T (3)
1933 – Murrayfield – Scotland 1T (3) to 0
1934 – Twickenham – England 2T (6) to 1T (3)
1935 – Murrayfield – Scotland 2G (10) to 1DG 1T (7)
1936 – Twickenham – England 3T (9) to 1G 1PG (8)
1937 – Murrayfield – England 2T (6) to 1PG (3)
1938 – Twickenham – Scotland 2PG 5T (21) to 1DG 3PG 1T (16)
1939 – Murrayfield – England 3PG (9) to 2T (6)
1947 – Twickenham – England 4G 1DG (24) to 1G (5)
1948 – Murrayfield – Scotland 2T (6) to 1PG (3)
1949 – Twickenham – England 2G 3T (19) to 1PG (3)
1950 – Murrayfield – Scotland 2G 1T (13) to 1G 1PG 1T (11)
1951 – Twickenham – England 1G (5) to 1T (3)
1952 – Murrayfield – England 2G 1DG 2T (19) to 1T (3)
1953 – Twickenham – England 4G 2T (26) to 1G 1T (8)
1954 – Murrayfield – England 2G 1T (13) to 1T (3)
1955 – Twickenham – England 1PG 2T (9) to 1PG 1T (6)
1956 – Murrayfield – England 1G 2PG (11) to 1PG 1T (6)
1957 – Twickenham – England 2G 1PG 1T (16) to 1PG (3)
1958 – Murrayfield – Draw 1PG (3) each
1959 – Twickenham – Draw 1PG (3) each
1960 – Murrayfield – England 3G 1DG 1PG (21) to 3PG 1T (12)
1961 – Twickenham – England 1PG 1T (6) to 0
1962 – Murrayfield – Draw 1PG (3) each
1963 – Twickenham – England 2G (10) to 1G 1DG (8)
1964 – Murrayfield – Scotland 3G (15) to 1PG 1T (6)
1965 – Twickenham – Draw England 1T (3) Scotland 1DG (3)
1966 – Murrayfield – Scotland 1PG 1T (6) to 1DG (3)
1967 – Twickenham – England 3G 2PG 1DG 1T (27) to 1G 2PG
1T (14)
1968 – Murrayfield – England 1G 1PG (8) to 1PG 1DG (6)
1969 – Twickenham – England 1G 1T (8) to 1PG (3)
1970 – Murrayfield – Scotland 1G 2PG 1T (14) to 1G (5)
1971 – Twickenham – Scotland 2G 1DG 1T (16) to 3PG 2T (15)
1971 – Murrayfield – (Centenary Match – non-championship) Scotland 4G 1PG 1T (26) to 1PG
1DG (6)
1972 – Murrayfield – Scotland 4PG 1DG 2T (23) to 3PG (9)
1973 – Twickenham – England 2G 2T (20) to 1G 1PG 1T (13)
1974 – Murrayfield – Scotland 1G 2PG 1T (16) to 1DG 1PG 2T (14)
1975 – Twickenham – England 1PG 1T (7) to 2PG (6)
1976 – Murrayfield – Scotland 2G 2PG 1T (22) to 1G 2PG (12)
1977 – Twickenham – England 2G 2PG 2T (26) to 2PG (6)
1978 – Murrayfield – England 2G 1PG (15) to 0
1979 – Twickenham – Draw 1PG 1T (7) each
1980 – Murrayfield – England 2G 2PG 3T (30) to 2G 2PG (18)
1981 – Twickenham – England 1G 3PG 2T (23) to 1G 1PG 2T (17)
1982 – Murrayfield – Draw Scotland 2PG 1DG (9) to England 3PG
(9)
1983 – Twickenham – Scotland 1G 3PG 1DG 1T (22) to 3PG 1DG
(12)
1984 – Murrayfield – Scotland 2G 2PG (18) to 2PG (6)
1985 – Twickenham – England 2PG 1T (10) to 1PG 1T (7)
1986 – Murrayfield – Scotland 3G 5PG (33) to 2PG (6)
1987 – Twickenham – England 2G 3PG (21) to 1G 2PG (12)
1988 – Murrayfield – England 2PG 1DG (9) to 2PG (6)
1989 – Twickenham – Draw England 4PG (12) to Scotland 1G 3PG
(12)
1990 – Murrayfield – Scotland 3PG 1T (13) to 1PG 1T (7)
1991 – Twickenham – England 1G 5PG (21) to 4PG (12)

SCOTLAND v WALES
Played 95 – Scotland 41, Wales 52, Drawn 2

1883 – Raeburn Place – Scotland 3G to 1G
1884 – Newport – Scotland 1DG 1T to 0
1885 – Hamilton Crescent – Draw no scoring
1886 – Cardiff – Scotland 2G 1T to 0
1887 – Raeburn Place – Scotland 4G 8T to 0
1888 – Newport – Wales 1T to 0
1889 – Raeburn Place – Scotland 2T to 0
1890 – Cardiff – Scotland 1G 2T (8) to 1T (2)
1891 – Raeburn Place – Scotland 1G 2DG 6T (15) to 0
1892 – Swansea – Scotland 1G 1T (7) to 1T (2)

1893 – Raeburn Place – Wales 1PG 3T (9) to 0
1894 – Newport – Wales 1DG 1T (7) to 0
1895 – Raeburn Place – Scotland 1G (5) to 1GM (4)
1896 – Cardiff – Wales 2T (6) to 0
1897 – No Match
1898 – No Match
1899 – Inverleith – Scotland 1G 2DG 3T (21) to 2G (10)
1900 – Swansea – Wales 4T (12) to 1T (3)
1901 – Inverleith – Scotland 3G 1T (18) to 1G 1T (8)
1902 – Cardiff – Wales 1G 3T (14) to 1G (5)
1903 – Inverleith – Scotland 1PG 1T (6) to 0
1904 – Swansea – Wales 3G 1PG 1T (21) to 1T (3)
1905 – Inverleith – Wales 2T (6) to 1T (3)
1906 – Cardiff – Wales 3T (9) to 1PG (3)
1907 – Inverleith – Scotland 2T (6) to 1PG (3)
1908 – Swansea – Wales 2T (6) to 1G (5)
1909 – Inverleith – Wales 1G (5) to 1PG (3)
1910 – Cardiff – Wales 1G 3T (14) to 0
1911 – Inverleith – Wales 2G 1DG 6T (32) to 1DG 2T (10)
1912 – Swansea – Wales 2G 2DG 1T (21) to 2T (6)
1913 – Inverleith – Wales 1G 1T (8) to 0
1914 – Cardiff – Wales 2G 2DG 1PG 1T (24) to 1G (5)
1920 – Inverleith – Scotland 2PG 1T (9) to 1G (5)
1921 – Swansea – Scotland 1G 1PG 2T (14) to 2DG (8)
1922 – Inverleith – Draw Scotland 1PG 2T (9) Wales 1G 1DG (9)
1923 – Cardiff – Scotland 1G 2T (11) to 1G 1PG (8)
1924 – Inverleith – Scotland 4G 1PG 4T (35) to 2G (10)
1925 – Swansea – Scotland 1G 1DG 5T (24) to 1G 1PG 2T (14)
1926 – Murrayfield – Scotland 1G 1PG (8) to 1G (5)
1927 – Cardiff – Scotland 1G (5) to 0
1928 – Murrayfield – Wales 2G 1T (13) to 0
1929 – Swansea – Wales 1G 3T (14) to 1DG 1PG (7)
1930 – Murrayfield – Scotland 1G 1DG 1T (12) to 1G 1DG (9)
1931 – Cardiff – Wales 2G 1T (13) to 1G 1T (8)
1932 – Murrayfield – Wales 1PG 1T (6) to 0
1933 – Swansea – Scotland 1G 1PG 1T (11) to 1T (3)
1934 – Murrayfield – Wales 2G 1T (13) to 1PG 1T (6)
1935 – Cardiff – Wales 1DG 2T (10) to 2T (6)
1936 – Murrayfield – Wales 2G 1T (13) to 1T (3)
1937 – Swansea – Scotland 2G 1T (13) to 2T (6)
1938 – Murrayfield – Scotland 1G 1PG (8) to 2T (6)
1939 – Cardiff – Wales 1G 1PG 1T (11) to 1PG (3)
1947 – Murrayfield – Wales 2G 1PG 3T (22) to 1G 1PG (8)
1948 – Cardiff – Wales 1G 1PG 2T (14) to 0
1949 – Murrayfield – Scotland 2T (6) to 1G (5)
1950 – Swansea – Wales 1DG 1PG 2T (12) to 0
1951 – Murrayfield – Scotland 2G 1DG 1PG 1T (19) to 0
1952 – Cardiff – Wales 1G 2PG (11) to 0
1953 – Murrayfield – Wales 1PG 3T (12) to 0
1954 – Swansea – Wales 1PG 4T (15) to 1T (3)
1955 – Murrayfield – Scotland 1G 1DG 1PG 1T (14) to 1G 1T (8)
1956 – Cardiff – Wales 3T (9) to 1PG (3)
1957 – Murrayfield – Scotland 1DG 1PG 1T (9) to 1PG 1T (6)
1958 – Cardiff – Wales 1G 1T (8) to 1PG (3)
1959 – Murrayfield – Scotland 1PG 1T (6) to 1G (5)
1960 – Cardiff – Wales 1G 1PG (8) to 0
1961 – Murrayfield – Scotland 1T (3) to 0
1962 – Cardiff – Scotland 1G 1T (8) to 1DG (3)
1963 – Murrayfield – Wales 1DG 1PG (6) to 0
1964 – Cardiff – Wales 1G 1PG 1T (11) to 1T (3)
1965 – Murrayfield – Wales 1G 2PG 1T (14) to 2DG 2PG (12)
1966 – Cardiff – Wales 1G 1T (8) to 1PG (3)
1967 – Murrayfield – Scotland 1G 1DG 1T (11) to 1G (5)
1968 – Cardiff – Wales 1G (5) to 0
1969 – Murrayfield – Wales 1G 2PG 2T (17) to 1PG (3)
1970 – Cardiff – Wales 3G 1T (18) to 1DG 1PG 1T (9)
1971 – Murrayfield – Wales 2G 1PG 2T (19) to 4PG 2T (18)
1972 – Cardiff – Wales 3G 3PG 2T (35) to 1G 2PG (12)
1973 – Murrayfield – Scotland 1G 1T (10) to 3PG (9)
1974 – Cardiff – Wales 1G (6) to 0
1975 – Murrayfield – Scotland 3PG 1DG (12) to 2PG 1T (10)
1976 – Cardiff – Wales 2G 3PG 1T (28) to 1G (6)
1977 – Murrayfield – Wales 2G 2PG (18) to 1G 1DG (9)

1978 – Cardiff – Wales 1PG 1DG 4T (22) to 2PG 2T (14)
1979 – Murrayfield – Wales 1G 3PG 1T (19) to 3PG 1T (13)
1980 – Cardiff – Wales 1G 1PG 2T (17) to 1G (6)
1981 – Murrayfield – Scotland 2G* 1PG (15) to 2PG (6)
           *includes one penalty try
1982 – Cardiff – Scotland 4G 2DG 1T (34) to 1G 4PG (18)
1983 – Murrayfield – Wales 1G 3PG 1T (19) to 1G 3PG (15)
1984 – Cardiff – Scotland 2G 1PG (15) to 1G 1PG (9)
1985 – Murrayfield – Wales 1G 1DG 4PG 1T (25) to 2G 2DG 1PG
           (21)
1986 – Cardiff – Wales 5PG 1DG 1T (22) to 1PG 3T (15)
1987 – Murrayfield – Scotland 2G 2PG 1DG (21) to 1G 2PG 1DG
           (15)
1988 – Cardiff – Wales 2G 2DG 1PG 1T (25) to 2T 4PG (20)
1989 – Murrayfield – Scotland 1G 2PG 1DG 2T (23) to 1PG 1T (7)
1990 – Cardiff – Scotland 3PG 1T (13) to 1G 1PG (9)
1991 – Murrayfield – Scotland 2G 3PG 1DG 2T (32) to 1G 2PG (12)

SCOTLAND v IRELAND
Played 102 – Scotland 52, Ireland 45, Drawn 4, Abandoned 1

1877 – Ormeau (Belfast) – Scotland 4G 2DG 2T to 0
1878 – No Match
1879 – Ormeau (Belfast) – Scotland 1G 1DG 1T to 0
1880 – Hamilton Crescent – Scotland 1G 2DG 2T to 0
1881 – Ormeau (Belfast) – Ireland 1DG to 1T
1882 – Hamilton Crescent – Ireland 2T to 0
1883 – Ormeau (Belfast) – Scotland 1G 1T to 0
1884 – Raeburn Place – Scotland 2G 2T to 1T
1885 – Ormeau (Belfast) – Abandoned Scotland 1T Ireland 0
1885 – Raeburn Place – Scotland 1G 2T to 0
1886 – Raeburn Place – Scotland 3G 1DG 2T to 0
1887 – Ormeau (Belfast) – Scotland 1G 1GM 2T to 0
1888 – Raeburn Place – Scotland 1G to 0
1889 – Ormeau (Belfast) – Scotland 1DG to 0
1890 – Raeburn Place – Scotland 1DG 1T (5) to 0
1891 – Ballynafeigh (Belfast) – Scotland 3G 1DG 2T (14) to 0
1892 – Raeburn Place – Scotland 1T (2) to 0
1893 – Ballynafeigh (Belfast) – Draw no score
1894 – Lansdowne Road – Ireland 1G (5) to 0
1895 – Raeburn Place – Scotland 2T (6) to 0
1896 – Lansdowne Road – Draw no score
1897 – Powderhall (Edinburgh) – Scotland 1G 1PG (8) to 1T (3)
1898 – Balmoral (Belfast) – Scotland 1G 1T (8) to 0
1899 – Inverleith – Ireland 3T (9) to 1PG (3)
1900 – Lansdowne Road – Draw no score
1901 – Inverleith – Scotland 3T (9) to 1G (5)
1902 – Balmoral (Belfast) – Ireland 1G (5) to 0
1903 – Inverleith – Scotland 1T (3) to 0
1904 – Lansdowne Road – Scotland 2G 3T (19) to 1T (3)
1905 – Inverleith – Ireland 1G 2T (11) to 1G (5)
1906 – Lansdowne Road – Scotland 2G 1GM (13) to 2T (6)
1907 – Inverleith – Scotland 3G (15) to 1PG (3)
1908 – Lansdowne Road – Ireland 2G 2T (16) to 1G 1PG 1T (11)
1909 – Inverleith – Scotland 3T (9) to 1PG (3)
1910 – Balmoral (Belfast) – Scotland 1G 3T (14) to 0
1911 – Inverleith – Ireland 2G 2T (16) to 1DG 2T (10)
1912 – Lansdowne Road – Ireland 1DG 1PG 1T (10) to 1G 1T (8)
1913 – Inverleith – Scotland 4G 3T (29) to 2G 1DG (14)
1914 – Lansdowne Road – Ireland 2T (6) to 0
1920 – Inverleith – Scotland 2G 1PG 2T (19) to 0
1921 – Lansdowne Road – Ireland 3T (9) to 1G 1T (8)
1922 – Inverleith – Scotland 2T (6) to 1T (3)
1923 – Lansdowne Road – Scotland 2G 1T (13) to 1T (3)
1924 – Inverleith – Scotland 2G 1T (13) to 1G 1T (8)
1925 – Lansdowne Road – Scotland 2G 1DG (14) to 1G 1PG (8)
1926 – Murrayfield – Ireland 1T (3) to 0
1927 – Lansdowne Road – Ireland 2T (6) to 0
1928 – Murrayfield – Ireland 2G 1T (13) to 1G (5)
1929 – Lansdowne Road – Scotland 2G 2T (16) to 1DG 1T (7)
1930 – Murrayfield – Ireland 1G 3T (14) to 1G 2T (11)
1931 – Lansdowne Road – Ireland 1G 1T (8) to 1G (5)
1932 – Murrayfield – Ireland 4G (20) to 1G 1T (8)

1933 – Lansdowne Road – Scotland 2DG (8) to 2T (6)
1934 – Murrayfield – Scotland 2G 1PG 1T (16) to 3T (9)
1935 – Lansdowne Road – Ireland 4T (12) to 1G (5)
1936 – Murrayfield – Ireland 1DG 2T (10) to 1DG (14)
1937 – Lansdowne Road – Ireland 1G 2T (11) to 1DG (4)
1938 – Murrayfield – Scotland 2G 1DG 1PG 2T (23) to 1G 3T (14)
1939 – Lansdowne Road – Ireland 1PG 1GM 2T (12) to 1T (3)
1947 – Murrayfield – Ireland 1T (3) to 0
1948 – Lansdowne Road – Ireland 2T (6) to 0
1949 – Murrayfield – Ireland 2G 1PG (13) to 1PG (3)
1950 – Lansdowne Road – Ireland 3G 2PG (21) to 0
1951 – Murrayfield – Ireland 1DG 1T (6) to 1G (5)
1952 – Lansdowne Road – Ireland 1PG 3T (12) to 1G 1PG (8)
1953 – Murrayfield – Ireland 4G 2T (26) to 1G 1PG (8)
1954 – Ravenhill (Belfast) – Ireland 2T (6) to 0
1955 – Murrayfield – Scotland 2PG 1DG 1T (12) to 1PG (3)
1956 – Lansdowne Road – Ireland 1G 3T (14) to 2G (10)
1957 – Murrayfield – Ireland 1G (5) to 1PG (3)
1958 – Lansdowne Road – Ireland 2PG 2T (12) to 2T (6)
1959 – Murrayfield – Ireland 1G 1PG (8) to 1PG (3)
1960 – Lansdowne Road – Scotland 1DG 1T (6) to 1G (5)
1961 – Murrayfield – Scotland 2G 1PG 1T (16) to 1G 1T (8)
1962 – Lansdowne Road – Scotland 1G 1DG 2PG 2T (20) to 1PG 1T (6)
1963 – Murrayfield – Scotland 1PG (3) to 0
1964 – Lansdowne Road – Scotland 2PG (6) to 1PG (3)
1965 – Murrayfield – Ireland 2G 1DG 1T (16) to 1DG 1PG (3)
1966 – Lansdowne Road – Scotland 1G 2T (11) to 1PG (3)
1967 – Murrayfield – Ireland 1G (5) to 1PG (3)
1968 – Lansdowne Road – Ireland 1G 1PG 2T (14) to 2PG (6)
1969 – Murrayfield – Ireland 2G 2T (16) to 0
1970 – Lansdowne Road – Ireland 2G 2T (16) to 1G 1DG 1T (11)
1971 – Murrayfield – Ireland 1G 2PG 2T (17) to 1G (5)
1972 – No Match
1973 – Murrayfield – Scotland 2PG 3DG 1T (19) to 2PG 2T (14)
1974 – Lansdowne Road – Ireland 1G 1PG (9) to 2PG (6)
1975 – Murrayfield – Scotland 2PG 2DG 2T (20) to 1G 1PG 1T (13)
1976 – Lansdowne Road – Scotland 4PG 1DG (15) to 2PG (6)
1977 – Murrayfield – Scotland 2PG 1DG 3T (21) to 1G 3PG 1DG (18)
1978 – Lansdowne Road – Ireland 1G 2PG (12) to 3PG (9)
1979 – Murrayfield – Draw 1PG 2T (11) each
1980 – Lansdowne Road – Ireland 1G 3PG 1DG 1T (22) to 2G 1PG (15)
1981 – Murrayfield – Scotland 1PG 1DG 1T (10) to 1G 1PG (9)
1982 – Lansdowne Road – Ireland 6PG 1DG (21) to 1G 2PG (12)
1983 – Murrayfield – Ireland 1G 3PG (15) to 2PG 1DG 1T (13)
1984 – Lansdowne Road – Scotland 3G* 2PG 2T (32) to 1G 1PG (9)
       * includes one penalty try
1985 – Murrayfield – Ireland 2G 1DG 1PG (18) to 4PG 1DG (15)
1986 – Lansdowne Road – Scotland 2PG 1T (10) to 1G 1PG (9)
1987 – Murrayfield – Scotland 1G 2DG 1T (16) to 1G 1PG 1DG (12)
1988 – Lansdowne Road – Ireland 2G 1PG 1DG 1T (22) to 2G 2PG (18)
1989 – Murrayfield – Scotland 4G 3PG 1T (37) to 3G 1PG (21)
1990 – Lansdowne Road – Scotland 1G 1PG 1T (13) to 2PG 1T (10)
1991 – Murrayfield – Scotland 2G 4PG 1T (28) to 3G 1DG 1T (25)

SCOTLAND v FRANCE
Played 62 – Scotland 29, France 30, Drawn 3

1910 – Inverleith – Scotland 3G 4T (27) to 0
1911 – Colombes – France 2G 2T (16) to 1G 1DG 2T (15)
1912 – Inverleith – Scotland 5G 1PG 1T (31) to 1T (3)
1913 – Parc des Princes – Scotland 3G 2T (21) to 1T (3)
1920 – Parc des Princes – Scotland 1G (5) to 0
1921 – Inverleith – France 1T (3) to 0
1922 – Colombes – Draw 1T (3) each
1923 – Inverleith – Scotland 2G 2T (16) to 1GM (3)
1924 – Stade Pershing – France 4T (12) to 1DG 1PG 1T (10)
1925 – Inverleith – Scotland 2G 5T (25) to 1DG (4)
1926 – Colombes – Scotland 1G 1PG 4T (20) to 1PG 1T (6)
1927 – Murrayfield – Scotland 4G 1PG (23) to 2T (6)

1928 – Colombes – Scotland 5T (15) to 2T (6)
1929 – Murrayfield – Scotland 1PG 1T (6) to 1T (3)
1930 – Colombes – France 1DG 1T (7) to 1T (3)
1931 – Murrayfield – Scotland 2PG (6) to 1DG (4)
1947 – Colombes – France 1G 1T (8) to 1PG (3)
1948 – Murrayfield – Scotland 2PG 1T (9) to 1G 1PG (8)
1949 – Colombes – Scotland 1G 1T (8) to 0
1950 – Murrayfield – Scotland 1G 1T (8) to 1G (5)
1951 – Colombes – France 1G 2PG 1T (14) to 2PG 2T (12)
1952 – Murrayfield – France 2G 1PG (13) to 1G 2PG (11)
1953 – Colombes – France 1G 1DG 1PG (11) to 1G (5)
1954 – Murrayfield – France 1T (3) to 0
1955 – Colombes – France 1PG 4T (15) to 0
1956 – Murrayfield – Scotland 2PG 2T (12) to 0
1957 – Colombes – Scotland 1DG 1PG (6) to 0
1958 – Murrayfield – Scotland 1G 1PG 1T (11) to 2PG 1T (9)
1959 – Colombes – France 2DG 1T (9) to 0
1960 – Murrayfield – France 2G 1T (13) to 1G 1PG 1T (11)
1961 – Colombes – France 1G 1DG 1PG (11) to 0
1962 – Murrayfield – France 1G 2PG (11) to 1PG (3)
1963 – Colombes – Scotland 1G 1DG 1PG (11) to 1DG 1PG (6)
1964 – Murrayfield – Scotland 2G (10) to 0
1965 – Colombes – France 2G 2T (16) to 1G 1T (8)
1966 – Murrayfield – Draw Scotland 1T (3) France 1PG (3)
1967 – Colombes – Scotland 2PG 1DG (9) to 1G 1T (8)
1968 – Murrayfield – France 1G 1T (8) to 1PG 1T (6)
1969 – Colombes – Scotland 1PG 1T (6) to 1PG (3)
1970 – Murrayfield – France 1G 1DG 1T (11) to 2PG 1T (9)
1971 – Colombes – France 2G 1PG (13) to 1G 1PG (8)
1972 – Murrayfield – Scotland 1G 1PG 1DG 2T (20) to 1G 1PG (9)
1973 – Parc des Princes – France 3PG 1DG 1T (16) to 2PG 1DG
          1T (13)
1974 – Murrayfield – Scotland 1G 3PG 1T (19) to 1PG 1DG (6)
1975 – Parc des Princes – France 1PG 1DG 1T (10) to 3PG (9)
1976 – Murrayfield – France 3PG 1T (13) to 1PG 1DG (6)
1977 – Parc des Princes – France 2G 1PG 2T (23) to 1PG (3)
1978 – Murrayfield – France 1G 3PG 1T (19) to 1G 1PG 1DG 1T
          (16)
1979 – Parc des Princes – France 2PG 1DG 3T (21) to 1G 1PG 2T
          (17)
1980 – Murrayfield – Scotland 2G 2PG 1T (22) to 1PG 1DG 2T (14)
1981 – Parc des Princes – France 1G 2PG 1T (16) to 1G 1PG (9)
1982 – Murrayfield – Scotland 3PG 1DG 1T (16) to 1PG 1T (7)
1983 – Parc des Princes – France 1G 1T 3PG (19) to 1G 2DG 1PG
          (15)
1984 – Murrayfield – Scotland 1G 5PG (21) to 1G 1DG 1PG (12)
1985 – Parc des Princes – France 1PG 2T (11) to 1PG (3)
1986 – Murrayfield – Scotland 6PG (18) to 1DG 2PG 2T (17)
1987 – Parc des Princes – France 3PG 1DG 4T (28) to 1G 4PG 1T
          (22)
1987 – Christchurch (World Cup) – Draw Scotland 2T 4PG (20) France
          1G 2T 2PG (20)
1988 – Murrayfield – Scotland 4PG 1DG 2T (23) to 1G 1PG 1DG (12)
1989 – Parc des Princes – France 2G 1PG 1T (19) to 1PG (3)
1990 – Murrayfield – Scotland 2G 3PG (21) to 0
1991 – Parc des Princes – France 2PG 3DG (15) to 2PG 1DG (9)

SCOTLAND v NEW ZEALAND
Played 15 – New Zealand 13, Drawn 2

1905 – Inverleith – New Zealand 4T (12) to 1DG 1T (7)
1935 – Murrayfield – New Zealand 3G 1T (18) to 1G 1T (8)
1954 – Murrayfield – New Zealand 1PG (3) to 0
1964 – Murrayfield – Draw no scoring
1967 – Murrayfield – New Zealand 1G 2PG 1T (14) to 1DG (3)
1972 – Murrayfield – New Zealand 1G 2T (14) to 1DG 2PG (9)
1975 – Auckland – New Zealand 4G (24) to 0
1976 – Murrayfield – New Zealand 2G 2PG (18) to 1G 1DG (9)
1979 – Murrayfield – New Zealand 2G 2T (20) to 2PG (6)
1981 – Dunedin – New Zealand 1PG 2T (11) to 1T (4)
1981 – Auckland – New Zealand 6G 1T (40) to 1G 2PG 1DG (15)
1983 – Murrayfield – Draw Scotland 5PG 2DG 1T (25) New
          Zealand 2G 3PG 1T (25)

1987 – Christchurch (World Cup) – New Zealand 2G 6PG (30) to 1PG (3)
1990 – Dunedin – New Zealand 4G 1PG 1T (31) to 2G 1T (16)
1990 – Auckland – New Zealand 1G 5PG (21) to 2G 2PG (18)

SCOTLAND v SOUTH AFRICA
Played 8 – Scotland 3, South Africa 5

1906 – Hampden Park – Scotland 2T (6) to 0
1912 – Inverleith – South Africa 2G 2T (16) to 0
1932 – Murrayfield – South Africa 2T (6) to 1T (3)
1951 – Murrayfield – South Africa 7G 1DG 2T (44) to 0
1960 – Port Elizabeth – South Africa 3G 1T (18) to 2G (10)
1961 – Murrayfield – South Africa 2PG 2T (12) to 1G (5)
1965 – Murrayfield – Scotland 1G 1DG (8) to 1G (5)
1969 – Murrayfield – Scotland 1PG 1T (6) to 1PG (3)

SCOTLAND v NEW SOUTH WALES

1927 – Murrayfield – Scotland 2G (10) to 1G 1T (8)

SCOTLAND v AUSTRALIA
Played 11 – Scotland 6, Australia 5

1947 – Murrayfield – Australia 2G 2T (16) to 1DG 1PG (7)
1958 – Murrayfield – Scotland 2PG 2T (12) to 1G 1T (8)
1966 – Murrayfield – Scotland 1G 1PG 1T (11) to 1G (5)
1968 – Murrayfield – Scotland 2PG 1T (9) to 1PG (3)
1970 – Sydney CG – Australia 1G 1PG 5T (23) to 1PG (3)
1975 – Murrayfield – Scotland 1G 1T (10) to 1PG (3)
1981 – Murrayfield – Scotland 1G 5PG 1DG (24) to 1PG 3T (15)
1982 – Ballymore (Brisbane) – Scotland 1G 1PG 1DG (12) to 1PG 1T (7)
1982 – Sydney CG – Australia 3G 5PG (33) to 3PG (9)
1984 – Murrayfield – Australia 3G 5PG 1T (37) to 4PG (12)
1988 – Murrayfield – Australia 3G 2PG 2T (32) to 1G 1PG 1T (13)

SCOTLAND v ROMANIA
Played 5 – Scotland 4, Romania 1

1981 – Murrayfield – Scotland 4PG (12) to 2PG (6)
1984 – Bucharest – Romania 2G 3PG 1DG 1T (28) to 1G 3PG 1DG 1T (22)
1986 – Bucharest – Scotland 3G 5PG (33) to 5PG 1DG (18)
1987 – Dunedin (World Cup) – Scotland 8G 1PG 1T (55) to 2G 4PG 1T (28)
1989 – Murrayfield – Scotland 3G 2PG 2T (32) to 0

SCOTLAND v ZIMBABWE

1987 – Wellington (World Cup) – Scotland 8G 3T (60) to 1G 5PG (21)

(A Scotland XV and Zimbabwe met twice in 1988, but Scotland did not award caps)

SCOTLAND v FIJI

1989 – Murrayfield – Scotland 4G 2PG 2T (38) to 3PG 2T (17)

(A Scotland XV and Fiji met in 1982, but Scotland did not award caps)

SCOTLAND v ARGENTINA

1990 – Murrayfield – Scotland 5G 1PG 4T (49) to 1PG (3)

(A Scotland XV met Argentina twice in 1969 and once in 1973, but Scotland did not award caps)

SCOTLAND v S.R.U. PRESIDENT'S XV

1973 – Murrayfield – Scotland 2G 1PG 3T (27) to 2G 2T (16)

1946 'VICTORY' INTERNATIONALS

Scotland 11, New Zealand Army 6 (Murrayfield)
Wales 6, Scotland 25 (Swansea)
Scotland 9, Ireland 0 (Murrayfield)
England 12, Scotland 8 (Twickenham)

Scotland 13, Wales 11 (Murrayfield)
Scotland 27, England 0 (Murrayfield)

SCOTLAND XV v ARGENTINA

1969 – Argentina 20–3 (Buenos Aires)
1969 – Scotland XV 6–3 (Buenos Aires)
1973 – Scotland XV 12–11 (Murrayfield)

SCOTLAND XV v BARBARIANS

1970 – Barbarians 33–17 (Murrayfield)
1983 – Barbarians 26–13 (Murrayfield)

SCOTLAND XV v FIJI

1982 – Scotland XV 32–12 (Murrayfield)

SCOTLAND XV v JAPAN

1976 – Scotland XV 34–9 (Murrayfield)
1977 – Scotland XV 74–9 (Tokyo)
1986 – Scotland XV 33–18 (Murrayfield)
1989 – Japan 28–24 (Tokyo)

SCOTLAND XV v NETHERLANDS

1974 – Scotland XV 17–9 (Hughenden)
1975 – Scotland XV 29–3 (Hilversum)
1978 – Scotland XV 19–0 (Hilversum)

SCOTLAND XV v SPAIN

1986 – Scotland XV 39–17 (Cornella, Barcelona)
1987 – Scotland XV 25–7 (Murrayfield)

SCOTLAND XV v TONGA

1974 – Scotland XV 44–8 (Murrayfield)

SCOTLAND XV v ZIMBABWE

1988 – Scotland XV 31–10 (Bulawayo)
1988 – Scotland XV 34–7 (Harare)

SCOTLAND'S 'B' INTERNATIONALS
SCOTLAND v FRANCE
Played 19 – Scotland 8, France 11

1971 – France 23–9 (Oyonnax)
1972 – France 17–15 (Bught Park, Inverness)
1974 – France 13–9 (Bayonne)
1975 – Scotland 19–6 (Greenyards)
1976 – France 14–6 (Rheims)
1977 – France 19–16 (Hughenden)
1978 – France 11–3 (Le Havre)
1979 – Match at Ayr cancelled because of snow
1980 – Scotland 6–0 (Aurillac)
1981 – Scotland 18–4 (Millbrae)
1982 – France 44–4 (Bourgoin-Jallieu)
1983 – France 26–12 (Mayfield, Dundee)
1984 – Scotland 13–10 (Albi)
1985 – Scotland 21–12 (Murrayfield)
1986 – Scotland 12–10 (Villefranche-sur-Saone)
1987 – France 15–9 (University Park, St Andrews)
1988 – Scotland 18–12 (Chalon-sur-Saone)
1989 – Scotland 14–12 (Greenyards)
1990 – France 31–9 (Oyonnax)
1991 – France 31–10 (Hughenden)

SCOTLAND v IRELAND
Played 6 – Scotland 2, Ireland 3, Drawn 1

1977 – Ireland 7–3 (Murrayfield)
1979 – Scotland 20-13 (Lansdowne Road)
1983 – Scotland 22–13 (Greenyards)
1984 – Ireland 23–20 (Galway)

1989 – Draw 22–22 (Murrayfield)
1990 – Ireland 16–0 (Ravenhill, Belfast)

SCOTLAND v ITALY
Played 4 – Scotland 4, Italy 0

1985 – Scotland 9–0 (Old Anniesland)
1986 – Scotland 24–6 (Benevento)
1987 – Scotland 37–0 (Seafield, Aberdeen)
1988 – Scotland 26–3 (L'Aquila)

UNDER–21 INTERNATIONALS
SCOTLAND v ITALY

1986 – Scotland 22–6 (Piacenza)
1987 – Draw 17–17 (New Anniesland)

SCOTLAND v NETHERLANDS

1984 – Scotland 24–9 (Hilversum)
1985 – Scotland 18–6 (Hughenden)

SCOTLAND v NEW ZEALAND *RUGBY NEWS* YOUTH XV

1988 – New Zealand Youth XV 21–15 (Murrayfield)

SCOTLAND v WALES

1987 – Wales 39–19 (Wrexham)
1988 – Wales 20–13 (Murrayfield)
1989 – Wales 26–18 (The Gnoll, Neath)
1990 – Wales 24–10 (Millbrae)
1991 – Wales 23–15 (Stradey Park, Llanelli)

UNDER–19 INTERNATIONALS
SCOTLAND v ITALY

1986 – Scotland 22–6 (Piacenza)
1987 – Italy 26–6 (Meggetland)
1988 – Italy 21–18 (Villorba, Treviso)
1989 – Scotland 29–13 (Millbrae)

SCOTLAND v ENGLAND

1990 – England 17–9 (Millbrae)
1991 – Scotland 24–7 (Bridgehaugh)

SCOTLAND v WALES

1991 – Wales 23–20 (Stradey Park, Llanelli)

SCOTLAND v AUSTRALIAN SCHOOLS

1991 – Australian Schools 17–12 (Murrayfield)

UNDER–18 INTERNATIONALS
SCOTLAND v BELGIUM

1984 – Scotland 35–10 (Brussels)

SCOTLAND v ITALY

1988 – Draw 25–25 (Villorba, Treviso)
1989 – Scotland 21–12 (Millbrae, Ayr)

SCOTLAND v JAPAN SCHOOLS

1990 – Scotland 28–23 (Murrayfield)

SCOTLAND v NETHERLANDS

1985 – Scotland 36–0 (Hilversum)
1990 – Scotland 32–0 (Hilversum)
1991 – Scotland 21–7 (Greenyards)

SCOTLAND v SPAIN

1991 – Spain 24–19 (Madrid)

SCOTLAND v SWEDEN

1985 – Scotland 32–0 (Malmö)
1986 – Scotland 43–4 (Murrayfield)
1989 – Scotland 85–6 (Trelleborg)

SCOTLAND v WEST GERMANY

1982 – West Germany 15–12 (Berlin)
1984 – Scotland 9–7 (Meggetland)
1987 – Scotland 50–9 (Hanover)

INTER-DISTRICT CHAMPIONS

1953–54	Edinburgh	W3
1954–55	South	W3
1955–56	Glasgow	W2:D1
1956–57	Edinburgh-South	W2:L1
1957–58	Edinburgh-South	W2:D1
1958–59	Edinburgh-South	W2:L1
1959–60	Edinburgh-North and Midlands-South	W2:L1
1960–61	Edinburgh	W3
1961–62	Edinburgh-South	W2:D1
1962–63	Edinburgh	W3
1963–64	South	W3
1964–65	Glasgow-South	W2:L1
1965–66	South	W3
1966–67	South	W2:D1
1967–68	Edinburgh-Glasgow-South	W2:L1
1968–69	South	W3
1969–70	South	W2:D1
1970–71	South	W3
1971–72	Edinburgh	W2:L1
	(Edinburgh beat Glasgow 20–16 in a play-off at Murrayfield)	
1972–73	Edinburgh-Glasgow	W2:L1
1973–74	Glasgow	W3
1974–75	Glasgow-North and Midlands	W2:L1
1975–76	Edinburgh-Glasgow-South	W2:L1
1976–77	South	W3
1977–78	Edinburgh-Glasgow-South	W2:L1
1978–79	South	W3
1979–80	Edinburgh	W3
1980–81	South	W3
1981–82	Edinburgh-South	W3:D1
1982–83	South	W4
1983–84	South	W4
1984–85	South	W4
1985–86	South	W4
1986–87	Edinburgh	W4
1987–88	Edinburgh	W4
1988–89	Edinburgh	W4
1989–90	Glasgow	W3:D1
1990–91	South	W3:D1

INTER-CITY SERIES
(since the first match in 1872)

Edinburgh won 57, Glasgow won 36, with 18 drawn

UNDER–21 INTER-DISTRICT CHAMPIONS

1979–80	Edinburgh	W3
1980–81	South	W3
1981–82	Edinburgh	W2:D1
1982–83	South	W3
1983–84	South	W2:D1
1984–85	South	W3
1985–86	South	W3

1986–87	Glasgow	W3
1987–88	South	W3
1988–89	Unfinished	
1989–90	South	W3:D1
1990–91	South-Glasgow	W3:L1

UNDER–18 INTER-DISTRICT CHAMPIONS

1982–83	Edinburgh	W3
1983–84	Edinburgh	W3
1984–85	South	W3
1985–86	South	W3
1986–87	South	W3
1987–88	Glasgow	W2:D1
1988–89	Glasgow	W3
1989–90	South	W3
1990–91	North and Midlands	W3

SCOTTISH UNOFFICIAL CLUB CHAMPIONS

1865–66 Edinburgh Academicals
1866–67 Edinburgh Academicals
1867–68 Edinburgh Academicals
1868–69 Edinburgh Academicals
1869–70 Edinburgh Academicals
1870–71 Edinburgh Academicals
1871–72 Glasgow Academicals and Edinburgh University
1872–73 Glasgow Academicals
1873–74 Glasgow Academicals and Edinburgh Academicals
1874–75 Edinburgh Academicals
1875–76 Glasgow Academicals
1876–77 Glasgow Academicals
1877–78 Edinburgh Academicals
1878–79 Edinburgh Academicals
1879–80 Edinburgh Academicals
1880–81 Edinburgh Institution FP
1881–82 Edinburgh Institution FP
1882–83 Glasgow Academicals and West of Scotland
1883–84 Royal High School FP
1884–85 West of Scotland
1885–86 Edinburgh Academicals and West of Scotland
1986–87 Edinburgh Academicals
1887–88 Edinburgh Academicals
1888–89 West of Scotland
1889–90 Edinburgh Academicals and West of Scotland
1890–91 West of Scotland
1891–92 Watsonians and West of Scotland
1892–93 Watsonians
1893–94 Watsonians
1894–95 Watsonians and West of Scotland
1895–96 Hawick
1896–97 Clydesdale, Jed-Forest and Watsonians
1897–98 Edinburgh Academicals
1898–99 Edinburgh Academicals
1899–1900 Edinburgh Academicals and Edinburgh University
1900–01 Edinburgh Academicals
1901–02 Edinburgh University
1902–03 Edinburgh University and Watsonians
1903–04 Edinburgh University and Glasgow Academicals
1904–05 Glasgow Academicals
1905–06 Edinburgh Academicals
1906–07 Jed-Forest
1907–08 Edinburgh University
1908–09 Hawick and Watsonians
1909–10 Watsonians
1910–11 Watsonians
1911–12 Edinburgh University and Watsonians
1912–13 Glasgow Academicals
1913–14 Watsonians
1914–19 No competition (First World War)
1919–20 Heriot's FP
1920–21 Watsonians
1921–22 Glasgow Academicals

1922–23 Heriot's FP
1923–24 Glasgow Academicals and Glasgow High School FP
1924–25 Glasgow Academicals
1925–26 Glasgow Academicals
1926–27 Hawick
1927–28 Heriot's FP
1928–29 Heriot's FP
1929–30 Glasgow Academicals
1930–31 Dunfermline
1931–32 Gala
1932–33 Dunfermline and Hawick
1933–34 Hillhead High School FP and Royal High School FP
1934–35 Watsonians
1935–36 Glasgow High School FP
1936–37 Hillhead High School FP and Watsonians
1937–38 Stewart's College FP
1938–39 Allan Glen's FP
1939–46 No competition (Second World War)
1946–47 Stewart's College FP
1947–48 Aberdeen GS FP and Kelso
1948–49 Hawick
1949–50 Heriot's FP
1950–51 Glasgow High School FP
1951–52 Melrose
1952–53 Selkirk
1953–54 Glasgow High School FP
1954–55 Boroughmuir
1955–56 Edinburgh Academicals
1956–57 Edinburgh Academicals and Jed-Forest
1957–58 Stewart's College FP
1958–59 Langholm
1959–60 Hawick
1960–61 Hawick
1961–62 Glasgow High School FP
1962–63 Melrose
1963–64 Hawick
1964–65 Hawick and West of Scotland
1965–66 Hawick
1966–67 Melrose
1967–68 Hawick
1968–69 Jordanhill College
1969–70 Watsonians
1970–71 West of Scotland
1971–72 Hawick
1972–73 Boroughmuir

SRU CLUB CHAMPIONSHIP WINNERS

1973–74 Hawick
1974–75 Hawick
1975–76 Hawick
1976–77 Hawick (play-off with Gala)
1977–78* Hawick
1978–79 Heriot's FP
1979–80 Gala
1980–81 Gala
1981–82 Hawick
1982–83 Gala
1983–84 Hawick
1984–85 Hawick
1985–86 Hawick
1986–87** Hawick
1987–88 Kelso
1988–89 Kelso
1989–90 Melrose
1990–91 Boroughmuir

(* Championship sponsored by Schweppes for nine years)
(** McEwan's sponsorship introduced)

BORDER LEAGUE CHAMPIONS

1901–02 Hawick
1902–03 Jed-Forest

1903–04 Jed-Forest
1904–05 Jed-Forest
1905–06 Gala
1906–07 Jed-Forest (first season of cup)
1907–08 Jed-Forest
1908–09 Hawick
1909–10 Hawick and Jed-Forest
1910–11 Melrose (after play-off with Hawick at Riverside Park)
1911–12 Hawick
1912–13 Hawick
1913–14 Hawick
1914–19 First World War
1919–20 Jed-Forest
1920–21 Hawick (after play-off with Jed-Forest at the Greenyards)
1921–22 Gala
1922–23 Hawick
1923–24 Hawick
1924–25 Hawick
1925–26 Hawick (after play-off with Kelso at the Greenyards)
1926–27 Hawick
1927–28 Hawick
1928–29 Hawick
1929–30 Hawick
1930–31 Kelso
1931–32 Hawick
1932–33 unfinished
1933–34 Kelso
1934–35 Selkirk
1935–36 unfinished
1936–37 Kelso
1937–38 Selkirk
1938–39 Melrose
1939–46 Second World War
1946–47 unfinished
1947–48 unfinished
1948–49 Hawick
1949–50 Gala and Melrose
1950–51 Hawick
1951–52 unfinished
1952–53 Selkirk
1953–54 Melrose
1954–55 Hawick
1955–56 Hawick
1956–57 Jed-Forest
1957–58 Melrose
1958–59 Langholm
1959–60 Hawick
1960–61 Hawick
1961–62 Hawick
1962–63 Melrose
1963–64 Hawick
1964–65 Hawick
1965–66 Hawick
1966–67 Gala
1967–68 Hawick
1968–69 Hawick
1969–70 Hawick
1970–71 Melrose
1971–72 Hawick
1972–73 Hawick
1973–74 Hawick
1974–75 Hawick
1975–76 Hawick
1976–77 Hawick
1977–78 Hawick
1978–79 Hawick
1979–80 Gala
1980–81 Gala
1981–82 Hawick
1982–83 Hawick
1983–84 Hawick
1984–85 Hawick
1985–86 Kelso

1986–87 Kelso
1987–88* Jed-Forest
1988–89 Hawick
1989–90 Melrose
1990–91** Melrose

(* Sponsored by Scotch Beef for three seasons)
(** Sponsored by Bank of Scotland)

S.R.U. YOUTH LEAGUE CHAMPIONS

1980–81* Kirkcaldy
1981–82 Kirkcaldy
1982–83 Melrose Colts
1983–84 Melrose Colts
1984–85 Jed Thistle
1985–86 Stirling County
1986–87 Hawick PSA
1987–88 Melrose Colts
1988–89 Stirling County
1989–90** Gala Wanderers
1990–91 West of Scotland

(* Royal Bank sponsors for 10 years)
(** Digital sponsorship started)

SCOTLAND'S INTERNATIONAL PLAYERS

Abbreviations: A – Australia; Arg – Argentina; E – England; EC – Centenary match against England (non-championship); F – France; Fj – Fiji; I – Ireland; NSW – New South Wales; NZ – New Zealand; P – SRU President's Overseas XV; R – Romania; SA – South Africa; W – Wales; WC – World Cup; Z – Zimbabwe; (r) – Replacement.

When Scotland played against a country more than once in one year the figures (1) and/or (2) denote whether the player appeared in the first and/or second match.

Abercrombie, C.H., United Services, London Scottish – 1910 I,E, 1911 F,W, 1913 F,W.
Abercrombie, J.G., Edinburgh U. – 1949 F,W,I, 1950 F,W,I,E.
Agnew, W.C.C., Stewart's Coll. FP – 1930 W,I.
Ainslie, R., Edinburgh Inst. FP – 1879 I,E, 1880, I,E, 1881 E, 1882 I,E.
Ainslie, T., Edinburgh Inst. FP – 1881 E, 1882 I,E, 1883 W,I,E, 1884 W,I,E, 1885 W,I (1,2).
Aitchison, G.R., Edinburgh Wands. – 1883 I.
Aitchison, T.G. Gala – 1929 W,I,E.
Aitken, A.I., Edinburgh Inst. FP – 1889 I.
Aitken, G.G. Oxford U. – 1924 W,I,E, 1925 F,W,I,E, 1929 F.
Aitken, J., Gala – 1977 E,I,F, 1981 F,W,E,I,NZ (1,2), R,A, 1982 E,I,F,W, 1983 F,W,E,NZ, 1984 W,E,I,F,R.
Aitken, R., London Scottish, Royal Navy – 1947 W.
Allan, B., Glasgow Acads. – 1881 I.
Allan, J., Edinburgh Acads. – 1990 NZ (1), 1991 W,I.
Allan, J.L., Melrose – 1952 F,W,I, 1953 W.
Allan, J.L.F., Cambridge U. – 1957 I,E.
Allan, J.W., Melrose – 1927 F, 1928 I, 1929 F,W,I,E, 1930 F,E, 1931 F,W,I,E, 1932 SA,W,I, 1934 I,E.
Allan, R.C., Hutchesons' GS FP – 1969 I.
Allardice, W.D., Aberdeen GS FP – 1948 A,F,W,I, 1949 F,W,I,E.
Allen, H.W., Glasgow Acads. – 1873 E.
Anderson, A.H., Glasgow Acads. – 1894 I.
Anderson, D.G., London Scottish – 1889 I, 1890 W,I,E, 1891 W,E, 1892 W,E.
Anderson, E., Stewart's Coll. FP – 1947 I,E.
Anderson, J.W., West of Scotland – 1872 E.
Anderson, T., Merchistonians – 1882 I.
Angus, A.W., Watsonians – 1909 W, 1910 F,W,E, 1911 W,I, 1912 F,W,I,E,SA, 1913 F,W, 1914 E, 1920 F,W,I,E.
Anton, P.A., St Andrew's U. – 1873 E.
Armstrong, G., Jed-Forest – 1988 A, 1989 W,E,I,F,Fj,R, 1990 I,F,W,E,NZ(1,2) Arg, 1991 F,W,E,I.
Arneil, R.J., Edinburgh Acads., Leicester, Northampton – 1968 I,E,A, 1969 F,W,I,E,SA, 1970 F,W,I,E,A, 1971 F,W,I,E,EC, 1972 F,W,E, 1973 NZ.
Arthur, A., Glasgow Acads. – 1875 E, 1876 E.
Arthur, J.W., Glasgow Acads. – 1871 E, 1872 E.
Asher, A.G.G., Oxford U., Fettesian–Lorettonians, Edinburgh Wands. – 1882 I, 1884 W,I,E, 1885 W, 1886 I,E.
Auld, W., West of Scotland – 1889 W, 1890 W.
Auldjo, L.J., Abertay – 1878 E.

Bain, D.McL., Oxford U. – 1911 E, 1912 F,W,E,SA, 1913 F,W,I,E, 1914 W,I.
Baird, G.R.T., Kelso – 1981 A, 1982 E,I,F,W,A (1,2), 1983 I,F,W,E,NZ, 1984 W,E,I,F,A, 1985 I,W,E, 1986 F,W,E,I,R, 1987 E, 1988 I.
Balfour, A., Watsonians – 1896 W,I,E, 1897 E.
Balfour, L.M., Edinburgh Acads. – 1872 E.
Bannerman, E.M., Edinburgh Acads. – 1872 E, 1873 E.
Bannerman, J.M., Glasgow HS FP, Oxford U. – 1921 F,W,I,E, 1922 F,W,I,E, 1923 F,W,I,E, 1924 F,W,I,E, 1925 F,W,I,E, 1926 F,W,I,E, 1927 F,W,I,E,NSW, 1928 F,W,I,E, 1929 F,W,I,E.
Barnes, I.A., Hawick – 1972 W, 1974 F (r), 1975 E (r),NZ, 1977 I,F,W.
Barrie, R.W., Hawick – 1936 E.
Bearne, K.R.F., Cambridge U., London Scottish – 1960 F,W.
Beattie, J.A., Hawick – 1929 F,W, 1930 W, 1931 F,W,I,E, 1932 SA, W,I,E, 1933 W,E,I, 1934 I,E, 1935 W,I,E,NZ, 1936 W,I,E.
Beattie, J.R., Glasgow Acads. – 1980 I,F,W,E, 1981 F,W,E,I, 1983 F,W,E,NZ, 1984 E (r), R,A, 1985 I, 1986 F,W,E,I,R, 1987 I,F,W,E.
Bedell-Sivright, D.R., Cambridge U., West of Scotland, Edinburgh U. – 1900 W, 1901 W,I,E, 1902 W,I,E, 1903 W,I, 1904 W,I,E, 1905 NZ, 1906 W,I,E,SA, 1907 W,I,E, 1908 W,I.
Bedell-Sivright, J.V., Cambridge U. – 1902 W.
Begbie, T.A., Edinburgh Wands. – 1881 I,E.
Bell, D.L., Watsonians – 1975 I,F,W,E.
Bell, J.A., Clydesdale – 1901 W,I,E, 1902 W,I,E.
Bell, L.H.I., Edinburgh Acads. – 1900 E, 1904 W,I.
Berkeley, W.V., Oxford U., London Scottish – 1926 F, 1929 F,W,I.

Berry, C.W., Fettesian-Lorettonians, Edinburgh Wanderers – 1884 I,E, 1885 W,I (1) 1887 I,W,E, 1888 W,I.

Bertram, D.M., Watsonians – 1922, F,W,I,E, 1923 F,W,I,E, 1924 W,I,E.

Biggar, A.G., London Scottish – 1969 SA, 1970 F,I,E,A, 1971 F,W,I,E,EC, 1972 F,W.

Biggar, M.A., London Scottish – 1975 I,F,W,E, 1976 W,E,I, 1977 I,F,W, 1978 I,F,W,E,NZ, 1979 W,E,I,F,NZ, 1980 I,F,W,E.

Birkett, G.A., Harlequins, London Scottish – 1975 NZ.

Bishop, J.M., Glasgow Acads. – 1893 I.

Bisset, A.A., RIE Coll. – 1904 W.

Black, A.W., Edinburgh U. – 1947 F,W, 1948 E, 1950 W,I,E.

Black, W.P., Glasgow HS FP – 1948 F,W,I,E, 1951 E.

Blackadder, W.F., West of Scotland – 1938 E.

Blaikie, C.F., Heriot's FP – 1963 I,E, 1966 E, 1968 A, 1969 F,W,I,E.

Blair, P.C.B., Cambridge U. – 1912 SA, 1913 F,W,I,E.

Bolton, W.H., West of Scotland – 1876 E.

Borthwick, J.B., Stewart's Coll. FP – 1938 W,I.

Bos, F.H. ten, Oxford U., London Scottish – 1959 E, 1960 F,W,SA, 1961 F,SA,W,I,E, 1962 F,W,I,E, 1963 F,W,I,E.

Boswell, J.D., West of Scotland – 1889 W,I, 1890 W,I,E, 1891 W,I,E, 1892 W,I,E, 1893 I,E, 1894 I,E.

Bowie, T.C., Watsonians – 1913 I,E, 1914 I,E.

Boyd, G.M., Glasgow HS FP – 1926 E.

Boyd, J.L., United Services – 1912 E, SA.

Boyle, A.C.W., London Scottish – 1963 F,W,I.

Boyle, A.H.W., St Thomas's Hospital, London Scottish – 1966 A, 1967 F,NZ, 1968 F,W,I.

Brash, J.C., Cambridge U. – 1961 E.

Breakey, R.W., Gosforth – 1978 E.

Brewis, N.T., Edinburgh Inst. FP – 1876 E, 1878 E, 1879 I,E, 1880 I,E.

Brewster, A.K., Stewart's Melville FP – 1977 E, 1980 I,F, 1986 E,I,R.

Brown, A.H., Heriot's FP – 1928 E, 1929 F,W.

Brown, A.R., Gala – 1971 E,EC, 1972 F,W,E.

Brown, C.H.C., Dunfermline – 1929 E.

Brown, D.I., Cambridge U. – 1933 W,E,I.

Brown, G.L., West of Scotland – 1969 SA, 1970 F,W(r),I,E,A, 1971 F,W,I,E,EC, 1972 F,W,E,NZ, 1973 E(r)P, 1974 W,E,I,F, 1975 I,F,W,E,A, 1976 F,W,E,I.

Brown, J.A., Glasgow Acads. – 1908 W,I.

Brown, J.B., Glasgow Acads. – 1879 I,E, 1880 I,E, 1881 I,E, 1882 I,E, 1883 W,I,E, 1884 W,I,E, 1885 I(1,2), 1886 W,I,E.

Brown P.C., West of Scotland, Gala – 1964 F,NZ,W,I,E, 1965 I,E,SA, 1966 A, 1969 I,E, 1970 W,E, 1971 F,W,I,E,EC, 1972 F,W,E,NZ, 1973 F,W,I,E,P.

Brown, T.G., Heriot's FP – 1929 W.

Brown, W.D., Glasgow Acads. – 1871 E, 1872 E, 1873 E, 1874 E, 1875 E.

Brown, W.S., Edinburgh Inst. FP – 1880, I,E, 1882, I,E, 1883 W,I,E.

Browning, A., Glasgow HS FP – 1920 I, 1922 F,W,I, 1923 W,I,E.

Bruce, C.R., Glasgow Acads. – 1947, F,W,I,E, 1949 F,W,I,E.

Bruce, N.S., Blackheath, Army, London Scottish – 1958 F,A,I,E, 1959 F,W,I,E, 1960 F,W,I,E,SA, 1961 F,SA,W,I,E, 1962 F,W,I,E, 1963 F,W,I,E, 1964 F,NZ,W,I,E.

Bruce, R.M., Gordonians – 1947 A, 1948 F,W,I.

Bruce Lockhart, J.H., London Scottish – 1913 W, 1920 E.

Bruce Lockhart, L., London Scottish – 1948 E, 1950 F,W, 1953 I,E.

Bruce Lockhart, R.B., Cambridge U., London Scottish – 1937 I, 1939 I,E.

Bryce, C.C., Glasgow Acads. – 1873 E, 1874 E.

Bryce, R.D.H., West of Scotland – 1973 I(r).

Bryce, W.E., Selkirk – 1922 W,I,E, 1923 F,W,I,E, 1924 F,W,I,E.

Brydon, W.R.C., Heriot's FP – 1939 W.

Buchanan, A., Royal HS FP – 1871 E.

Buchanan, F.G., Kelvinside Acads., Oxford U. – 1910 F, 1911 F,W.

Buchanan, J.C.R., Stewart's Coll. FP., Exeter – 1921 W,I,E, 1922 W,I,E, 1923 F,W,I,E, 1924 F,W,I,E, 1925 F,I.

Buchanan-Smith, G.A.E., London Scottish – 1989 R(r), 1990 Arg.

Bucher, A.M., Edinburgh Acads. – 1897 E.

Budge, G.M., Edinburgh Wands. – 1950 F,W,I,E.

Bullmore, H.H., Edinburgh U. – 1902 I.

Burnell, A.P., London Scottish – 1989 E,I,F,Fj,R, 1990 I,F,W,E,Arg, 1991 F,W,E,I.

Burnet, P.J., London Scottish – 1960 SA.

Burnet, W., Hawick – 1912 E.

Burnet, W.A., West of Scotland – 1934 W, 1935 W,I,E,NZ, 1936 W,I,E.

Burnett, J.N., Heriot's FP – 1980 I,F,W,E.

Burrell, G., Gala – 1950 F,W,I, 1951 SA.

Cairns, A.G., Watsonians – 1903 W,I,E, 1904 W,I,E, 1905 W,I,E, 1906 W,I,E.

Calder, F., Stewart's Melville FP – 1986, F,W,E,I,R, 1987 I,F,W,E,WC-F,Z,R,NZ, 1988 I,F,W,E, 1989 W,E,I,F,R, 1990 I,F,W,E,NZ(1,2).

Calder, J.H., Stewart's Melville FP – 1981 F,W,E,I,NZ(1,2),R,A, 1982 E,I,F,W,A(1,2), 1983 I,F,W,E,NZ, 1984 W,E,I,F,A, 1985 I,F,W.

Callander, G.J., Kelso – 1984 R, 1988 I,F,W,E,A.

Cameron, A., Glasgow HS FP – 1948 W, 1950 I,E, 1951 F,W,I,E,SA, 1953 I,E, 1955 F,W,I,E, 1956 F,W,I.

Cameron, A.D., Hillhead HS FP – 1951 F, 1954 F,W.

Cameron, A.W., Watsonians – 1887 W, 1893 W, 1894 I.

Cameron D., Glasgow HS FP – 1953 I,E, 1954 F,NZ,I,E.

Cameron N.W., Glasgow U. – 1952 E, 1953 F,W.

Campbell, A.J., Hawick – 1984 I,F,R, 1985 I,F,W,E, 1986 F,W,E,I,R, 1988 F,W,A.

Campbell, G.T., London Scottish – 1892 W,I,E, 1893 I,E, 1894 W,I,E, 1895 W,I,E, 1896 W,I,E, 1897 I, 1899 I, 1900 I.

Campbell, H.H., Cambridge U., London Scottish – 1947 I,E, 1948 I,E.

Campbell, J.A., Merchistonians, West of Scotland – 1878 E, 1879 I,E, 1881 I,E.

Campbell, J.A., Cambridge U. – 1900 I.

Campbell, N.M., London Scottish – 1956 F,W.

Campbell-Lamerton, J.R.E., London Scottish – 1986 F, 1987 WC-Z,R(r).

Campbell-Lamerton, M.J., Halifax, Army, London Scottish – 1961 F,SA,W,I, 1962 F,W,I,E, 1963 F,W,I,E, 1964 I,E, 1965 F,W,I,E,SA, 1966 F,W,I,E.

Carmichael, A.B., West of Scotland – 1967 I,NZ, 1968 F,W,I,E,A, 1969 F,W,I,E,SA, 1970 F,W,I,E,A, 1971 F,W,I,E,EC, 1972 F,W,E,NZ, 1973 F,W,I,E,P, 1974 W,E,I,F, 1975 I,F,W,E,NZ,A, 1976 F,W,E,I, 1977 E,I(r),F,W, 1978 I.

Carmichael, J.H., Watsonians – 1921 F,W,I.

Carrick, J.S., Glasgow Acads. – 1876 E, 1877 E.

Cassels, D.Y., West of Scotland – 1880 E, 1881 I, 1882 I,E, 1883 W,I,E.

Cathcart, C.W., Edinburgh U. – 1872 E, 1873 E, 1876 E.

Cawkwell, G.L., Oxford U. – 1947 F.

Chalmers, C.M., Melrose – 1989 W,E,I,F,Fj, 1990 I,F,W,E,NZ(1,2), Arg, 1991 F,W,E,I.

Chalmers T., Glasgow Acads. – 1871 E, 1872 E, 1873 E, 1874 E, 1875 E, 1876 E.

Chambers, H.F.T., Edinburgh U. – 1888 W,I, 1889 W,I.

Charters, R.G., Hawick – 1955 W,I,E.

Chisholm, D.H., Melrose – 1964 I,E, 1965 E,SA, 1966 F,I,E,A, 1967 F,W,NZ, 1968 F,W,I.

Chisholm, R.W.T., Melrose – 1955 I,E, 1956 F,W,I,E, 1958 F,W,A,I, 1960 SA.

Church, W.C., Glasgow Acads. – 1906 W.

Clark, R.L., Edinburgh Wands., Royal Navy – 1972 F,W,E,NZ, 1973 F,W,I,E,P.

Clauss, P.R.A., Oxford U., Birkenhead Park – 1891 W,I,E, 1892 W,E, 1895 I.

Clay, A.T., Edinburgh Acads. – 1886 W,I,E, 1887 I,W,E, 1888 W.

Clunies-Ross, A., St Andrews U. – 1871 E.

Coltman, S., Hawick – 1948 I, 1949 F,W,I,E.

Colville, A.G., Merchistonians – 1871 E, 1872 E.

Connell, G.C., Trinity Acads., London Scottish – 1968 E,A, 1969 F,E, 1970 F.

Cooper, M.McG., Oxford U. – 1936 W,I.

Cordial, I.F., Edinburgh Wands. – 1952 F,W,I,E.

Cotter, J.L., Hillhead HS FP – 1934 I,E.

Cottington, G.S., Kelso – 1934 I,E, 1935 W,I, 1936 E.

Coughtrie, S., Edinburgh Acads. – 1959 F,W,I,E, 1962 W,I,E, 1963 F,W,I,E.

Couper, J.H., West of Scotland – 1896 W,I, 1899 I.

Coutts, F.H., Melrose, Army – 1947 W,I,E.

Coutts, I.D.F., Old Alleynians – 1951 F, 1952 E.

Cowan, R.C., Selkirk – 1961 F, 1962 F,W,I,E.

Cowie, W.L.K., Edinburgh Wands. – 1953 E.

Cownie, W.B., Watsonians – 1893 W,I,E, 1894 W,I,E, 1895 W,I,E.

Crabbie, G.E., Edinburgh Acads. – 1904 W.

Crabbie, J.E., Edinburgh Acads., Oxford U. – 1900 W, 1902 I, 1903 W,I, 1904 E, 1905 W.

Craig, J.B., Heriot's FP – 1939 W.

Cramb, R.I., Harlequins – 1987 WC-R(r), 1988 I,F,A.

Cranston, A.G., Hawick – 1976 W,E,I, 1977 E,W, 1978 F(r),W,E,NZ, 1981 NZ (1,2).

Crawford, J.A., Army, London Scottish – 1934 I.

Crawford, W.H., United Services, RN – 1938 W,I,E, 1939 W,E.

Crichton-Miller, D., Gloucester – 1931 W,I,E.

Crole, G.B., Oxford U. – 1920 F,W,I,E.

Cronin, D.F., Bath – 1988 I,F,W,E,A, 1989 W,E,I,F,Fj,R, 1990 I,F,W,E,NZ(1,2), 1991 F,W,E,I.

Cross, M., Merchistonians – 1875 E, 1876 E, 1877 I,E, 1878 E, 1879 I,E, 1880 I,E.

Cross, W. Merchistonians – 1871 E, 1872 E.

Cumming, R.S., Aberdeen U. – 1921 F,W.

Cunningham, G., Oxford U., London Scottish – 1908 W,I, 1909 W,E, 1910 F,I,E, 1911 E.

Cunningham, R.F., Gala – 1978 NZ, 1979 W,E.

Currie, L.R., Dunfermline – 1947 A, 1948 F,W,I, 1949 F,W,I,E.

Cuthbertson, W., Kilmarnock, Harlequins – 1980 I, 1981 W,E,I,NZ(1,2),R,A, 1982 E,I,F,W,A(1,2), 1983 I,F,W,NZ, 1984 W,E,A.

Dalgleish, A., Gala – 1890 W,E, 1891 W,I, 1892 W, 1893 W, 1894 W,I.

Dalgleish, K.J., Edinburgh Wands., Cambridge U. – 1951 I,E, 1953 F,W.

Dallas, J.D., Watsonians – 1903 E.
Davidson, J.A., London Scottish, Edinburgh Wands. – 1959 E, 1960 I,E.
Davidson, J.N.G., Edinburgh U. – 1952 F,W,I,E, 1953 F,W, 1954 F.
Davidson, J.P., RIE Coll. – 1873 E, 1874 E.
Davidson, R.S., Royal HS FP – 1893 E.
Davies, D.S., Hawick – 1922 F,W,I,E, 1923 F,W,I,E, 1924 F,E, 1925 W,I,E, 1926 F,W,I,E,
    1927 F,W,I.
Dawson, J.C., Glasgow Acads. – 1947 A, 1948 F,W, 1949 F,W,I, 1950 F,W,I,E, 1951 F,W,I,E,SA,
    1952 F,W,I,E, 1953 E.
Deans, C.T., Hawick – 1978 F,W,E,NZ, 1979 W,E,I,F,NZ, 1980 I,F, 1981 F,W,E,I,NZ (1,2),R,A,
    1982 E,I,F,W,A(1,2), 1983 I,F,W,E,NZ, 1984 W,E,I,F,A, 1985 I,F,W,E, 1986 F,W,E,I,R,
    1987 I,F,W,E,WC-F,Z,R,NZ.
Deans, D.T., Hawick – 1968 E.
Deas, D.W., Heriot's FP – 1947 F,W.
Dick, L.G., Loughborough Colls., Jordanhill, Swansea – 1972 W(r),E, 1974 W,E,I,F, 1975
    I,F,W,E,NZ,A, 1976 F, 1977 E.
Dick, R.C.S., Cambridge U., Guy's Hospital – 1934 W,I,E, 1935 W,I,E,NZ, 1936 W,I,E, 1937 W,
    1938 W,I,E.
Dickson, G., Gala – 1978 NZ, 1979 W,E,I,F,NZ, 1980 W, 1981 F, 1982 W(r).
Dickson, M.R., Edinburgh U. – 1905 I.
Dickson, W.M., Blackheath, Oxford U. – 1912 F,W,E,SA, 1913 F,W,I.
Dobson, J., Glasgow Acads. – 1911 E, 1912 F,W,I,E,SA.
Dobson, J.D., Glasgow Acads. – 1901 I.
Dobson, W.G., Heriot's FP – 1922 W,I,E.
Docherty, J.T., Glasgow HS FP – 1955 F,W, 1956 E, 1958 F,W,A,I,E.
Dods, F.P., Edinburgh Acads. – 1901 I.
Dods, J.H., Edinburgh Acads., London Scottish – 1895 W,I,E, 1896 W,I,E, 1897 I,E.
Dods, P.W., Gala – 1983 I,F,W,E,NZ, 1984 W,E,I,F,R,A, 1985 I,F,W,E, 1989 W,E,I,F, 1991 I(r).
Donald, D.G., Oxford U. – 1914 W,I.
Donald R.L.H., Glasgow HS FP – 1921 W,I,E.
Donaldson, W.P., Oxford U., West of Scotland – 1893 I, 1894 I, 1895 E, 1896 I,E, 1899 I.
Don Wauchope, A.R., Cambridge U., Fettesian-Lorettonians – 1881 E, 1882 E, 1883 W, 1884
    W,I,E, 1885 W,I(1,2), 1886 W,I,E, 1888 I.
Don Wauchope, P.H., Fettesian-Lorettonians, Edinburgh Wands. – 1885 I(1,2), 1886 W, 1887
    I,W,E.
Dorward, A.F., Cambridge U., Gala – 1950 F, 1951 SA, 1952 W,I,E, 1953 F,W,E, 1955 F, 1956
    I,E, 1957 F,W,I,E.
Dorward, T.F., Gala – 1938 W,I,E, 1939 I,E.
Douglas, G., Jed-Forest – 1921 W.
Douglas, J., Stewart's Coll. FP – 1961 F,SA,W,I,E, 1962 F,W,I,E, 1963 F,W,I.
Douty, P.S., London Scottish – 1927 NSW, 1928 F,W.
Drew, D., Glasgow Acads. – 1871 E, 1876 E.
Druitt, W.A.H., London Scottish – 1936 W,I.E.
Drummond, A.H., Kelvinside Acads. – 1938 W,I.
Drummond, C.W., Melrose – 1947 F,W,I,E, 1948 F,I,E, 1950 F,W,I,E.
Drybrough, A.S., Edinburgh Wands., Merchistonians – 1902 I, 1903 I.
Dryden, R.H., Watsonians – 1937 E.
Drysdale, D., Heriot's FP, Oxford U., London Scottish – 1923 F,W,I,E, 1924 F,W,I,E, 1925
    F,W,I,E, 1926 F,W,I,E, 1927 F,W,I,E,NSW, 1928 F,W,I,E, 1929 F.
Duff, P.L., Glasgow Acads. – 1936 W,I, 1938 W,I,E, 1939 W.
Duffy, H., Jed-Forest – 1955 F.
Duke, A., Royal HS FP – 1888 W,I, 1889 W,I, 1890 W,I.
Duncan, A.W., Edinburgh U. – 1901 W,I,E, 1902 W,I,E.
Duncan, D.D., Oxford U. – 1920 F,W,I,E.
Duncan, M.D.F., West of Scotland – 1986 F,W,E,R, 1987 I,F,W,E,WC-F,Z,R,NZ, 1988 I,F,W,E,A,
    1989 W.
Duncan, M.M., Fettesian-Lorettonians – 1888 W.
Dunlop, J.W., West of Scotland – 1875 E.
Dunlop, Q., West of Scotland – 1971 E,EC.
Dykes, A.S., Glasgow Acads. – 1932 E.
Dykes, J.C., Glasgow Acads. – 1922 F,E, 1924 I, 1925 F,W,I, 1926 F,W,I,E, 1927 F,W,I,E,NSW,
    1928 F,I, 1929 F,W,I.
Dykes, J.M., Clydesdale, London Scottish, Glasgow HS FP – 1898 I,E, 1899 W,E, 1900 W,I, 1901
    W,I,E, 1902 E.

Edwards, D.B., Heriot's FP – 1960 I,E,SA.
Elgie, M.K., London Scottish – 1954 NZ,I,E,W, 1955 F,W,I,E.
Elliot, C., Langholm – 1958 E, 1959 F, 1960 F, 1963 E, 1964 F,NZ,W,I,E, 1965 F,W,I.
Elliot, M., Hawick – 1895 W, 1896 E, 1897 I,E, 1899 I,E.
Elliot, T., Gala – 1905 E.
Elliot, T., Gala – 1955 W,I,E, 1956 F,W,I,E, 1957 F,W,I,E, 1958 W,A,I.
Elliot, T.G., Langholm – 1968 W,A, 1969 F,W, 1970 E.
Elliot, W.I.D., Edinburgh Acads. – 1947 F,W,E,A, 1948 F,W,I,E, 1949 F,W,I,E, 1950 F,W,I,E, 1951

F,W,I,E,SA, 1952, F,W,I,E, 1954 NZ,I,E,W.
Emslie, W.D., Royal HS FP – 1930 F, 1932 I.
Evans, H.L., Edinburgh U. – 1885 I(1,2).
Ewart, E.N., Glasgow Acads. – 1879 E, 1880 I,E.

Fahmy, E.C., Abertillery – 1920 F,W,I,E.
Fasson, F.H., London Scottish, Edinburgh U. – 1900 W, 1901 W,I, 1902 W,E.
Fell, A.N., Edinburgh U. – 1901 W,I,E, 1902 W,E, 1903 W,E.
Ferguson, J.H., Gala – 1928 W.
Ferguson, W.G., Royal HS FP – 1927 NSW, 1928 F,W,I,E.
Fergusson, E.A.J., Oxford U. – 1954 F,NZ,I,E,W.
Finlay, A.B., Edinburgh Acads. – 1875 E.
Finlay, J.F., Edinburgh Acads. – 1871 E, 1872 E, 1874 E, 1875 E.
Finlay, N.J., Edinburgh Acads. – 1875 E, 1876 E, 1878 E, 1879 I,E, 1880 I,E, 1881 I,E.
Finlay, R., Watsonians – 1948 E.
Fisher, A.T., Waterloo, Watsonians – 1947 I,F.
Fisher, C.D., Waterloo – 1975 NZ,A, 1976 W,E,I.
Fisher, D., West of Scotland – 1893 I.
Fisher, J.P., Royal HS FP, London Scottish – 1963 E, 1964 F,NZ,W,I,E, 1965 F,W,I,E,SA. 1966
    F,W,I,E,A, 1967 F,W,I,E,NZ, 1968 F,W,I,E.
Fleming, C.J.N., Edinburgh Wands. – 1896 I,E, 1897 I.
Fleming, G.R., Glasgow Acads. – 1875 E, 1876 E.
Fletcher, H.N., Edinburgh U. – 1904 E, 1905 W.
Flett, A.B., Edinburgh U. – 1901 W,I,E, 1902 W,I.
Forbes, J.L., Watsonians – 1905 W, 1906 I,E.
Ford, D.St.C., United Services, RN – 1930 I,E, 1931 E, 1932 W,I.
Ford, J.R., Gala – 1893 I.
Forrest, J.E., Glasgow Acads. – 1932 SA, 1935 E,NZ.
Forrest, J.G.S., Cambridge U. – 1938 W,I,E.
Forrest, W.T., Hawick – 1903 W,I,E, 1904 W,I,E, 1905 W,I.
Forsayth, H.H., Oxford U. – 1921 F,W,I,E, 1922 W,I,E.
Forsyth, I.W., Stewart's Coll. FP – 1972 NZ, 1973 F,W,I,E,P.
Forsyth, J., Edinburgh U. – 1871 E.
Foster, R.A., Hawick – 1930 W, 1932 SA,I,E.
Fox, J., Gala – 1952 F,W,I,E.
Frame, J.N.M., Edinburgh U., Gala – 1967 NZ, 1968 F,W,I,E, 1969 W,I,E,SA, 1970 F,W,I,E,A,
    1971 F,W,I,E,EC, 1972 F,W,E, 1973 P(r).
France, C., Kelvinside Acads. – 1903 I.
Fraser, C.F.P., Glasgow U. – 1888 W, 1889 W.
Fraser, J.W., Edinburgh Inst. FP – 1881 E.
Fraser, R., Cambridge U. – 1911 F,W,I,E.
French, J., Glasgow Acads. – 1886 W, 1887 I,W,E.
Frew, A., Edinburgh U. – 1901 W,I,E.
Frew, G.M., Glasgow HS FP – 1906 SA, 1907 W,I,E, 1908 W,I,E, 1909 W,I,E, 1910 F,W,I,
    1911 E.
Friebe, J.P., Glasgow HS FP – 1952 E.
Fulton, A.K., Edinburgh U., Dollar Acads. – 1952 F, 1954 F.
Fyfe, K.C., Cambridge U., Sale, London Scottish – 1933 W,E, 1934 E, 1935 W,I,E,NZ, 1936 W,E,
    1939 I.

Gallie, G.H. Edinburgh Acads. – 1939 W.
Gallie, R.A., Glasgow Acads. – 1920 F,W,I,E, 1921 F,W,I,E.
Gammell, W.B.B., Edinburgh Wands. – 1977 I,F,W, 1978 W,E.
Geddes, I.C., London Scottish – 1906 SA, 1907 W,I,E, 1908 W,E.
Geddes, K.I., London Scottish – 1947 F,W,I,E.
Gedge, H.T.S., London Scottish, Edinburgh Wands. – 1894 W,I,E, 1896 E, 1899 W,E.
Gedge, P.M.S., Edinburgh Wands. – 1933 I.
Gemmill, R., Glasgow HS FP – 1950 F,W,I,E, 1951 F,W,I.
Gibson, W.R., Royal HS FP – 1891 I,E, 1892 W,I,E, 1893 W,I,E, 1894 W,I,E, 1895 W,I,E.
Gilbert-Smith, D.S., London Scottish – 1952 E.
Gilchrist, J., Glasgow Acads. – 1925 F.
Gill, A.D., Gala – 1973 P, 1974 W,E,I,F.
Gillespie, J.I., Edinburgh Acads. – 1899 E, 1900 W,E, 1901 W,I,E, 1902 W,I, 1904 I,E.
Gillies, A.C., Watsonians, Carlisle – 1924 W,I,E, 1925 F,W,E, 1926 F,W, 1927 F,W,I,E.
Gilray, C.M., Oxford U., London Scottish – 1908 E, 1909 W,E, 1912 I.
Glasgow, R.J.C., Dunfermline – 1962 F,W,I,E, 1963 I,E, 1964 I,E, 1965 W,I.
Glen, W.S., Edinburgh Wands. – 1955 W.
Gloag, L.G., Cambridge U. – 1949 F,W,I,E.
Goodfellow, J., Langholm – 1928 W,I,E.
Goodhue, F.W.J., London Scottish – 1890 W,I,E, 1891 W,I,E, 1892 W,I,E.
Gordon, R., Edinburgh Wands. – 1951 W, 1952 F,W,I,E, 1953 W.
Gordon, R.E., Royal Artillery – 1913 F,W,I.
Gordon, R.J., London Scottish – 1982 A(1,2).

Gore, A.C., London Scottish – 1882 I.
Gossman, B.M., West of Scotland – 1980 W, 1983 F,W.
Gossman, J.S., West of Scotland – 1980 E(r).
Gowans, J.J., Cambridge U., London Scottish – 1893 W, 1894 W,E, 1895 W,I,E, 1896 I,E.
Gowlland, G.C., London Scottish – 1908 W, 1909 W,E, 1910 F,W,I,E.
Gracie, A.L., Harlequins – 1921 F,W,I,E, 1922 F,W,I,E, 1923 F,W,I,E, 1924 F.
Graham, I.N., Edinburgh Acads. – 1939 I,E.
Graham, J., Kelso – 1926 I,E, 1927 F,W,I,E,NSW, 1928 F,W,I,E, 1930 I,E, 1932 SA,W.
Graham, J.H.S., Edinburgh Acads. – 1876 E, 1877 I,E, 1878 E, 1879 I,E, 1880 I,E, 1881 I,E.
Grant, D., Hawick – 1965 F,E,SA, 1966 F,W,I,E,A, 1967 F,W,I,E,NZ, 1968 F.
Grant, D.M., East Midlands – 1911 W,I.
Grant, M.L., Harlequins – 1955 F, 1956 F,W, 1957 F.
Grant, T.O., Hawick – 1960 I,E,SA, 1964 F,NZ,W.
Grant, W.St.C., Craigmount – 1873 E, 1874 E.
Gray, C.A., Nottingham – 1989 W,E,I,F,Fj,R, 1990 I,F,W,E,NZ (1,2), Arg, 1991 F,W,E,I.
Gray, D., West of Scotland – 1978 E, 1979 I,F,NZ, 1980 I,F,W,E, 1981 F.
Gray, G.L., Gala – 1935 NZ, 1937 W,I,E.
Gray, T., Northampton, Heriot's FP – 1950 E, 1951 F,E.
Greenlees, H.D., Leicester – 1927 NSW, 1928 F,W, 1929 I,E, 1930 E.
Greenlees, J.R.C., Cambridge U., Kelvinside Acads. – 1900 I, 1902 W,I,E, 1903 W,I,E.
Greenwood, J.T., Dunfermline, Perthshire Acads. – 1952 F, 1955 F,W,I,E, 1956 F,W,I,E, 1957
      F,W,E, 1958 F,W,A,I,E, 1959 F,W,I.
Greig, A., Glasgow HS FP – 1911 I.
Greig, L.L., Glasgow Acads., United Services – 1905 NZ, 1906 SA, 1907 W, 1908 W,I.
Greig, R.C., Glasgow Acads., – 1893 W, 1897 I.
Grieve, C.F., Oxford U. – 1935 W, 1936 E.
Grieve, R.M., Kelso – 1935 W,I,E,NZ, 1936 W,I,E.
Gunn, A.W., Royal HS FP – 1912 F,W,I,SA, 1913 F.

Hamilton, A.S., Headingley – 1914 W, 1920 F.
Hamilton, H.M., West of Scotland – 1874 E, 1875 E.
Hannah, R.S.M., West of Scotland – 1971 I.
Harrower, P.R., London Scottish – 1885 W.
Hart, J.G.M., London Scottish – 1951 SA.
Hart, T.M., Glasgow U. – 1930 W,I.
Hart, W., Melrose – 1960 SA.
Harvey, L., Greenock Wands. – 1899 I.
Hastie, A.J., Melrose – 1961 W,I,E, 1964 I,E, 1965 E,SA, 1966 F,W,I,E,A, 1967 F,W,I,NZ,
      1968 F,W.
Hastie, I.R., Kelso – 1955 F, 1958 F,E, 1959 F,W,I.
Hastie, J.D.H., Melrose – 1938 W,I,E.
Hastings, A.G., Cambridge U., Watsonians, London Scottish – 1986 F,W,E,I,R, 1987 I,F,W,E,WC-
      F,Z,R,NZ, 1988 I,F,W,E,A, 1989 Fj,R, 1990 I,F,W,E,NZ(1,2), Arg, 1991 F,W,E,I.
Hastings, S., Watsonians – 1986 F,W,E,I,R, 1987 I,F,W,WC-R, 1988 I,F,W,A, 1989 W,E,I,F,Fj,R,
      1990 I,F,W,E,NZ(1,2), Arg, 1991 F,W,E,I.
Hay, B.H., Boroughmuir – 1975 NZ,A, 1976 F, 1978 I,F,W,E,NZ, 1979 W,E,I,F,NZ, 1980
      I,F,W,E, 1981 F,W,E,I,NZ(1,2).
Hay-Gordon, J.R., Edinburgh Acads. – 1875 E, 1877 I,E.
Hegarty, C.B., Hawick – 1978 I,F,W,E.
Hegarty, J.J., Hawick – 1951 F, 1953 F,W,I,E, 1955 F.
Henderson, B.C., Edinburgh Wands. – 1963 E, 1964 F,I,E, 1965 F,W,I,E, 1966 F,W,I,E.
Henderson, F.W., London Scottish – 1900 W,I.
Henderson, I.C., Edinburgh Acads. – 1939 I,E, 1947 F,W,E,A, 1948 I,E.
Henderson, J.H., Oxford U., Richmond – 1953 F,W,I,E, 1954 F,NZ,I,E,W.
Henderson, J.M., Edinburgh Acads. – 1933 W,E,I.
Henderson, J.Y.M., Watsonians – 1911 E.
Henderson, M.M., Dunfermline – 1937 W,I,E.
Henderson, N.F., London Scottish – 1892 I.
Henderson, R.G., Newcastle Northern – 1924 I,E.
Hendrie, K.G.P., Heriot's FP – 1924 F,W,I.
Hendry, T.L., Clydesdale – 1893 W,I,E, 1895 I.
Henriksen, E.H., Royal HS FP – 1953 I.
Hepburn, D.P., Woodford – 1947 A, 1948 F,W,I,E, 1949 F,W,I,E.
Heron, G., Glasgow Acads. – 1874 E, 1875 E.
Hill, C.C.P., St. Andrews U. – 1912 F,I.
Hinshelwood, A.J.W., London Scottish – 1966 F,W,I,E,A, 1967 F,W,I,E,NZ, 1968 F,W,I,E,A, 1969
      F,W,I,SA, 1970 F,W.
Hodgson, C.G., London Scottish – 1968 I,E.
Hogg, C.G., Boroughmuir – 1978 F(r),W(r).
Holms, W.F., RIE Coll. – 1886 W,E, 1887 I,E, 1889 W,I.
Horsburgh, G.B., London Scottish – 1937 W,I,E, 1938 W,I,E, 1939 W,I,E.
Howie, D.D., Kirkcaldy – 1912 F,W,I,E,SA, 1913 F,W.
Howie, R.A., Kirkcaldy – 1924 F,W,I,E, 1925 W,I,E.

Hoyer-Millar, G.C., Oxford U. – 1953 I.
Huggan, J.L., London Scottish – 1914 E.
Hume, J., Royal HS FP – 1912 F, 1920 F, 1921 F,W,I,E, 1922 F.
Hume, J.W.G., Oxford U., Edinburgh Wands. – 1928 I, 1930 F.
Hunter, F., Edinburgh U. – 1882 I.
Hunter, I.G., Selkirk – 1984 I(r), 1985 F(r),W,E.
Hunter, J.M., Cambridge U. – 1947 F.
Hunter, M.D., Glasgow High – 1974 F.
Hunter, W.J., Hawick – 1964 F,NZ,W, 1967 F,W,I,E.
Hutchison, W.R., Glasgow HS FP – 1911 E.
Hutton, A.H.M., Dunfermline – 1932 I.
Hutton, J.E., Harlequins – 1930 E, 1931 F.

Inglis, H.M., Edinburgh Acads. – 1951 F,W,I,E,SA, 1952 W,I.
Inglis, J.M., Selkirk – 1952 E.
Inglis, W.M., Cambridge U., Royal Engineers – 1937 W,I,E, 1938 W,I,E.
Innes, J.R.S., Aberdeen GS FP – 1939 W,I,E, 1947 A, 1948 F,W,I,E.
Ireland, J.C.H., Glasgow HS FP – 1925 W,I,E, 1926 F,W,I,E, 1927 F,W,I,E.
Irvine, A.R., Heriot's FP – 1972 NZ, 1973 F,W,I,E,P, 1974 W,E,I,F, 1975 I,F,W,E,NZ,A,
    1976 F,W,E,I, 1977 E,I,F,W, 1978 I,F,E,NZ, 1979 W,E,I,F,NZ, 1980 I,F,W,E, 1981
    F,W,E,I,NZ(1,2),R,A, 1982 E,I,F,W,A(1,2).
Irvine, D.R., Edinburgh Acads. – 1878 E, 1879 I,E.
Irvine, R.W., Edinburgh Acads. – 1871 E, 1872 E, 1873 E, 1874 E, 1875 E, 1876 E, 1877 I,E,
    1878 E, 1879 I,E, 1880 I,E.
Irvine, T.W., Edinburgh Acads. – 1885 I(1,2), 1886 W,I,E, 1887 I,W,E, 1888 W,I, 1891 I.

Jackson, K.L.T., Oxford U. – 1933 W,E,I, 1934 W.
Jackson, T.G.H., Army, London Scottish – 1947 F,W,E,A, 1948 F,W,I,E, 1949 F,W,I,E.
Jackson, W.D., Hawick – 1964 I, 1965 E,SA, 1968 A, 1969 F,W,I,E.
Jamieson, J., West of Scotland – 1883 W,I,E, 1884 W,I,E, 1885 W,I(1,2).
Jeffrey, J., Kelso – 1984 A, 1985 I,E, 1986 F,W,E,I,R, 1987 I,F,W,E,WC-F,Z,R, 1988 I,W,A, 1989
    W,E,I,F,Fj,R, 1990 I,F,W,E,NZ(1,2),Arg, 1991 F,W,E,I.
Johnston, D.I., Watsonians – 1979 NZ, 1980 I,F,W,E, 1981 R,A, 1982 E,I,F,W,A(1,2), 1983
    I,F,W,NZ, 1984 W,E,I,F,R, 1986 F,W,E,I,R.
Johnston, H.H., Edinburgh Collegians – 1877 I,E.
Johnston, J., Melrose – 1951 SA, 1952 F,W,I,E.
Johnston, W.G.S., Cambridge U., Richmond – 1935 W,I, 1937 W,I,E.
Johnston, W.C., Glasgow HS FP – 1922 F.
Junor, J.E., Glasgow Acads. – 1876 E, 1877 I,E, 1878 E, 1879 E, 1881 I.

Keddie, R.R., Watsonians – 1967 NZ.
Keith, G.J., Wasps – 1968 F,W.
Keller, D.H., London Scottish, Sheffield – 1949 F,W,I,E, 1950 F,W,I.
Kelly, R.F., Watsonians – 1927 NSW, 1928 F,W,E.
Kemp, J.W.Y., Glasgow GS FP – 1954 W, 1955 F,W,I,E, 1956 F,W,I,E, 1957 F,W,I,E, 1958
    F,W,A,I,E, 1959 F,W,I,E, 1960 F,W,I,E,SA.
Kennedy, A.E., Watsonians – 1983 NZ, 1984 W,E,A.
Kennedy, F., Stewart's Coll. FP – 1920 F,W,I,E, 1921 E.
Kennedy, N., West of Scotland – 1903 W,I,E.
Ker, A.B.M., Kelso – 1988 W,E.
Ker, H.T., Glasgow Acads. – 1887 I,W,E, 1888 I, 1889 W, 1890 I,E.
Kerr, D.S., Heriot's FP – 1923 F,W, 1924 F, 1926 I,E, 1927 W,I,E, 1928 I,E.
Kerr, G.C., Durham, Old Dunelmians, Edinburgh Wands. – 1898 I,E, 1899 I,W,E, 1900 W,I,E.
Kerr, J.M., Heriot's FP – 1935 NZ, 1936 I,E, 1937 W,I.
Kerr, J.R. Greenock Wanderers – 1905 E.
Kerr, W., London Scottish – 1953 E.
Kidston, D.W., Glasgow Acads. – 1883 W,E.
Kidston, W.H., West of Scotland – 1874 E.
Kilgour, I.J., RMC Sandhurst – 1921 F.
King, J.H.F., Selkirk – 1953 F,W,E, 1954 E.
Kininmonth, P.W., Oxford U., Richmond – 1949 F,W,I,E, 1950 F,W,I,E, 1951 F,W,I,E,SA, 1952
    F,W,I 1954 F,NZ,I,E,W.
Kinnear, R.M., Heriot's FP – 1926 F,W,I.
Knox, J., Kelvinside Acads. – 1903 W,I,E.
Kyle, W.E., Hawick – 1902 W,I,E, 1903 W,I,E, 1904 W,I,E, 1905 W,I,E,NZ, 1906 W,I,E, 1908 E,
    1909 W,I,E, 1910 W.

Laidlaw, A.S., Hawick – 1897 I.
Laidlaw, F.A.L., Melrose – 1965 F,W,I,E,SA, 1966 F,W,I,E,A, 1967 F,W,I,E,NZ, 1968 F,W,I,A,
    1969 F,W,I,E,SA, 1970 F,W,I,E,A, 1971 F,W,I.
Laidlaw, R.J., Jed-Forest – 1980 I,F,W,E, 1981 F,W,E,I,NZ(1,2),R,A, 1982 E,I,F,W,A,(1,2), 1983
    I,F,W,E,NZ, 1984 W,E,I,F,R,A, 1985 I,F, 1986 F,W,E,I,R, 1987 I,F,W,E,WC-F,R,NZ, 1988
    I,F,W,E.
Laing, A.D., Royal HS FP – 1914 W,I,E, 1920 F,W,I, 1921 F.

Lambie, I.K., Watsonians – 1978 NZ(r), 1979 W,E,NZ.
Lambie, L.B., Glasgow HS FP – 1934 W,I,E, 1935 W,I,E,NZ.
Lamond, G.A.W., Kelvinside Acads., Bristol – 1899 W,E, 1905 E.
Lang, D., Paisley – 1876 E, 1877 I.
Langrish, R.W., London Scottish – 1930 F, 1931 F,W,I.
Lauder, W., Neath – 1969 I,E,SA, 1970 F,W,I,A, 1973 F, 1974 W,E,I,F, 1975 I,F,NZ,A, 1976 F,
    1977 E.
Laughland, I.H.P., London Scottish – 1959 F, 1960 F,W,I,E, 1961 SA,W,I,E, 1962 F,W,I,E, 1963
    F,W,I, 1964 F,NZ,W,I,E, 1965 F,W,I,E,SA, 1966 F,W,I,E, 1967 E.
Lawrie, J.R., Melrose, Leicester – 1922 F,W,I,E, 1923 F,W,I,E, 1924 W,I,E.
Lawrie, K.G., Gala – 1980 F(r),W,E.
Lawson, A.J.M., Edinburgh Wands., London Scottish, Heriot's FP – 1972 F(r),E, 1973 F, 1974
    W,E, 1976 E,I, 1977 E, 1978 NZ, 1979 W,E,I,F,NZ, 1980 W(r).
Lawther, T.H.B., Old Millhillians – 1932 SA,W.
Ledingham, G.A., Aberdeen GS FP – 1913 F.
Lees, J.B., Gala – 1947 I,A, 1948 F,W,E.
Leggatt, H.T.O., Watsonians – 1891 W,I,E, 1892 W,I, 1893 W,E, 1894 I,E.
Lely, W.G., Cambridge U., London Scottish – 1909 I.
Leslie, D.G., Dundee HS FP., West of Scotland, Gala – 1975 I,F,W,E,NZ,A, 1976 F,W,E,I, 1978
    NZ, 1980 E, 1981 W,E,I,NZ(1,2),R,A, 1982 E, 1983 I,F,W,E, 1984 W,E,I,F,R, 1985 F,W,E.
Liddell, E.H., Edinburgh U. – 1922 F,W,I, 1923 F,W,I,E.
Lind, H., Dunfermline, London Scottish – 1928 I, 1931 F,W,I,E, 1932 SA,W,E, 1933 W,E,I, 1934
    W,I,E, 1935 I, 1936 E.
Lindsay, A.B., London Hospital – 1910 I, 1911 I.
Lindsay, G.C., London Scottish – 1884 W, 1885 I(1), 1887 W,E.
Lindsay-Watson, R.H., Hawick – 1909 I.
Lineen, S.R.P., Boroughmuir – 1989 W,E,I,F,Fj,R, 1990 I,F,W,E,NZ(1,2),Arg, 1991 F,W,E,I.
Little, A.W., Hawick – 1905 W.
Logan, W.R., Edinburgh U., Edinburgh Wands. – 1931 E, 1932 SA,W,I, 1933 W,E,I, 1934 W,I,E,
    1935 W,I,E,NZ, 1936 W,I,E, 1937 W,I,E.
Lorraine, H.D.B., Oxford U. – 1933 W,E,I.
Loudoun-Shand, E.G., Oxford U. – 1913 E.
Lowe, J.D., Heriot's FP – 1934 W.
Lumsden, I.J., Bath, Watsonians – 1947 F,W,A, 1949 F,W,I,E.
Lyall, G.G., Gala – 1947 A, 1948 F,W,I,E.
Lyall, W.J.C., Edinburgh Acads. – 1871 E.

Mabon, J.T., Jed-Forest – 1898 I,E, 1899 I, 1900 I.
Macarthur, J.P., Waterloo – 1932 E.
MacCallum, J.C., Watsonians – 1905 E,NZ, 1906 W,I,E,SA, 1907 W,I,E, 1908 W,I,E, 1909 W,I,E,
    1910 F,W,I,E, 1911 F,I,E, 1912 F,W,I,E.
McClung, T., Edinburgh Acads. – 1956 I,E, 1957 W,I,E, 1959 F,W,I, 1960 W.
McClure, G.B., West of Scotland – 1873 E.
McClure, J.H., West of Scotland – 1872 E.
McCowan, D., West of Scotland – 1880 I,E, 1881 I,E, 1882 I,E, 1883 I,E, 1884 I,E.
McCowat, R.H., Glasgow Acads. – 1905 I.
McCrae, I.G., Gordonians – 1967 E, 1968 I, 1969 F(r),W, 1972 F,NZ.
McCrow, J.W.S., Edinburgh Acads. – 1921 I.
McDonald, C., Jed-Forest – 1947 A.
Macdonald, D.C., Edinburgh U. – 1953 F,W, 1958 I,E.
Macdonald, D.S.M., Oxford U., London Scottish, West of Scotland – 1977 E,I,F,W, 1978 I,W,E.
Macdonald, J.D., London Scottish, Army – 1966, F,W,I,E, 1967 F,W,I,E.
Macdonald, J.M., Edinburgh Wands. – 1911 W.
Macdonald, J.S., Edinburgh U. – 1903 E, 1904 W,I,E, 1905 W.
Macdonald, K.R., Stewart's Coll. FP – 1956 F,W,I, 1957 W,I,E.
Macdonald, R., Edinburgh U. – 1950 F,W,I,E.
McDonald, W.A., Glasgow U. – 1889 W, 1892 I,E.
Macdonald, W.G., London Scottish – 1969 I(r).
Macdougall, J.B., Greenock Wands., Wakefield – 1913 F, 1914 I, 1921 F,I,E.
McEwan, M.C., Edinburgh Acads. – 1886 E, 1887 I,W,E, 1888 W,I, 1889 W,I, 1890 W,I,E, 1891
    W,I,E, 1892 E.
MacEwan, N.A., Gala, Highland – 1971 F,W,I,E,EC, 1972 F,W,E,NZ, 1973 F,W,I,E,P, 1974
    W,E,I,F, 1975 W,E.
McEwan, W.M.C., Edinburgh Acads. – 1894 W,E, 1895 W,E, 1896 W,I,E, 1897 I,E, 1898 I,E,
    1899 I,W,E, 1900 W,E.
MacEwen, R.K.G., Cambridge U., London Scottish, Lansdowne – 1954 F,NZ,I,W, 1956 F,W,I,E,
    1957 F,W,I,E, 1958 W.
Macfarlan, D.J., London Scottish – 1883 W, 1884 W,I,E, 1886 W,I, 1887 I, 1888 I.
McFarlane, J.L.H., Edinburgh U. – 1871 E, 1872 E, 1873 E.
McGaughey, S.K., Hawick – 1984 R.
McGeechan, I.R., Headingley – 1972 NZ, 1973 F,W,I,E,P, 1974 W,E,I,F, 1975 I,F,W,E,NZ,A,
    1976 F,W,E,I, 1977 E,I,F,W, 1978 I,F,W,NZ, 1979 W,E,I,F.
McGlashan, T.P.L., Royal HS FP – 1947 F,I,E, 1954 F,NZ,I,E,W.

MacGregor, D.G., Watsonians, Pontypridd – 1907 W,I,E.
MacGregor, G., Cambridge U. – 1890 W,I,E, 1891 W,I,E, 1893 W,I,E, 1894 W,I,E, 1896 E.
MacGregor, I.A.A., Hillhead HS FP, Llanelli – 1955 I,E, 1956 F,W,I,E, 1957 F,W,I.
MacGregor, J.R., Edinburgh U. – 1909 I.
McGuinness, G.M., West of Scotland – 1982 A(1,2), 1983 I, 1985 I,F,W,E.
McHarg, A.F., West of Scotland, London Scottish – 1968 I,E,A, 1969 F,W,I,E, 1971 F,W,I,E,EC,
    1972 F,E,NZ, 1973 F,W,I,E,P, 1974 W,E,I,F, 1975 I,F,W,E,NZ,A, 1976 F,W,E,I, 1977
    E,I,F,W, 1978 I,F,W,NZ, 1979 W,E.
McIndoe, F., Glasgow Acads. – 1886 W,I.
MacIntyre, I., Edinburgh Wands. – 1890 W,I,E, 1891 W,I,E.
Mackay, E.B., Glasgow Acads. – 1920 W, 1922 E.
McKeating, E., Heriot's FP – 1957 F,W, 1961 SA,W,I,E.
Mckendrick, J.G., West of Scotland – 1889 I.
Mackenzie, A.D.G., Selkirk – 1984 A.
Mackenzie, C.J.G., United Services – 1921 E.
Mackenzie, D.D., Edinburgh U. – 1947 W,I,E, 1948 F,W,I.
Mackenzie, D.K.A., Edinburgh Wands. – 1939 I,E.
Mackenzie, J.M., Edinburgh U. – 1905 NZ, 1909 W,I,E, 1910 W,I,E, 1911 W,I.
Mackenzie, R.C., Glasgow Acads. – 1877 I,E, 1881 I,E.
Mackie, G.Y., Highland – 1975 A, 1976 F,W, 1978 F.
MacKinnon, A., London Scottish – 1898 I,E, 1899 I,W,E, 1900 E.
Mackintosh, C.E.W.C., London Scottish   1924 F.
Mackintosh, H.S., Glasgow U., West of Scotland – 1929 F,W,I,E, 1930 F,W,I,E, 1931 F,W,I,E,
    1932 SA,W,I,E.
MacLachlan, L.P., Oxford U., London Scottish – 1954 NZ,I,E,W.
Maclagan, W.E., Edinburgh Acads. – 1878 E, 1879 I,E, 1880 I,E, 1881 I,E, 1882 I,E, 1883 W,I,E,
    1884 W,I,E, 1885 W,I(1,2), 1887 I,W,E, 1888 W,I, 1890 W,I,E.
McLaren, A., Durham County – 1931 F.
McLaren, E., London Scottish, Royal HS FP – 1923 F,W,I,E, 1924 F.
McLauchlan, J., Jordanhill – 1969 E,SA, 1970 F,W, 1971 F,W,I,E,EC, 1972 F,W,E,NZ, 1973
    F,W,I,E,P, 1974 W,E,I,F, 1975 I,F,W,E,NZ,A, 1976 F,W,E,I, 1977 W, 1978 I,F,W,E,NZ,
    1979 W,E,I,F,NZ.
McLean, D.I., Royal HS FP – 1947 I,E.
Maclennan, W.D., Watsonians – 1947 F,I.
MacLeod, D.A., Glasgow U. – 1886 I,E.
MacLeod, G., Edinburgh Acads. – 1878 E, 1882 I.
McLeod, H.F., Hawick – 1954 F,NZ,I,E,W, 1955 F,W,I,E, 1956 F,W,I,E, 1957 F,W,I,E, 1958
    F,W,A,I,E, 1959 F,W,I,E, 1960 F,W,I,E,SA, 1961 F,SA,W,I,E, 1962 F,W,I,E.
MacLeod, K.G., Cambridge U. – 1905 NZ, 1906 W,I,E,SA, 1907 W,I,E, 1908 I,E.
MacLeod, W.M., Fettesian-Lorettonians, Edinburgh Wands. – 1886 W,I.
McMillan, K.H.D., Sale – 1953 F,W,I,E.
MacMillan, R.G., London Scottish, West of Scotland – 1887 W,I,F, 1890 W,I,E, 1891 W,E, 1892
    W,I,E, 1893 W,E, 1894 W,I,E, 1895 W,I,E, 1897 I,E.
MacMyn, D.J., Cambridge U., London Scottish – 1925 F,W,I,E, 1926 F,W,I,E, 1927 E,NSW,
    1928 F.
McNeil, A.S.B., Watsonians – 1935 I.
McPartlin, J.J., Harlequins, Oxford U. – 1960 F,W, 1962 F,W,I,E.
Macphail, J.A.R., Edinburgh Acads. – 1949 E, 1951 SA.
Macpherson, D.G., London Hospital – 1910 I,E.
Macpherson, G.P.S., Oxford U., Edinburgh Acads. – 1922 F,W,I,E, 1924 W,E, 1925 F,W,E, 1927
    F,W,I,E, 1928 F,W,E, 1929 I,E, 1930 F,W,I,E, 1931 W,E, 1932 SA,E.
Macpherson, N.C., Newport, Mon – 1920 W,I,E, 1921 F,E, 1923 I,E.
McQueen, S.B., Waterloo – 1923 F,W,I,E.
Macrae, D.J., St. Andrews U. – 1937 W,I,E, 1938 W,I,E, 1939 W,I,E.
Madsen, D.F., Gosforth – 1974 W,E,I,F, 1975 I,F,W,E, 1976 F, 1977 E,I,F,W, 1978 I.
Mair, N.G.R., Edinburgh U. – 1951 F,W,I,E.
Maitland, G., Edinburgh Inst. FP – 1885 W,I(2).
Maitland, R., Edinburgh Inst. FP – 1881 E, 1882 I,E, 1884 W, 1885 W.
Maitland, R.P., Royal Artillery – 1872 E.
Malcolm, A.G. Glasgow U. – 1881 I.
Marsh, J., Edinburgh Inst. FP – 1889 W,I.
Marshall, A., Edinburgh Acads. – 1875 E.
Marshall, G.R., Selkirk – 1988 A(r), 1989 Fj, 1990 Arg.
Marshall, J.C., London Scottish – 1954 F,NZ,I,E,W.
Marshall, K.W., Edinburgh Acads. – 1934 W,I,E, 1935 W,I,E, 1936 W, 1937 E.
Marshall, T.R., Edinburgh Acads. – 1871 E, 1872 E, 1873 E, 1874 E.
Marshall, W., Edinburgh Acads. – 1872 E.
Martin, H., Edinburgh Acads., Oxford U. – 1908 W,I,E, 1909 W,E.
Masters, W.H., Edinburgh Inst. FP – 1879 I, 1880 I,E.
Maxwell, F.T., Royal Engineers – 1872 E.
Maxwell, G.H.H.P., Edinburgh Acads., RAF, London Scottish – 1913 I,E, 1914 W,I,E, 1920 W,E,
    1921 F,W,I,E, 1922 F,E.
Maxwell, J.M., Langholm – 1957 I.

Mein, J., Edinburgh Acads. – 1871 E, 1872 E, 1873 E, 1874 E, 1875 E.
Melville, C.L., Army – 1937 W,I,E.
Menzies, H.F., West of Scotland – 1893 W,I, 1894 W,E.
Methuen, A., London Scottish – 1889 W,I.
Michie, E.J.S., Aberdeen U., London Scottish – 1954 F,NZ,I,E, 1955 W,I,E, 1956 F,W,I,E, 1957
    F,W,I,E.
Millar, J.N., West of Scotland – 1892 W,I,E, 1893 W, 1895 I,E.
Millar, R.K., London Scottish – 1924 I.
Millican, J.G., Edinburgh U. – 1973 W,I,E.
Milne, C.J.B., Fettesian-Lorettonians, West of Scotland – 1886 W,I,E.
Milne, I.G., Heriot's FP, Harlequins – 1979 I,F,NZ, 1980 I,F, 1981 NZ(1,2),R,A, 1982
    E,I,F,W,A(1,2), 1983 I,F,W,E,NZ, 1984 W,E,I,F,A, 1985 F,W,E, 1986 F,W,E,I,R, 1987
    I,F,W,E,WC-F,Z,NZ, 1988 A, 1989 W, 1990 NZ(1,2)
Milne, K.S., Heriot's FP – 1989 W,E,I,F,Fj,R, 1990 I,F,W,E,NZ(2),Arg, 1991 F,W(r),E.
Milne, W.M., Glasgow Acads. – 1904 I,E, 1905 W,I.
Milroy, E., Watsonians – 1910 W, 1911 E, 1912 W,I,E,SA, 1913 F,W,I,E, 1914 I,E.
Mitchell, G.W.E., Edinburgh Wands. – 1967 NZ, 1968 F,W.
Mitchell, J.G., West of Scotland – 1885 W,I(1,2).
Moncrieff, F.J., Edinburgh Acads. – 1871 E, 1872 E, 1873 E.
Monteith, H.G., Cambridge U., London Scottish – 1905 E, 1906 W,I,E,SA, 1907 W,I, 1908 E.
Monypenny, D.B., London Scottish – 1899 I,W,E.
Moodie, A.R., St. Andrews U. – 1909 E, 1910 F, 1911 F.
Moore, A., Edinburgh Acads. – 1990 NZ(2),Arg, 1991 F,W,E.
Morgan, D.W., Stewart's Melville FP – 1973 W,I,E,P, 1974 I,F, 1975 I,F,W,E,NZ,A, 1976 F,W,
    1977 I,F,W, 1978 I,F,W,E.
Morrison, M.C., Royal HS FP – 1896 W,I,E, 1897 I,E, 1898 I,E, 1899 I,W,E, 1900 W,E, 1901
    W,I,E, 1902 W,I,E, 1903 W,I, 1904 W,I,E.
Morrison, R.H., Edinburgh U. – 1886 W,I,E.
Morrison, W.H., Edinburgh Acads. – 1900 W.
Morton, D.S., West of Scotland – 1887 I,W,E, 1888 W,I, 1889 W,I, 1890 I,E.
Mowat, J.G., Glasgow Acads. – 1883 W,E.
Muir, D.E., Heriot's FP – 1950 F,W,I,E, 1952 W,I,E.
Munnoch, N.M., Watsonians – 1952 F,W,I.
Munro, P., Oxford U., London Scottish – 1905 W,I,E,NZ, 1906 W,I,E,SA, 1907 E, 1911 F,W,I.
Munro, R., St. Andrews U. – 1871 E.
Munro, S., Ayr, West of Scotland – 1980 I,F, 1981 F,W,E,I,NZ(1,2),R, 1984 W.
Munro, W.H., Glasgow HS FP – 1947 I,E.
Murdoch, W.C.W., Hillhead HS FP – 1935 E,NZ, 1936 W,I, 1939 E, 1948 F,W,I,E.
Murray, G.M., Glasgow Acads. – 1921 I, 1926 W.
Murray, H.M., Glasgow U. – 1936 W,I.
Murray, K.T., Hawick – 1985 I,F,W.
Murray, R.O., Cambridge U. – 1935 W,E.
Murray, W.A.K., London Scottish – 1920 F,I, 1921 F.

Napier, H.M., West of Scotland – 1877 I,E, 1878 E, 1879 I,E.
Neill, J.B., Edinburgh Acads. – 1963 E, 1964 F,NZ,W,I,E, 1965 F.
Neill, R.M., Edinburgh Acads. – 1901 E, 1902 I.
Neilson, G.T., West of Scotland – 1891 W,I,E, 1892 W,E, 1893 W, 1894 W,I, 1895 W,I,E,
    1896 W,I,E.
Neilson, J.A., Glasgow Acads. – 1878 E, 1879 E.
Neilson, R.T., West of Scotland – 1898 I,E, 1899 I,W, 1900 I,E.
Neilson, T., West of Scotland – 1874 E.
Neilson, W., Merchistonians, Cambridge U., London Scottish – 1891 W,E, 1892 W,I,E, 1893 I,E,
    1894 E, 1895 W,I,E, 1896 I, 1897 I,E.
Neilson, W.G., Merchistonians – 1894 E.
Nelson, J.B., Glasgow Acads. – 1925 F,W,I,E, 1926 F,W,I,E, 1927 F,W,I,E, 1928 I,E, 1929 F,W,I,E,
    1930 F,W,I,E, 1931 F,W,I.
Nelson, T.A., Oxford U. – 1898 E.
Nichol, J.A., Royal HS FP – 1955 W,I,E.
Nimmo, C.S., Watsonians – 1920 E.

Ogilvy, C., Hawick – 1911 I,E, 1912 I.
Oliver, G.H., Hawick – 1987 WC-Z, 1990 NZ(2r).
Oliver, G.K., Gala – 1970 A.
Orr, C.E., West of Scotland – 1887 I,E,W, 1888 W,I, 1889 W,I, 1890 W,I,E, 1891 W,I,E,
    1891 W,I,E.
Orr, H.J., London Scottish – 1903 W,I,E, 1904 W,I.
Orr, J.E., West of Scotland – 1889 I, 1890 W,I,E, 1891 W,I,E, 1892 W,I,E, 1893 I,E.
Orr, J.H., Edinburgh City Police – 1947 F,W.
Osler, F.L., Edinburgh U. – 1911 F,W.

Park, J., Royal HS FP – 1934 W.
Paterson, D.S., Gala – 1969 SA, 1970 I,E,A, 1971 F,W,I,E,EC, 1972 W.

Paterson, G.Q., Edinburgh Acads. – 1876 E.
Paterson, J.R., Birkenhead Park – 1925 F,W,I,E, 1926 F,W,I,E, 1927 F,W,I,E,NSW, 1928 F,W,I,E,
    1929 F,W,I,E.
Patterson, D., Hawick – 1896 W.
Pattullo, G.L., Panmure – 1920 F,W,I,E.
Paxton, I.A.M., Selkirk – 1981 NZ(1,2),R,A, 1982 E,I,F,W,A(1,2), 1983 I,E,NZ, 1984 W,E,I,F,
    1985 I(r),F,W,F., 1986 W,E,I,R, 1987 I,F,W,E,WC-F,Z,R,NZ, 1988 I,E,A.
Paxton, R.E., Kelso – 1982 I,A(2r).
Pearson, J., Watsonians – 1909 I,E, 1910 F,W,I,E, 1911 F, 1912 F,W,SA, 1913 I,E.
Pender, I.M., London Scottish – 1914 E.
Pender, N.E.K., Hawick – 1977 I, 1978 F,W,E.
Penman, W.M., RAF – 1939 I.
Peterkin, W.A., Edinburgh U. – 1881 E, 1883 I, 1884 W,I,E, 1885 I(1,2),W.
Petrie, A.G., Royal HS FP – 1873 E, 1874 E, 1875 E, 1876 E, 1877 I,E, 1878 E, 1879 I,E,
    1880 I,E.
Philp, A., Edinburgh Inst. FP – 1882 E.
Pocock, E.I., Edinburgh Wands. – 1877 I,E.
Pollock, J.A., Gosforth – 1982 W, 1983 E,NZ, 1984 E(r),I,F,R, 1985 F.
Polson, A.H., Gala – 1930 E.
Purdie, W., Jed-Forest – 1939 W,I,E.
Purves, A.B.H.L., London Scottish – 1906 W,I,E,SA, 1907 W,I,E, 1908 W,I,E.
Purves, W.D.C.L., London Scottish – 1912 F,W,I,SA, 1913 I,E.

Rea, C.W.W., West of Scotland, Headingley – 1968 A, 1969 F,W,I,SA, 1970 F,W,I,A. 1971
    F,W,E,EC.
Reid, C., Edinburgh Acads. – 1881, I,E, 1882 I,E, 1883 W,I,E, 1884 W,I,E, 1885 W,I,(1,2), 1886
    W,I,E, 1887 I,W,E, 1888 W,I.
Reid, J., Edinburgh Wands. – 1874 E, 1875 E, 1876 E, 1877 I,E.
Reid, J.M., Edinburgh Acads. – 1898 I,E, 1899 I.
Reid, M.F., Loretto – 1883 I,E.
Ralph, W.K.L., Stewart's Coll. FP – 1955 F,W,I,E.
Renny-Tailyour, H.W., Royal Engineers – 1872 E.
Renwick, J.M., Hawick – 1972 F,W,E,NZ, 1973 F, 1974 W,E,I,F, 1975 I,F,W,E,NZ,A,
    1976 F,W,E(r), 1977 I,F,W, 1978 I,F,W,E,NZ, 1979 W,E,I,F,NZ, 1980 I,F,W,E, 1981
    F,W,E,I,NZ(1,2),R,A, 1982 E,I,F,W, 1983 I,F,W,E, 1984 R.
Renwick, W.L., London Scottish – 1989 R.
Renwick, W.N., London Scottish, Edinburgh Wands. – 1938 E, 1939 W.
Ritchie, G., Merchistonians – 1871 E.
Ritchie, G.F., Dundee HS FP – 1932 E.
Ritchie, J.M., Watsonians – 1933 W,E,I, 1934 W,I,E.
Ritchie, W.T., Cambridge U. – 1905 I,E.
Robb, G.H., Glasgow U. – 1881 I, 1885 W.
Roberts, G., Watsonians – 1938 W,I,E, 1939 W,E.
Robertson, A.H., West of Scotland – 1871 E.
Robertson, A.W., Edinburgh Acads. – 1897 E.
Robertson, D., Edinburgh Acads. – 1875 E.
Robertson, D.D., Cambridge U. – 1893 W.
Robertson, I., London Scottish, Watsonians – 1968 E, 1969 E,SA, 1970 F,W,I,E,A.
Robertson, I.P.M., Watsonians – 1910 F.
Robertson, J., Clydesdale – 1908 E.
Robertson, K.W., Melrose – 1978 NZ, 1979 W,E,I,F,NZ, 1980 W,E, 1981 F,W,E,I,R,A, 1982
    E,I,F,A(1,2), 1983 I,F,W,E, 1984 E,I,F,R,A, 1985 I,F,W,E, 1986 I, 1987 F(r),W,E,WC-
    F,Z,NZ, 1988 E,A, 1989 E,I,F.
Robertson, L., London Scottish, United Services – 1908 E, 1911 W, 1912 W,I,E,SA, 1913 W,I,E.
Robertson, M.A., Gala – 1958 F.
Robertson, R.D., London Scottish – 1912 F.
Robson, A., Hawick – 1954 F, 1955 F,W,I,E, 1956 F,W,I,E, 1957 F,W,I,E, 1958 W,A,I,E, 1959
    F,W,I,E, 1960 F.
Rodd, J.A.T., United Services, RN, London Scottish – 1958 F,W,A,I,E, 1960 F,W, 1962 F, 1964
    F,NZ,W, 1965 F,W,I.
Rogerson, J., Kelvinside Acads. – 1894 W.
Roland, E.T., Edinburgh Acads. – 1884 I,E.
Rollo, D.M.D., Howe of Fife – 1959 E, 1960 F,W,I,E,SA, 1961 F,SA,W,I,E, 1962 F,W,E, 1963
    F,W,I,E, 1964 F,NZ,W,I,E, 1965 F,W,I,E,SA, 1966 F,W,I,E,A, 1967 F,W,E,NZ, 1968 F,W,I.
Rose, D.M., Jed-Forest – 1951 F,W,I,E,SA, 1953 F,W.
Ross, A., Kilmarnock – 1924 F,W.
Ross, A., Royal HS FP – 1905 W,I,E, 1909 W,I.
Ross, A.R., Edinburgh U. – 1911 W, 1914 W,I,E.
Ross, E.J., London Scottish – 1904 W.
Ross, G.T., Watsonians – 1954 NZ,I,E,W.
Ross, I.A., Hillhead HS FP – 1951 F,W,I,E.
Ross, J., London Scottish – 1901 W,I,E, 1902 W, 1903 E.
Ross, K.I., Boroughmuir – 1961 SA,W,I,E, 1962 F,W,I,E, 1963 F,W,E.

Ross, W.A., Hillhead HS FP – 1937 W,E.
Rottenburg, H., Cambridge U., London Scottish – 1899 W,E, 1900 W,I,E.
Roughead, W.N., Edinburgh Acads., London Scottish – 1927 NSW, 1928 F,W,I,E, 1930 I,E, 1931
     F,W,I,E, 1932 W.
Rowan, N.A., Boroughmuir – 1980 W,E, 1981 F,W,E,I, 1984 R, 1985 I, 1987 WC-R, 1988
     I,F,W,E.
Rowand, R., Glasgow HS FP – 1930 F,W, 1932 E, 1933 W,E,I, 1934 W.
Roy, A., Waterloo – 1938 W,I,E, 1939 W,I,E.
Russell, W.L., Glasgow U., Glasgow Acads. – 1905 NZ, 1906 W,I,E.
Rutherford, J.Y., Selkirk – 1979 W,E,I,F,NZ, 1980 I,F,E, 1981 F,W,E,I,NZ(1,2), A, 1982
     E,I,F,W,A,(1,2), 1983 E,NZ, 1984 W,E,I,F,R, 1985 I,F,W,E, 1986 F,W,E,I,R, 1987
     I,F,W,E,WC-F.

Sampson, R.W.F., London Scottish – 1939 W, 1947 W.
Sanderson, G.A., Royal HS FP – 1907 W,I,E, 1908 I.
Sanderson, J.L.P., Edinburgh Acads. – 1873 E.
Schulze, D.G., London Scottish, Dartmouth RNC, Northampton – 1905 E, 1907 I,E, 1908 W,I,E,
     1909 W,I,E, 1910 W,I,E, 1911 W.
Scobie, R.M., Royal Military Coll. – 1914 W,I,E.
Scotland, K.J.F., Royal Signals, Heriot's FP, Cambridge U., London Scottish, Leicester,
     Aberdeenshire – 1957 F,W,I,E, 1958 E, 1959 F,W,I,E, 1960 F,W,I,E, 1961 F,SA,W,I,E, 1962
     F,W,I,E, 1963 F,W,I,E, 1965 F.
Scott, D.M., Langholm, Watsonians – 1950 I,E, 1951 W,I,E,SA, 1952 F,W,I, 1953 F.
Scott, H., St. Andrews U. – 1950 E.
Scott, J.M.B., Edinburgh Acads. – 1907 E, 1908 W,I,E, 1909 W,I,E, 1910 F,W,I,E, 1911 F,W,I,
     1912 W,I,E,SA, 1913 W,I,E.
Scott, J.W., Stewart's Coll. FP, Bradford, Waterloo – 1925 F,W,I,E, 1926 F,W,I,E, 1927
     F,W,I,E,NSW, 1928 F,W,E, 1929 E, 1930 F.
Scott, R., Hawick – 1898 I, 1900 I,E.
Scott, T., Langholm, Hawick – 1896 W, 1897 I,E, 1898 I,E, 1899 I,W,E, 1900 W,I,E.
Scott, T.M., Hawick, Melrose – 1893 E, 1895 W,I,E, 1896 W,E, 1897 I,E, 1898 I,E, 1900 W,I.
Scott, W.P., West of Scotland – 1900 I,E, 1902 I,E, 1903 W,I,E, 1904 W,I,E, 1905 W,I,E,NZ, 1906
     W,I,E,SA, 1907 W,I,E.
Scoular, J.G., Cambridge U. – 1905 NZ, 1906 W,I,E,SA.
Selby, J.A.R., Watsonians – 1920 W,I.
Shackleton, J.A.P., London Scottish – 1959 E, 1963 F,W, 1964 NZ,W, 1965 I,SA.
Sharp, G., Stewart's FP, Army – 1960 F, 1964 F,NZ,W.
Shaw, G.D., Gala, Sale – 1935 NZ, 1936 W, 1937 W,I,E, 1939 I.
Shaw, I., Glasgow HS FP – 1937 I.
Shaw, J.N., Edinburgh Acads. – 1921 W,I.
Shaw, R.W., Glasgow HS FP – 1934 W,I,E, 1935 W,I,E,NZ, 1936 W,I,E, 1937 W,I,E, 1938 W,I,E,
     1939 W,I,E.
Shedden, D., West of Scotland – 1972 NZ, 1973 F,W,I,E,P, 1976 W,E,I, 1977 I,F,W, 1978 I,F,W.
Shillinglaw, R.B., Gala, Army – 1960 I,E,SA, 1961 F,SA.
Simmers, B.M., Glasgow Acads. – 1965 F,W, 1966 A, 1967 F,W,I, 1971 F(r).
Simmers, W.M., Glasgow Acads. – 1926 W,I,E, 1927 F,W,I,E,NSW, 1928 F,W,I,E, 1929 F,W,I,E,
     1930 F,W,I,E, 1931 F,W,I,E, 1932 SA,W,I,E.
Simpson, J.W., Royal HS FP – 1893 I,E, 1894 W,I,E, 1985 W,I,E, 1896 W,I, 1897 E, 1898 W,E.
Simpson, R.S., Glasgow Acads. – 1923 I.
Simson, E.D., Edinburgh U., London Scottish – 1902 E, 1903 W,I,E, 1904 W,I,E, 1905 W,I,E,NZ,
     1906 W,I,E, 1907 W,I,E.
Simson, J.T., Watsonians – 1905 NZ, 1909 W,I,E, 1910 F,W, 1911 I.
Simson, R.F., London Scottish – 1911 E.
Sloan, A.T., Edinburgh Acads. – 1914 W, 1920 F,W,I,E, 1921 F,W,I,E.
Sloan, D.A., Edinburgh Acads., London Scottish – 1950 F,W,E, 1951 W,I,E, 1953 F.
Sloan, T., Glasgow Acads., London Scottish – 1905 NZ, 1906 W,SA, 1907 W,E, 1908 W, 1909 I.
Smeaton, P.W., Edinburgh Acads. – 1881 I, 1883 I,E.
Smith, A.R., Oxford U. – 1895 W,I,E, 1896 W,I, 1897 I,E, 1898 I,E, 1900 I,E.
Smith, A.R., Cambridge U., Gosforth, Ebbw Vale, Edinburgh Wands. – 1955 W,I,E, 1956 F,W,I,E,
     1957 F,W,I,E, 1958 F,W,A,I, 1959 F,W,I,E, 1960 F,W,I,E,SA, 1961 F,SA,W,I,E, 1962 F,W,I,E.
Smith, D.W.C., Army, London Scottish – 1949 F,W,I,E, 1950 F,W,I, 1953 I.
Smith, E.R., Edinburgh Acads. – 1879 I.
Smith, G.K., Kelso – 1957 I,E, 1958 F,W,A, 1959 F,W,I,E, 1960 F,W,I,E, 1961 F,SA,W,I,E.
Smith, H.O., Watsonians – 1895 W, 1896 W,I,E, 1898 I,E, 1899 W,I,E, 1900 E, 1902 E.
Smith, I.S., Oxford U., Edinburgh U., London Scottish – 1924 W,I,E, 1925 F,W,I,E, 1926 F,W,I,E,
     1927 F,I,E, 1929 F,W,I,E, 1930 F,W,I, 1931 F,W,I,E, 1932 SA,W,I,E, 1933 W,E,I.
Smith, I.S.G., London Scottish – 1969 SA, 1970 F,W,I,E, 1971 F,W,I.
Smith, M.A., London Scottish – 1970 W,I,E,A.
Smith, R.T., Kelso – 1929 F,W,I,E, 1930 F,W,I.
Smith, S.H., Glasgow Acads. – 1877 I, 1878 E.
Smith, T.J., Gala – 1983 E,NZ, 1985 I,F,
Sole, D.M.B., Bath, Edinburgh Acads. – 1986 F,W, 1987 I,F,W,E,WC-F,Z,R,NZ, 1988 I,F,W,E,A,
     1989 W,E,I,F,Fj,R, 1990 I,F,W,E,NZ(1,2),Arg, 1991 F,W,E,I.

Somerville, D., Edinburgh Inst. FP – 1879 I, 1882 I, 1883 W,I,E, 1884 W.

Spence, K.M., Oxford U. – 1953 I.

Spencer, E., Clydesdale – 1898 I.

Spiers, L.M., Watsonians – 1906 SA, 1907 W,I,E, 1908 W,I,E, 1910 F,W,E.

Stagg, P.K., Sale – 1965 F,W,E,SA, 1966 F,W,I,E,A, 1967 F,W,I,E,NZ, 1968 F,W,I,E,A, 1969 F,W,I(r),SA, 1970 F,W,I,E,A.

Stanger, A.G., Hawick – 1989 Fj,R, 1990 I,F,W,E,NZ(1,2),Arg, 1991 F,W,E,I.

Steele, W.C.C., Bedford, RAF, London Scottish – 1969 E, 1971 F,W,I,E,EC, 1972 F,W,E,NZ, 1973 F,W,I,E, 1975 I,F,W,E,NZ(r), 1976 W,E,I, 1977 E.

Stephen, A.E., West of Scotland – 1885 W, 1886 I.

Steven, P.D., Heriot's FP – 1984 A, 1985 F,W,E.

Steven, R., Edinburgh Wands. – 1962 I.

Stevenson, A.K., Glasgow Acads. – 1922 F, 1923 F,W,E.

Stevenson, A.M., Glasgow U. – 1911 F.

Stevenson, G.D., Hawick – 1956 E, 1957 F, 1958 F,W,A,I,E, 1959 W,I,E, 1960 W,I,E,SA, 1961 F,SA,W,I,E, 1963 F,W,I, 1964 E, 1965 F.

Stevenson, H.J., Edinburgh Acads. – 1888 W,I, 1889 W,I, 1890 W,I,E, 1891 W,I,E, 1892 W,I,E, 1893 I,E.

Stevenson, L.E., Edinburgh U. – 1888 W.

Stevenson, R.C., London Scottish – 1897 I,E, 1898 E, 1899 I,W,E.

Stevenson, R.C., St. Andrews U. – 1910 F,I,F, 1911 F,W,I.

Stevenson, W.H., Glasgow Acads. – 1925 F.

Stewart, A.K., Edinburgh U. – 1874 E, 1876 E.

Stewart, A.M., Edinburgh Acads. – 1914 W.

Stewart, C.A.R., West of Scotland – 1880 I,E.

Stewart, C.E.B., Kelso – 1960 W, 1961 F.

Stewart, J., Glasgow HS FP – 1930 F.

Stewart, J.L., Edinburgh Acads. – 1921 I.

Stewart, M.S., Stewart's Coll. FP – 1932 SA,W,I, 1933 W,E,I, 1934 W,I,E.

Stewart, W.A., London Hospital – 1913 F,W,I, 1914 W.

Steyn, S.S.L., Oxford U. – 1911 E, 1912 I.

Strachan, G.M., Jordanhill – 1971 E(r), 1973 W,I,E,P.

Stronach, R.S., Glasgow Acads. – 1901 W,E, 1905 W,I,E.

Stuart, C.D., West of Scotland – 1909 I, 1910 F,W,I,E, 1911 I,E.

Stuart, L.M., Glasgow HS FP – 1923 F,W,I,E, 1924 F, 1928 E, 1930 I,E.

Suddon, N., Hawick – 1965 W,I,E,SA, 1966 A, 1968 E,A, 1969 F,W,I, 1970 I,E,A.

Sutherland, W.R., Hawick – 1910 W,E, 1911 F,E, 1912 F,W,E,SA, 1913 F,W,I,E, 1914 W.

Swan, J.S., Army, London Scottish, Leicester, Coventry – 1953 E, 1954 F,NZ,I,E,W, 1955 F,W,I,E, 1956 F,W,I,E, 1957 F,W, 1958 F.

Swan, M.W., Oxford U., London Scottish – 1958 F,W,A,I,E, 1959 F,W,I.

Sweet, J.B., Glasgow HS FP – 1913 E, 1914 I.

Symington, A.W., Cambridge U. – 1914 W,E.

Tait, A.V., Kelso – 1987 WC-F(r),Z,R,NZ, 1988 I,F,W,E.

Tait, J.G., Edinburgh Acads., Cambridge U. – 1880 I, 1885 I(2).

Tait, P.W., Royal HS FP – 1935 E.

Taylor, E.G., Oxford U. – 1927 W,NSW.

Taylor, R.C., Kelvinside-West – 1951 W,I,E,SA.

Telfer, C.M., Hawick – 1968 A, 1969 F,W,I,E, 1972 F,W,E, 1973 W,I,E,P, 1974 W,E,I, 1975 A, 1976 F.

Telfer, J.W., Melrose – 1964 F,NZ,W,I,E, 1965 F,W,I, 1966 F,W,I,E, 1967 W,I,E, 1968 E,A, 1969 F,W,I,E,SA, 1970 F,W,I.

Tennent, J.M., West of Scotland – 1909 W,I,E, 1910 F,W,E.

Thom, D.A., London Scottish – 1932 W, 1935 W,I,E,NZ.

Thom, G., Kirkcaldy – 1920 F,W,I,E.

Thom, J.R., Watsonians – 1933 W,E,I.

Thomson, A.E., United Services – 1921 F,W,E.

Thomson, A.M., St. Andrews U. – 1949 I.

Thomson, B.E., Oxford U. – 1953 F,W,I.

Thomson, I.H.M., Heriot's FP, Army – 1951 W,I, 1952 F,W,I, 1953 I,E.

Thomson, J.S., Glasgow Acads. – 1871 E.

Thomson, R.H., London Scottish – 1960 I,E,SA, 1961 F,SA,W,I,E, 1963 F,W,I,E, 1964 F,NZ,W.

Thomson, W.H., West of Scotland – 1906 SA.

Thomson, W.J., West of Scotland – 1899 W,E, 1900 W.

Timms, A.B., Edinburgh U., Edinburgh Wands., Cardiff – 1896 W, 1900 W,I, 1901 W,I,E, 1902 W,E, 1903 W,E, 1904 I,E, 1905 I,E.

Tod, H.B., Gala – 1911 F.

Tod, J., Watsonians – 1884 W,I,E, 1885 W,I(1,2), 1886 W,I,E.

Todd, J.K., Glasgow Acads. – 1874 E, 1875 E.

Tolmie, J.M., Glasgow HS FP – 1922 E.

Tomes, A.J., Hawick – 1976 E,I, 1977 E, 1978 I,F,W,E,NZ, 1979 W,E,I,F,NZ, 1980 F,W,E, 1981 F,W,E,I,NZ(1,2),R,A, 1982 E,I,F,W,A(1,2), 1983 I,F,W, 1984 W,E,I,F,R,A, 1985 W,E, 1987 I,F,E(r),WC-F,Z,R,NZ.

Torrie, T.J., Edinburgh Acads. – 1877 E.
Tukalo, I., Selkirk – 1985 I, 1987 I,F,W,E,WC-F,Z,R,NZ, 1988 F,W,E,A, 1989 W,E,I,F,Fj, 1990
    I,F,W,E,NZ(1), 1991 I.
Turk, A.S., Langholm – 1971 E(r).
Turnbull, F.O., Kelso – 1951 F,SA.
Turnbull, D.J., Hawick – 1987 WC-NZ, 1988 F,E, 1990 E(r), 1991 F,W,E,I.
Turnbull, G.O., West of Scotland, London Scottish, Edinburgh Wands. – 1896 I,E, 1897 I,E,
    1904 W.
Turnbull, P., Edinburgh Acads. – 1901 W,I,E, 1902 W,I,E.
Turner, F.H., Oxford U., Liverpool – 1911 F,W,I,E, 1912 F,W,I,E,SA, 1913 F,W,I,E, 1914 I,E.
Turner, J.W.C., Gala – 1966 W,A, 1967 F,W,I,E,NZ, 1968 F,W,I,E,A, 1969 F, 1970 E,A, 1971
    F,W,I,E,EC.

Usher, C.M., London Scottish, United Services, Edinburgh Wands. – 1912 E, 1913 F,W,I,E, 1914
    E, 1920 F,W,I,E, 1921 W,E, 1922 F,W,I,E.

Valentine, A.R., RNAS, Anthorn – 1953 F,W,I.
Valentine, D.D., Hawick – 1947 I,E.
Veitch, J.P., Royal HS FP – 1882 E, 1883 I, 1884 W,I,E, 1885 I(1,2), 1886 E.
Villar, C., Edinburgh Wands. – 1876 E, 1877 I,E.

Waddell, G.H., London Scottish, Devonport Services, Cambridge U. – 1957 E, 1958 F,W,A,I,E,
    1959 F,W,I,E, 1960 I,E,SA, 1961 F, 1962 F,W,I,E.
Waddell, H., Glasgow Acads. – 1924 F,W,I,E, 1925 I,E, 1926 F,W,I,E, 1927 F,W,I,E, 1930 W.
Wade, A.L., London Scottish – 1908 E.
Walker, A., West of Scotland – 1881 I, 1882 E, 1883 W,I,E.
Walker, A.W., Cambridge U., Birkenhead Park – 1931 F,W,I,E, 1932 I.
Walker, J.G., Fettesian-Lorettonians, West of Scotland – 1882 E, 1883 W.
Walker, M., Oxford U. – 1952 F.
Wallace, A.C., Oxford U. – 1923 F, 1924 F,W,E, 1925 F,W,I,E, 1926 F.
Wallace, W.M., Cambridge U. – 1913 E, 1914 W,I,E.
Walls, W.A., Glasgow Acads. – 1882 E, 1883 W,I,E, 1884 W,I,E, 1886 W,I,E.
Walter, M.W., London Scottish – 1906 I,E,SA, 1907 W,I, 1908 W,I, 1910 I.
Warren, J.R., Glasgow Acads. – 1914 I.
Warren, R.C., Glasgow Acads. – 1922 W,I, 1930 W,I,E.
Waters, F.H. Cambridge U., London Scottish – 1930 F,W,I,E, 1932 SA,W,I.
Waters, J.A., Selkirk – 1933 W,E,I, 1934 W,I,E, 1935 W,I,E,NZ, 1936 W,I,E, 1937 W,I,E.
Waters, J.B., Cambridge U., – 1904 I,E.
Watherston, J.G., Edinburgh Wands. – 1934 I,E.
Watherston, W.R.A., London Scottish – 1963 F,W,I.
Watson, D.H., Glasgow Acads. – 1876 E, 1877 I,E.
Watson, W.S., Boroughmuir – 1974 W,E,I,F, 1975 NZ, 1977 I,F,W, 1979 I,F.
Watt, A.G.M., Edinburgh Acads., Army – 1947 F,W,I,A, 1948 F,W.
Weatherstone, T.G., Stewart's Coll. FP – 1952 E, 1953 I,E, 1954 F,NZ,I,E,W, 1955 F, 1958
    W,A,I,E, 1959 W,I,E.
Weir, G.W., Melrose – 1990 Arg.
Welsh, R., Watsonians – 1895 W,E,I, 1896 W.
Welsh, R.B., Hawick – 1967 I,E.
Welsh, W.B., Hawick – 1927 NSW, 1928 F,W,I, 1929 I,E, 1930 F,W,I,E, 1931 F,W,I,E, 1932
    SA,W,I,E, 1933 W,E,I.
Welsh, W.H., Edinburgh U. – 1900 I,E, 1901 W,I,E, 1902 W,I,E.
Wemyss, A., Gala, Edinburgh Wands. – 1914 W,I, 1920 F,E, 1922 F,W,I.
West, L., Edinburgh U., Carlisle, London Scottish, West Hartlepool – 1903 W,I,E, 1905 I,E,NZ,
    1906 W,I,E.
Weston, V.G., Kelvinside Acads. – 1936 I,E.
White, D.B., Gala, London Scottish – 1982 F,W,A(1,2), 1987 W,E,WC-F,R,NZ, 1988 I,F,W,E,A,
    1989 W,E,I,F,Fj,R, 1990 I,F,W,E,NZ(1,2), 1991 F,W,E,I.
White, D.M., Kelvinside Acads. – 1963 F,W,I,E.
White, T.B., Edinburgh Acads. – 1886 W,I, 1889 W.
Whittington, T.P., Merchistonians – 1873 E.
Whitworth, R.J.E., London Scottish – 1936 I.
Whyte, D.J., Edinburgh Wands. – 1965 W,I,E,SA, 1966 F,W,I,E,A, 1967 F,W,I,E.
Will, J.G., Cambridge U. – 1912 F,W,I,E, 1914 W,I,E.
Wilson, A.W., Dunfermline – 1931 F,I,E.
Wilson, G.A., Oxford U. – 1949 F,W,E.
Wilson, G.R., Royal HS FP – 1886 E, 1890 W,I,E, 1891 I.
Wilson, J.H., Watsonians – 1953 I.
Wilson, J.S., St. Andrews U. – 1931 F,W,I,E, 1932 E.
Wilson, J.S., United Services, London Scottish – 1908 I, 1909 W.
Wilson, R., London Scottish – 1976 E,I, 1977 E,I,F, 1978 I,F, 1981 R, 1983 I.
Wilson, R.L., Gala – 1951 F,W,I,E,SA, 1953 F,W,E.
Wilson, R.W., West of Scotland – 1873 E, 1874 E.

Wilson, S., Oxford U., London Scottish – 1964 F,NZ,W,I,E, 1965 W,I,E,SA, 1966 F,W,I,A, 1967
    F,W,I,E,NZ, 1968 F,W,I,E.
Wood, A., Royal HS FP – 1873 E, 1874 E, 1875 E.
Wood, G., Gala – 1931 W,I, 1932 W,I,E.
Woodburn, J.C., Kelvinside Acads. – 1892 I.
Woodrow, A.N., Glasgow Acads. – 1887 I,W,E.
Wotherspoon, W., West of Scotland – 1891 I, 1892 I, 1893 W,E, 1894 W,I,E.
Wright, F.A., Edinburgh Acads. – 1932 E.
Wright, H.B., Watsonians – 1894 W.
Wright, K.M., London Scottish – 1929 F,W,I,E.
Wright, R.W.J., Edinburgh Wands. – 1973 F.
Wright, S.T.H., Stewart's Coll. FP – 1949 E.
Wright, T., Hawick – 1947 A.
Wyllie, D.S., Stewart's Melville FP – 1984 A, 1985 W(r),E, 1987 I,F,WC-F,Z,R,NZ, 1989 R.

Young, A.H., Edinburgh Acads. – 1874 E.
Young, E.T., Glasgow Acads. – 1914 E.
Young, R.G., Watsonians – 1970 W.
Young, T.E.B., Durham – 1911 F.
Young, W.B., Cambridge U., King's College Hospital, London Scottish – 1937 W,I,E, 1938 W,I,E,
    1939 W,I,E, 1948 E.

SCOTLAND B PLAYERS

*Abbreviations: A – Australia; Arg – Argentina; E – England; F – France; Fj – Fiji; I – Ireland; It
– Italy; NZ – New Zealand; W – Wales; WC – World Cup; Z – Zimbabwe; (r) – Replacement.*

*Matches are listed by the second half of the season in which the games were played, i.e. 1974
indicates season 1973–74 even if the match was played in December, 1973*

Aitchison, W.D., Highland – 74 F, 75 F, 77 F, 78 I(r).
Aitken, J., Gala – 75 F, 76 F (capped v E 77).
Armstrong, A.D., Jordanhill – 81 F, 82 F.
Armstrong, G., Jed-Forest – 88 It,F (capped v A 88)
Ashton, D.M., Ayr – 77 F.

Baird, G.R.T., Kelso – 80 I,F, 81 F (capped v A 82).
Balfour, R.F.A., Glasgow HS FP – 74 F, 75 F.
Barnes, I.A., Hawick – 72 F (capped v W 72)
Barrett, D.N., West of Scotland – 90 I,F, 91 I.
Beattie, J.R., Glasgow Acads. – 80 I,F, (capped v I 80).
Bell, D.L., Watsonians – 74 F, 75 F (capped v I 75).
Berthinussen, J.M., Gala – 81 F.
Biggar, M.A., London Scottish – 75 F (capped v I 75).
Black, A.A., Boroughmuir – 72 F.
Blackwood, A.W., Stewart's Melville FP – 78 I.
Breakey, R.W., Gosforth – 76 F, 78 I (capped v E 78).
Breckenridge, G.M., Glasgow High/Kelvinside – 90 F.
Brown, J.F., Ayr – 78 F.
Bruce Lockhart, D.R.M., London Scottish – 84 I,F.
Bryce, R.D.H., London Scottish – 72 F, 73 F (capped v I 73).
Bryson, D., Gala – 82 F, 90 I,F.
Buchanan–Smith, G.A.E., London Scottish – 89 F (capped v Fj 90).
Burnell, A.P., London Scottish – 89 It (capped v E 89).
Burnett, H.M., Heriot's FP – 77 F, 78 I, 81 F.
Burnett, J.N., Heriot's FP – 78 I, 80 I,F (capped v I 80).
Busby, J.D., Glasgow High/Kelvinside – 90 I,F.
Butcher, D.J.D., Harlequins – 88 It,F.

Calder, F., Stewart's Melville FP – 84 I,F (capped v F 86).
Calder, J., Stewart's Melville FP – 83 F.
Calder, J.H. (Jim), Stewart's Melville FP – 80 I,F (capped v I 81).
Callander, G.J., Kelso – 82 F (capped v R 84).
Campbell, A.J., Hawick – 83 F, 84 I,F, (capped v I 84).
Campbell, H., Jordanhill – 78 I, 82 F.
Campbell-Lamerton, J.R.E., London Scottish – 85 F, 86 It (capped v F 86).
Chalmers, C.M., Melrose – 88 F, 89 It (capped v W 89).
Clark, R.L., Edinburgh Wands. – 72 F (capped v F 72).
Cockburn, D.G., Boroughmuir – 83 F.
Corcoran, I., Gala – 90 F.
Cramb, R.I., Harlequins – 86 It,F (capped v R 87WC).
Cranston, A.G., Hawick – 73 F, 74 F (capped v W 76).

Cronin, D.F., Bath – 88 It (capped v I 88).
Cunningham, R., Gosforth, Bath – 81 F, 83 F, 84 I,F, 85 I,F.
Cuthbertson, W., Kilmarnock – 80 I,F (capped v I 80).

Dall, F.N.F., Heriot's FP – 73 F.
Davies, W.S., Hawick – 76 F.
Deans, C.T., Hawick – 76 F, 77 F, 78 I (capped v F 78).
Dick, L.G., Loughborough Colleges – 72 F (capped v W 72).
Dickson, G., Gala – 77 F, 78 I,F (capped v NZ 79).
Dixon, J.R., Jordanhill – 78 F, 80 I,F.
Dods, P.W., Gala – 80 I,F, 81 F, 82 F (capped v I 83).
Dougall, A.G., Jordanhill – 78 F.
Duncan, M.D.F., West of Scotland – 85 F, 86 It (capped v F 86).
Dunlop, A.L., Highland – 80 I,F.
Dunlop, T.D., West of Scotland – 75 F, 78 I.

Edwards, B., Boroughmuir – 89 It,F, 90 I,F.
Exeter, T.J., Moseley – 88 It.

Flannigan, C.F., Melrose – 86 F, 87 F.
Flockhart, D.M., Highland – 83 F.
Fowler, S.G., Dunfermline – 72 F, 73 F.
Fraser, A.S., Madras College FP – 73 F.
Fraser, J.A., London Scottish – 81 F, 83 F, 84 I,F, 85 I.
Friell, A.P., London Scottish – 75 F, 76 F, 77 F, 78 F, 80 I,F.

Gammell, W.B.B., Edinburgh Wands. – 76 F, 77 F (capped v I 77).
Gass, C.W., Hawick – 83 F, 85 F.
Glasgow, I.C., Heriot's FP – 91 F.
Gill, A.D., Gala – 73 F (capped v P 73).
Gordon, R.J., London Scottish – 82 F (capped v A 82).
Gossman, B.M., West of Scotland – 80 I,F (capped v W 80).
Gossman, J.S., West of Scotland – 80 I,F (capped v E 80).
Graham, G., Stirling County – 88 It, 89 It, 90 I,F.
Grant, A.R., London Scottish – 76 F.
Gray, C.A., Nottingham – 87 It, 88 It,F, 89 It (capped v W 89).
Gray, D., West of Scotland – 78 I (capped v E 78).
Gray, I.A., West of Scotland – 75 F.
Grecian, N.J., London Scottish – 91 I.

Haldane, R., West of Scotland – 73 F 74 F.
Hall, R., Watsonians – 77 F.
Halliday, B.G., Boroughmuir – 78 F.
Hamilton, J.S., Heriot's FP – 86 F, 87 F.
Hardie, J.A., Aberdeen GS FP – 73 F.
Hastings, A.G., Watsonians – 83 F 84 I,F, 85 I,F (capped v F 86).
Hastings, S., Watsonians – 86 It (capped v F 86).
Hay, J.A., Hawick – 89 F, 91 F.
Hegarty, C.B., Hawick – 77 F (capped v I 78).
Hewitt, P.J., Heriot's FP – 83 F.
Hogarth, P.J., Hawick – 85 I,F, 86 It,F, 87 It,F.
Hogg, C.D., Melrose – 91 F.
Howie, W.H., Glasgow HS FP – 72 F.
Hume, J.H., London Scottish – 82 F, 83 F.
Hunter, I.G., Selkirk – 81 F, 83 F, 84 I,F (capped v I 84).
Hunter, M.D., Glasgow HS FP – 72 F, 73 F (capped v F 74).

Irvine, A.R., Heriot's FP – 73 F (capped v NZ 73).

Jardine, I.C., Stirling County – 90 I.
Jardine, S., Glamorgan Wands. – 91 I.
Jeffrey, J., Kelso – 83 F, 84 I,F (capped v A 85).
Johnston, S.G., Watsonians – 85 I,F, 86 It,F.
Jones, P., Gloucester – 91 I.

Kennedy, A.E., Watsonians – 76 F, 81 F (capped v NZ 84).
Ker, A.B.M., Kelso – 87 It,F, 88 It (capped v W 88).

Laidlaw, R.J., Jed-Forest – 75 F, 76 F, 77 F, 78 I,F, 80 I,F (capped v I 80).
Lambie, I.K., Watsonians – 76 F, 78 F (capped v NZ 79).
Lawrie, K.G., Gala – 78 F, 80 I,F (capped v F 80).
Leckie, D.E.W., Edinburgh Acads. – 87 F(r), 90 I.
Leslie, D.G., Dundee HS FP – 74 F, 75 F (capped v I 75).

Lillington, P.M., Durham U. – 81 F, 82 F.
Livingstone, E.J., Jordanhill – 76 F.

McAslan, S.W., Heriot's FP – 84 F, 86 It,F, 87 It F.
McCallum, D.S.D., Jordanhill – 73 F, 74 F.
MacDonald, A.E.D., Cambridge U. – 90 F, 91 I,F.
Macdonald, D.S.M., London Scottish – 76 F (capped v E 77).
McGauchie, S., Pontypool – 91 I.
McGaughey, S.K., Hawick – 84 F (capped v R 84).
MacGregor, G.T., Glasgow Acads. – 89 It.
McGuffie, A.C., Ayr – 89 It.
McGuinness, G.M., West of Scotland – 77 F, 78 F, 81 F, 82 F (capped v A 82).
McHardy, H.R., Kilmarnock – 74 F, 75 F(r).
McIvor, D.J., Edinburgh Acads. – 91 F.
McKenzie, K.D., Stirling County – 90 I.
Mackenzie, R.S., London Scottish – 74 F, 75 F.
Mackie, G.Y., Highland – 74 F (capped v A 76).
McKie, I.D., Sale – 81 F 84 I,F, 85 I.
Maclean, R.R.W., Gloucester, Moseley – 88 It,F, 89 F, 91 F.
McLeod, D.J., Hawick – 78 I,F.
Macklin, A.J., London Scottish – 85 F, 86 It,F, 87 It,F, 90 I,F.
Mair, C.D.R., West of Scotland – 78 I.
Marshall, G.R., Wakefield – 88 It,F (capped v A 88).
Millar, G.P., Heriot's FP – 83 F.
Milne, D.F., Heriot's FP – 86 F, 87 It,F, 88 F, 89 F, 91 F.
Milne, K.S., Heriot's FP – 86 It, 87 It,F, 88 It,F, 89 It (capped v W 89).
Moncrieff, M., Gala – 91 F.
Moore, A., Gala, Edinburgh Acads.), 87 It, 90 I,F (capped v NZ 90).
Morgan, D.W., Melville College FP – 72 F, 73 F (capped v W 73).
Morrison, K., Glasgow HS FP – 74 F.
Munro, D.S., Glasgow High/Kelvinside – 88 F, 89 F, 90 F.
Munro, S., Ayr – 80 I,F (capped v I 80).
Murray, H.M., Dunfermline – 87 It.
Murray, K.T., Hawick – 85 I,F (capped v I 85).
Murray, R.W., Hawick – 84 I,F, 85 I.

Nichol, R.A., Hawick – 85 F.
Nichol, S.A., Selkirk – 91 I,F.
Nicol, A.D., Dundee HS FP – 91 F.

Oliver, G.H., Hawick – 87 It,F (capped v Z 87WC).

Parker, H.M., Kilmarnock – 85 F, 86 It,F, 87 It, 88 It,F.
Paterson-Brown, T., London Scottish – 87 F, 88 It,F.
Paxton, R.E., Kelso – 81 F, 82 F (capped v I 82).
Pender, N.E.K., Hawick – 75 F, 76 F, 77 F (capped v I 77).
Porter, S.T.G., Malone – 90 I,F, 91 I,F.
Preston, A.J., Gosforth – 76 F.

Rafferty, K.P, Heriot's FP – 88 It,F, 89 It,F.
Ramsey, I.J., Melrose – 88 It,F.
Redpath, A.C., Melrose – 91 I,F.
Reid, S.J., Boroughmuir – 91 I,F.
Renwick, J.M., Hawick – 72 F (capped v F 72).
Renwick, W.L., London Scottish – 88 It,F, 89 It,F (capped v R 90).
Richardson, C.B.S., Edinburgh Acads. – 85 I, 86 It, 89 It,F.
Richardson, J.F., Edinburgh Acads. – 87 F, 89 It,F, 90 I,F, 91 I.
Roberts, H., London Scottish – 91 I.
Robertson, G.B., Stirling County – 91 I.
Robertson, K.W., Melrose – 78 F (capped v NZ 79).
Rose, W.B.N., Kilmarnock – 72 F.
Rouse, P.F., Dundee HS FP – 90 F.
Rowan, N.A., Boroughmuir – 78 F, 80 I,F (capped v W 80).
Runciman, J.G., Melrose – 86 F.
Rutherford, J.Y., Selkirk – 78 I,F (capped v W 79).

Scott, J.M., Stewart's Melville FP – 89 F.
Scott, S.H., Stewart's Melville FP – 86 It,F, 87 It,F.
Shedden, D., West of Scotland – 72 F, 73 F (capped v NZ 73).
Shiel, D.K., Jed-Forest – 89 F, 90 I.
Smith, D.J.M., West of Scotland – 77 F, 78 I.
Smith, I.R., Gloucester – 91 I,F.
Smith, T.J., Gala – 81 F, 82 F (capped v E 83).

Sole, D.M.B., Exeter U. – 84 I,F, 85 I,F, 86 It (capped v F 86).
Stark, D.A., Kilmarnock – 88 F, 89 It,F.
Steven, J., Edinburgh Wands. – 72 F.
Steven, P.D., Heriot's FP – 83 F, 84 I,F, 85 I (capped v A 85).
Stewart, A.A., London Scottish – 78 I.

Tait, A.V., Kelso – 85 I,F, 86 It,F, 87 It,F (capped v F 87WC).
Thomson, A.M., Kelso – 86 F.
Tolbert, R.S., Watsonians – 73 F.
Tomes, A.J., Hawick – 75 F (capped v F 76).
Tukalo, I., Royal High, Selkirk – 82 F, 84 I,F, 85 I,F (capped v I 85).
Turnbull, D.J., Hawick – 82 F, 85 I,F, 86 F, 87 It,F (capped v R 87wc).
Turnbull, G.W., Jed-Forest – 74 F.

Wainwright, R.I., Cambridge U. – 89 It, 91 I.
Waite, T.G., Kelso – 86 It,F, 87 It,F.
Walker, M., Boroughmuir – 89 F(r).
Watson, G.M., Boroughmuir – 76 F, 78 F.
Watson, W.S., Boroughmuir – 72 F (capped v W 72).
Watt, A.G.J., Glasgow High/Kelvinside – 91 F.
Weir, G.W., Melrose – 90 I (capped v Arg 91).
White, A.B., Hawick – 74 F, 75 F.
White, D.B., Gala – 82 F (capped v F 82).
Wilkinson, J.S., Gala – 72 F.
Williamson, C.J., West of Scotland – 83 F 84 I.
Wilson, A.C., West of Scotland – 74 F.
Wilson, G.D., Boroughmuir – 90 I,F.
Wilson, K.D.M., Boroughmuir – 77 F, 81 F, 82 F.
Wilson, R., London Scottish – 75 F (capped v E 76).
Wright, M., Kelso – 89 It,F.
Wright, P.H., Boroughmuir – 89 F.
Wright, R.W.J., Edinburgh U. – 73 F (capped v F 73).
Wyllie, D.S., Stewart's Melville FP – 84 I,F, 85 I (capped v A 85).
Wyroslawski, W., Jordanhill – 74 F, 77 F.